T0227400

Music Emotion Recognition

Multimedia Computing, Communication and Intelligence

Series Editors: Chang Wen Chen and Shiguo Lian

Music Emotion Recognition
Yi-Hsuan Yang and Homer H. Chen
ISBN: 978-1-4398-5046-6

TV Content Analysis: Techniques and Applications
Edited by Yiannis Kompatsiaris, Bernard Merialdo, and Shiguo Lian
ISBN: 978-1-4398-5560-7

Music Emotion Recognition

Yi-Hsuan Yang • Homer H. Chen

CRC Press
Taylor & Francis Group
Boca Raton   London   New York

CRC Press is an imprint of the
Taylor & Francis Group, an **informa** business
AN AUERBACH BOOK

MATLAB® is a trademark of The MathWorks, Inc. and is used with permission. The MathWorks does not warrant the accuracy of the text or exercises in this book. This book's use or discussion of MATLAB® software or related products does not constitute endorsement or sponsorship by The MathWorks of a particular pedagogical approach or particular use of the MATLAB® software.

CRC Press
Taylor & Francis Group
6000 Broken Sound Parkway NW, Suite 300
Boca Raton, FL 33487-2742

© 2011 by Taylor and Francis Group, LLC
CRC Press is an imprint of Taylor & Francis Group, an Informa business

No claim to original U.S. Government works

International Standard Book Number: 978-1-4398-5046-6 (Hardback)

This book contains information obtained from authentic and highly regarded sources. Reasonable efforts have been made to publish reliable data and information, but the author and publisher cannot assume responsibility for the validity of all materials or the consequences of their use. The authors and publishers have attempted to trace the copyright holders of all material reproduced in this publication and apologize to copyright holders if permission to publish in this form has not been obtained. If any copyright material has not been acknowledged please write and let us know so we may rectify in any future reprint.

Except as permitted under U.S. Copyright Law, no part of this book may be reprinted, reproduced, transmitted, or utilized in any form by any electronic, mechanical, or other means, now known or hereafter invented, including photocopying, microfilming, and recording, or in any information storage or retrieval system, without written permission from the publishers.

For permission to photocopy or use material electronically from this work, please access www.copyright.com (http://www.copyright.com/) or contact the Copyright Clearance Center, Inc. (CCC), 222 Rosewood Drive, Danvers, MA 01923, 978-750-8400. CCC is a not-for-profit organization that provides licenses and registration for a variety of users. For organizations that have been granted a photocopy license by the CCC, a separate system of payment has been arranged.

Trademark Notice: Product or corporate names may be trademarks or registered trademarks, and are used only for identification and explanation without intent to infringe.

Visit the Taylor & Francis Web site at
http://www.taylorandfrancis.com

and the CRC Press Web site at
http://www.crcpress.com

Contents

Preface

This book provides a comprehensive introduction to the research on modeling humans' emotion perception of music, a research topic that emerges in the face of the explosive growth of digital music. Automatic recognition of the perceived emotion of music allows users to retrieve and organize their music collections in a fashion that is more content-centric than conventional metadata-based methods.

Building such a music emotion recognition system, however, is challenging because of the subjective nature of emotion perception. One needs to deal with issues such as the reliability of ground truth data and the difficulty in evaluating the prediction result, which do not exist in other pattern recognition problems such as face recognition and speech recognition. This book provides the details of the methods that have been developed to address the issues related to the ambiguity and granularity of emotion description, the heavy cognitive load of emotion annotation, the subjectivity of emotion perception, and the semantic gap between low-level audio signal and high-level emotion perception.

Specifically, this book deals with a comprehensive introduction of the techniques developed for emotion description and emotion recognition in Chapters 2 and 3. Chapter 4 describes a regression-based computational framework that generalizes emotion recognition from categorical domain to real-valued 2D space and thereby resolves the issues related to emotion description. Chapter 5 describes a ranking-base emotion annotation and model training method that reduces the effort of emotion annotation and enhances the quality of ground truth. Chapters 6–9 describe how to take the subjective nature of emotion perception into account in the development of an automatic music emotion recognition system. Chapters 10–12 present methods that integrate information extracted from lyrics, chord sequence, and genre metadata to improve the accuracy of emotion recognition. After describing an emotion-based music retrieval system that is particularly useful for mobile devices in Chapter 13, we describe research directions that can be extended from the techniques introduced in this book in Chapter 14.

To the best of our knowledge, this is the first book dedicated to automatic music emotion recognition. It is aimed at students and researchers in the fields of computer science, engineering, psychology, and musicology and industrial practitioners in mobile multimedia, database management, digital home, computer–human interaction, and music information retrieval. The reader will learn from this book basic multidisciplinary knowledge of music and emotion and gain inspiration about next-generation multimedia retrieval systems.

In addition, this book provides the technical details of implementing the techniques introduced in this book, twelve example MATLAB® codes, and more than 360 useful references. Therefore, this book can be used as a guidebook for computer scientists and engineers in the development of automatic music emotion recognition systems.

We would like to thank many people who helped us during the course of our music emotion recognition research. First of all we would like to express our sincere thanks to the National Science Council of Taiwan, Chung-Hwa Telecom, Irving T. Ho Foundation, MediaTek Inc., and Microsoft Research Asia for their financial support. We also owe gratitude to many colleagues we worked with in the Multimedia Processing and Communication Lab of National Taiwan University, including Heng-Tze Cheng, Chun-Yu Ko, Ann Lee, Cheng-Te Lee, Chia-Kai Liang, Keng-Sheng Lin, Yu-Ching Lin, Chia-Chu Liu, Ming-Yan Su, and Ya-Fan Su. We are also grateful to Ching-Wei Chen, J. Stephen Downie, Winston Hsu, Olivier Lartillot, Lin-Shan Lee, Lie Lu, Jyh-Shing Roger Jang, Shyh-Kang Jeng, Christopher Raphael, Wen-Yu Su, Douglas Turnbull, George Tzanetakis, Hsin-Min Wang, Ja-Ling Wu, Tien-Lin Wu, and Su-Ling Yeh for helpful discussions and comments. We would also like to thank CRC Press for bringing this book to print.

Finally, this book could not have been finished without the strong support of our family members, especially our spouses, Wan-Hsin Liu and Mei-Hsun Wu.

Yi-Hsuan Yang

Homer H. Chen

Taipei, Taiwan

MATLAB® is a registered trademark of The Math Works, Inc. For product information, please contact:

The Math Works, Inc.
3 Apple Hill Drive
Natick, MA
Tel: 508-647-7000
Fax: 508-647-7001
E-mail: info@mathworks.com
Web: http://www.mathworks.com

Abbreviations

2DES	Two-dimensional emotion space
3DES	Three-dimensional emotion space
AMC	Audio mood classification
AO	Audio only
AP	Audio power
API	Application programming interface
BoU	Bag-of-users
BoW	Bag-of-words
BPM	Beat-per-minute
CH	Chord histogram
DCT	Discrete cosine transform
DWCH	Daubechies wavelets coefficient histogram
EFFC	Early-fusion-by-feature-concatenation
EM	Expectation maximization
FKNN	Fuzzy k-nearest neighbor
FNM	Fuzzy nearest mean
GMM	Gaussian mixture model
GPR	Gaussian process regression
GPS	Global positioning system
GWMER	Groupwise MER
HMM	Hidden Markov model
JS divergence	Jensen–Shannon divergence
KDE	Kernel density estimation
KL divergence	Kullback–Leibler divergence
LCCS	Longest common chord subsequence
LFLC	Late-fusion-by-linear-combination
LFSM	Late-fusion-by-subtask-merging
LOO	Leave-one-out
LPMCC	Linear predictive Mel cepstrum coefficients
MA toolbox	Music analysis toolbox
MER	Music emotion recognition

MEVD	Music emotion variation detection
MFCC	Mel-frequency cepstral coefficient
MIR	Music information retrieval
MIREX	Music information retrieval evaluation exchange
MLR	Multiple linear regression
MPEG	Moving picture experts group
MSE	Mean squared error
MV	Music video
NLP	Natural language processing
NN	Nearest neighbor
PCA	Principal component analysis
PCM	Pulse-code modulation
PCP	Pitch class profile
PLSA	Probabilistic latent semantic analysis
PMER	Personalized MER
QBAE	Query by artist and emotion
QBEP	Query by emotion point
QBET	Query by emotion trajectory
QBLE	Query by lyrics and emotion
RBF	Radial basis function
RM	Residual modeling
RMS	Root-mean-square
RP	Rhythm pattern
RRF	RReliefF
RSS	Really simple syndication
RT	Regression tree
SCF	Spectral crest factor
SDT	Sound description toolbox
SFM	Spectral flatness measure
SONE	Specific loudness sensation coefficients
SPL	Sound pressure level
STFT	Short-time Fourier transform
SVC	Support vector classification
SVM	Support vector machine
SVR	Support vector regression
SWIPE	Sawtooth waveform inspired pitch estimator
System ID	System identification
TF-IDF	Term-frequency inverse-document frequency
TL	Total loudness
TO	Text only
URL	Uniform resource locator
WAV	Waveform audio file format

1

Introduction

One of the most appealing functions of music is that it can convey emotion and modulate a listener's mood [90]. It is generally believed that music cannot be composed, performed, or listened to without affection involvement [159]. Music can bring us to tears, console us when we are grieving, and drive us to love. Music information behavior studies have also identified emotion as an important criterion used by people in music searching and organization. In this chapter, we describe the importance of music emotion recognition, with examples that illustrate the application of emotion-based music retrieval. After briefly describing the system components of a typical music emotion recognition system, we move on to discuss the issues one needs to consider when building the music emotion recognition system.

1.1 Importance of Music Emotion Recognition

Music plays an important role in human life, even more so in the digital age. Never before has such a large collection of music been created and accessed daily by people. The popularity of the Internet and the use of compact audio formats with near CD quality, such as MP3 (MPEG-1 Audio Layer 3), have greatly contributed to the tremendous growth of digital music libraries [340]. The prevailing context in which we encounter music is ubiquitous, including those in which the most routine activities of life take place: waking up, eating, housekeeping, shopping, studying, exercising, driving, and so forth [159]. Conventionally, the management of music collections is based on catalog metadata, such as artist name, album name, and song title. As the amount of content continues to explode, this conventional approach may be no longer sufficient. The way that music information is organized and retrieved has to evolve to meet the ever increasing demand for easy and effective information access [146, 149, 188, 193].

1

Music, as a complex acoustic and temporal structure, is rich in content and expressivity [33]. According to [159], when an individual engages with music as a composer, performer, or listener, a very board range of mental processes is involved, including *representational* and *evaluative*. The representational process includes the perception of meter, rhythm, tonality, harmony, melody, form, and style, whereas the evaluative process includes the perception of preference, aesthetic experience, mood, and emotion. The term *evaluative* is used because such processes are typically both *valenced* and *subjective*. Both the representational and the evaluative processes of music listening can be leveraged to enhance music retrieval. In [146], Huron specifically points out that since the preeminent functions of music are social and psychological, the most useful characterization of music for facilitating large-scale music access would be based on four types of information: style, emotion, genre, and similarity.

According to a study of social tagging on Last.fm [6], a popular commercial music website, emotion tag is the third most frequent type of tags (second to genre and locale) assigned to music pieces by online users [178]. Even though emotion-based music retrieval was a new idea at that time, a survey conducted in 2004 showed that about 28.2% of the participants identified emotion as an important criterion in music seeking and organization (see Table 1.1) [188, 193]. Since then, emotion-based music retrieval has received increasing attention in both academia and the industry [140, 145, 159, 217, 229, 364].

Table 1.1 Responses of 427 Subjects to the Question "When You Search for Music or Music Information, How Likely Are You to Use the Following Search/Browse Options?"

Search/Browse By	Positive Rate	Search/Browse By	Positive Rate
Singer/performer	96.2%	Popularity	31.0%
Title of work(s)	91.7%	**Mood/emotional state**	**28.2%**
Some words of the lyrics	74.0%	Time period	23.8%
Music style/genre	62.7%	Occasions to use	23.6%
Recommendations	62.2%	Instrument(s)	20.8%
Similar artist(s)	59.3%	Place/event where heard	20.7%
Similar music	54.2%	Storyline of music	17.9%
Associated usage (ad, etc.)	41.9%	Tempo	14.2%
Singing/humming	34.8%	Record label	11.7%
Theme (main subject)	33.4%	Publisher	6.0%

Source: Data from J.H. Lee and J.S. Down i.e. *Proc. Int. Conf. Music Information Retrieval* 2004: 441–446 [193].

Figure 1.1 Screen capture of a software media player that uses affective adjectives for music retrieval. For example, *Let's Groove* by the artist B5 is labeled "Edgy / Sexy," while *Cherish* by The Association is labeled "Tender." (courtesy of Gracenote®, Inc.)

Consider two examples that illustrate the application of emotion-based music retrieval. Figure 1.1 shows a PC media player using software and metadata provided by Gracenote®, Inc., an industry leader in music metadata and technology [5]. The Gracenote mood taxonomy consists of over 300 highly specific mood categories, which are organized hierarchically with broader mood categories at the top-level made up of several more specific sub-mood categories. Mood metadata is automatically derived by using Gracenote's proprietary content analysis and machine learning technologies, without any manual labeling or user input. This mood metadata provides an additional criterion by which users can organize and retrieve music in a content-based fashion. As shown in Figure 1.1, the users are able to organize their music collections by various mood categories represented by affective adjectives such as "Peaceful," "Romantic," "Defiant," "Fiery," and "Easygoing," to name a few.

Another music company that uses emotion labels for music organization and retrieval is All Music Guide (AMG) [1], which uses up to 183 emotion labels to describe the affective content of music. Nevertheless, because the emotion labels of AMG are assigned manually by musical experts, only the emotion labels for artists and albums, not for tracks, are provided. For example, the famous singer Michael Jackson is associated with emotion labels including *stylish, confident, rousing, romantic,* and *sentimental*, to name a few (see http://www.allmusic.com/). With these emotion labels, the user can retrieve/browse artists or albums by emotion.

Making computers capable of recognizing the emotion of music also enhances the way humans and computers interact. It is possible to play back music that matches the user's mood detected from physiological, prosodic, or facial cues [22, 154, 192, 210, 253]. A portable device such as an MP3 player or a cellular phone equipped with automatic music emotion recognition (MER) function can then play a song best suited to the emotional state of the user [77, 264]; a smart space (e.g., restaurant, conference room, residence) can play background music best suited the people inside it [148, 201]. For example, in [346] T.-L. Wu et al. proposed an interactive content presenter based on the perceived emotion of multimedia content and the physiological feedback of the user. Multimedia content (photos, music, and Web blog articles) are automatically classified into eight emotion classes (*happy, light, easy, touching, sad, sublime, grand,* and *exciting*) [344] and then organized in a tiling slideshow fashion [56] to create music videos (MVs) [55]. The user's preference of these MVs is detected from physiological signals such as blood pressure and skin conductance and then utilized to recommend the next MV. This retrieval paradigm is functionally powerful since people's criteria for music selection are often related to the emotional state at the moment of music selection [159].

1.2 Recognizing the Perceived Emotion of Music

The relationship between music and emotion has been the subject of much scholarly discussion and empirical research in many different disciplines, including philosophy, musicology, psychology, biology, anthropology, and sociology [159]. In psychology, the notion that music expresses emotion has a venerable history and its validity is rarely debated. A great amount of work has been done by psychologists to study the relationship between music and emotion (see [113, 159] for an exhaustive repository of theory and research in this domain). In these studies, emotions are often divided into three categories: *expressed* emotion, *perceived* emotion, and *felt* (or evoked) emotion [100, 113, 147, 159]. The first one refers to the emotion the performer tries to communicate with the listeners, while the latter two refer to the affective responses of the listeners. We may simply perceive an emotion being expressed in a song (emotion perception) or actually feel an emotion in response to the song (emotion induction). Both perceived emotion and felt emotion, especially the latter, are dependent on an interplay between the musical, personal, and situational factors [100]. We focus on the perceived emotion in this book, for it is relatively less influenced by the situational factors (environment, mood, etc.) of listening.

Engineering study of the problem, however, dates back only to the 2000s or so [90, 164, 203, 212]. From an engineering point of view, one of the main interests is to develop a computational model of music emotion and to facilitate emotion-based music retrieval and organization. Many efforts have been made in the music

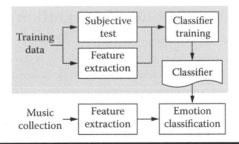

Figure 1.2 Schematic diagram of the categorical approach to MER.

information retrieval (MIR) community for automatic recognition of the perceived emotion of music. A typical approach to MER categorizes emotions into a number of classes (such as *happy, angry, sad,* and *relaxing*) and applies machine learning techniques to train a classifier [140, 164, 183, 203, 211, 214, 217, 288, 297, 316, 336, 344, 365]. Usually, timbre, rhythm, and harmony features of music are extracted to represent the acoustic property of a music piece. Some of the musical parameters controlling the perceived emotion of music have been mapped out by psychologists [156, 157, 159]. Typically a subjective test is conducted to collect the ground truth needed for training the computational model of emotion prediction. The subjects (annotators) are asked to report their emotion perceptions of the music pieces. Because emotion perception is subjective, each music piece is annotated by multiple subjects and the ground truth is set by majority voting. Several classification algorithms have been applied to learn the relationship between music features and emotion labels, such as support vector machines [34, 140, 203, 336], Gaussian mixture models [212], neural networks [90], and *k*-nearest neighbor [338, 365]. After training, the automatic model can be applied to classify the emotion of an input music piece. See Figure 1.2 for a schematic diagram of this *categorical* approach to MER.*

In this section we have only briefly described the system components of a typical music emotion recognition system. The details of the process of data preparation, subjective test, and model training are provided in Chapter 2, which presents an overview of emotion description and recognition. In Chapter 3, we focus on the music features that have been adopted for modeling our emotion perception of music, including features that represent the following five perceptual dimensions of music listening: energy, rhythm, temporal, spectrum, and harmony.

---

* It is noted that psychologists tend to use *emotion* to describe our affective response to music, while MIR researchers tend to use *mood*. While emotion is usually understood as a short-lived experience in response to an object (here music), mood is a longer experience without specific object connection [299]. We follow the psychologists in this book. Moreover, we use *music emotion* as a short term for "emotions that are perceived in music."

1.3 Issues of Music Emotion Recognition

As MER is still in its infancy, there are many open issues [357]. In this section, we describe the four major issues that are often discussed in research work on MER. As summarized in Table 1.2, the remainder of the book is dedicated to the methods that have been developed to address these issues.

1.3.1 Ambiguity and Granularity of Emotion Description

The aforementioned categorical approach to MER, though widely adopted, suffers from the imperfect relationship between emotions and the affective terms that denote emotions, and the problem of choosing which and how many affective terms to be included in the taxonomy. The former is referred to as the *ambiguity* issue, while the latter is referred to as the *granularity* issue.

Ambiguity, or fuzziness, is a characteristic of natural language categories in general [125]. Emotions, in particular, are very fuzzy concepts. As noted by J. A. Russell [260], a "human being usually is able to recognize emotional state but has difficulties with its proper defining." One of the main disadvantages of the categorical approach is thus the ambiguity associated with the affective terms. Comparing the affective terms is not trivial since there are semantic similarities between different terms. For example, for the affective terms *calm/peaceful, carefree, laid-back/mellow, relaxing,* and *soft,* one cannot simply quantify their similarity as zero just because they are different words or quantify their similarity as one because they are synonyms [294]. These terms can be used by people to either differentiate the subtlety of different emotion perceptions or describe the same emotion perception. Other examples include *cheerful, happy, joyous, party/celebratory* and *melancholy, gloomy, sad, somber,* to name a few.* Such ambiguity often confuses the subjects in the subjective test and the users who want to retrieve music according to emotion.

To avoid the ambiguity of affective terms and reduce the system development effort, many researchers use the basic emotions (e.g., happy, angry, sad, and relaxing) or emotion clusters as the classification taxonomy [90, 137, 203, 217, 352]. This approach faces the granularity issue; namely, the number of emotion classes included in the emotion taxonomy is too small in comparison with the richness of emotion perceived by humans. This is undesirable because a retrieval system with limited emotion vocabulary may not satisfy the user requirement in real-world music retrieval applications. Using a finer granularity for emotion description does not necessarily address the issue because it introduces a fuzzy boundary between the affective terms (the ambiguity issue) [27] and because developing an automatic system that precisely classifies music into a large number of classes is very difficult. It is often observed that the classification accuracy of an automatic model is inversely proportional to the number of classes considered [325].

---

* All these terms are used by All Music Guide [1].

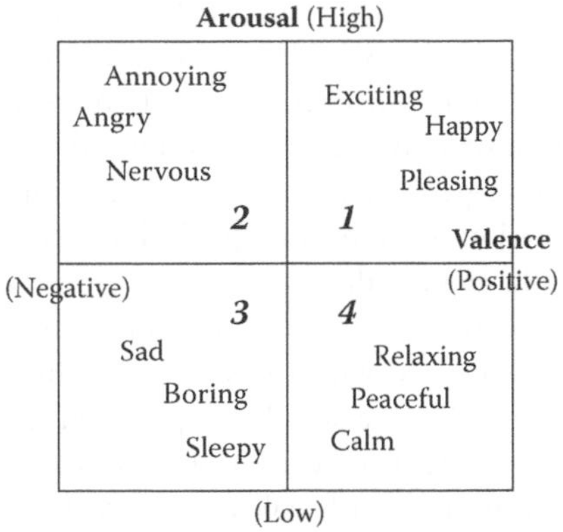

Arousal (High)

Annoying Angry Nervous **2**	Exciting Happy Pleasing **1**

(Negative)   **Valence**   (Positive)

3
Sad
   Boring
      Sleepy
	4
	Relaxing
	Peaceful
	Calm

(Low)

Figure 1.3   The 2D valence-arousal emotion plane (the positions of the affective terms are only approximated, not exact [272, 310]).

In Chapter 4, we describe a *dimensional* approach to MER that defines emotions as points in 2D space in terms of valence (how positive or negative) and arousal (how exciting or calming)—the two emotion dimensions found to be most fundamental by psychologists [272, 310]. For example, *happy* is an emotion of positive valence and high arousal, whereas *sad* is an emotion of negative valence and low arousal; see Figure 1.3. In this approach, MER becomes the prediction of the valence and arousal (VA) values of a song corresponding to an emotion point in the emotion plane [80, 167, 220, 355–357, 362, 364]. This way, the granularity and ambiguity issues associated with emotion classes no longer exist because no categorical class is needed and because the emotion plane implicitly offers an infinite number of emotion descriptions. This dimensional conceptualization of emotion has been found simple, highly reliable, and easily understood by participants in psychological experiments [159]. Moreover, because the 2D plane provides a simple means for user interface, novel emotion-based music organization, browsing, and retrieval methods can be easily created for mobile devices that have small display space. For example, a user can specify a point in the plane to retrieve songs of a certain emotion or draw a path to create a playlist of songs with various emotions corresponding to points on the trajectory [362]. See Chapter 4 for more technical descriptions and Chapter 13 for a user interface built on this idea.

1.3.2 Heavy Cognitive Load of Emotion Annotation

To collect the ground truth needed for training an automatic model, a subjective test is typically conducted by inviting human subjects to annotate the emotion of music pieces. To reduce the administrative effort, each music piece is often annotated by less than three subjects (often musical *experts* to gain consensus of the annotation result) [203, 217, 297, 316]. This practice is problematic because, as it has been argued, the everyday contexts in which musical experts experience music are so different from those of nonexperts (who form the vast bulk of the population) and require separate treatment [300]. Since an MER system is expected to be used in the everyday context, the emotion annotation should be carried out by *ordinary people*. The psychology literature suggests that each stimulus be annotated by more than 30 annotators for the annotation to be reliable [65]. This requires a great amount of annotations to develop a large-scale data set.

The cognitive load of collecting emotion labels for training a categorical MER system has recently been alleviated with the surge of online tagging websites such as AMG [1] and Last.fm [6]. With a simple script-based URL lookup, researchers can easily obtain the emotion tags from these websites. Many MER researchers have adopted this approach to ground truth collection [34, 139, 142, 189]. As the online tags may be inaccurate (e.g., in AMG the emotion labels are applied to artists and albums, not tracks) or noisy (e.g., in Last.fm users can tag music with arbitrary words) [207], social tagging games have been designed to harness the so-called human computation and make the annotation more engaging [26, 190, 224, 322]. When users play the Web-based games, they would in the meantime (unconsciously) contribute high-quality annotations to the system, with little administrative effort from the developer side.

The emotion annotation process of dimensional MER, however, requires emotion ratings in the valence and arousal dimensions. Such emotion ratings cannot be obtained from the online repository. Moreover, it has been found that rating emotion in a continuum, using either the standard ordinal rating scale or the graphic rating scale [364, 366], imposes a heavy cognitive load on the subjects [355, 356]. It is also difficult to ensure a consistent rating scale between different subjects and within the same subject [244]. As a result, the quality of the ground truth varies, which in turn degrades the accuracy of the MER system.

Chapter 5 provides the detail of a *ranking* approach that is developed to relieve the effort of collecting emotion annotations for dimensional MER. In this approach, a subject is asked to compare the affective content of two songs and determine, for example, which song has a higher arousal value, instead of the exact emotion values. It has been shown by experiments that this scheme reduces the cognitive load of emotion annotation and enhances the quality of the ground truth. Chapter 5 also describes a computational model that exploits the ranking-based annotations and is free of the multiple ties in the ground truth. It performs consistently well across different experiment settings.

1.3.3 Subjectivity of Emotional Perception

Music perception is intrinsically subjective and is under the influence of many factors such as cultural background, age, gender, personality, training, and so forth [16]. The interactions between music and listener may also involve the listener's familiarity with the music [150] and his/her musical preferences [132, 150]. Because of this subjectivity issue, it is difficult to achieve consensus regarding which affective term best characterizes the emotion perception of a music piece. Therefore, conventional categorical approaches that simply assign one emotion class to each music piece in a deterministic manner do not perform well in practice. The dimensional approach to MER also faces the subjectivity issue that people can respond differently to the same song. Despite that the subjective nature of emotion perception is well recognized, little effort has been made to take the subjectivity into account. Many researchers either assume a consensus can be achieved (particularly for classic music) [336], discard those songs for which a consensus cannot be achieved [211, 217], or simply leave this issue unaddressed [203].

To give the reader a clear picture of the research devoted to the subjectivity issue of MER, we divide the research work into fuzzy approach (Chapter 6), personalized MER and groupwise MER (Chapter 7), two-layer personalization (Chapter 8), and emotion distribution prediction (Chapter 9). We begin with the categorical approach to MER and describe a *fuzzy* approach that measures the strength of each emotion class in association with the song under classification [365]. By assigning each music piece a *soft* label that indicates how likely a certain emotion would be perceived when listening to the piece, the prediction result becomes less deterministic. For example, a song could be 70% likely to be relaxing and 30% likely to be sad.

The next three chapters present techniques that address the subjectivity issue of dimensional MER. Two relatively more intuitive methods are described in Chapter 7. The first one utilizes user feedback to train a personalized prediction model, whereas the second one utilizes the personal factors of the users (e.g., gender, music experience, and personality) to train prediction models that respond to different types of users. Chapter 8 discusses a more advanced two-layer personalization scheme that performs better than the aforementioned two methods.

In Chapter 9, we describe a computational framework that assigns *soft* emotion values to music pieces, like the fuzzy approach assigns the assignment of soft emotion labels in the fuzzy approach. This computational framework, which is called *music emotion distribution prediction*, models the perceived emotions of a song as a probabilistic distribution in the emotion plane and utilizes regression techniques to compute the probability of an emotion perceived in a song based on music features [354]. This computational framework provides a basis for personalized emotion-based retrieval and opens a new window to music understanding.

1.3.4 Semantic Gap between Low-Level Audio Signal and High-Level Human Perception

The viability of an MER system largely lies in the accuracy of emotion recognition. However, due to the so-called semantic gap between the object feature level and the human cognitive level of emotion perception, it is difficult to accurately compute the emotion values, especially the valence values [217, 282, 314, 364]. What

Table 1.2 Issues of MER and the Corresponding Methods

Chapter(s)	Issue	Method(s)
4	Ambiguity and granularity of emotion description	Regression approach
5	Heavy cognitive load of emotion annotation	Ranking approach
6–9	Subjectivity of emotion perception	Fuzzy approach, personalized MER, groupwise MER, two-layer personalization, emotion distribution prediction
10–12	Semantic gap between low-level features and high-level perception	Leveraging lyrics, chord progression, and genre metadata to improve MER

intrinsic element of music, if any, causes a listener to create a specific emotional perception is still far from well understood. In consequence, the performance of conventional methods that exploit only the low-level audio features seems to have reached a limit.

For example, the audio mood classification (AMC) task of the annual music information retrieval evaluation exchange (MIREX) has been held since 2007, aiming at promoting MER research and providing benchmark comparisons [140].* Five emotion clusters are used in this contest: *passionate, rollicking, literate, humorous,* and *aggressive* [137]. Table 1.3 shows the top three performers (in terms of raw mean classification accuracy) of this contest from 2007 to 2010. It can be observed that, despite that various low-level audio features and their combinations have been used [140], the classification accuracy never exceeds 70%.†

Chapters 10–12 deal with the use of mid-level features, including lyrics, chord progression, and genre metadata to improve the accuracy of categorical MER. Available data for MER are not limited to the raw audio signal. Complementary to music signal, lyrics are semantically rich and have profound impact on human perception of music [20]. Chord sequence, which describes harmonic progression and tonal structure of music, is often related to the emotion perception of music. Similar chord sequences can be observed in songs that are close in emotion. Chapters 10 and 11 show that the incorporation of lyrics and chord progression does improve the accuracy of emotion prediction, especially for valence prediction.

---

* [Online] http://music-ir.org/mirexwiki
† Note the performance is also influenced by the ambiguity issue inherent to the five-class emotion taxonomy used by MIREX [140] and the subjectivity issue inherent to emotion perception.

**Table 1.3   Top Three Performers
of Audio Mood Classification
(AMC) of MIREX from 2007 to 2010
(Retrieved from the Website of
MIREX [11])**

Contest	Top Three Accuracy
AMC 2007	65.67%, 65.50%, 63.67%
AMC 2008	63.67%, 56.00%, 55.00%
AMC 2009	61.50%, 60.50%, 59.67%
AMC 2010	64.17%, 63.83%, 63.17%

Genre, by which a song is classified into classical, jazz, hip-hop, etc., has been used to describe the intrinsic form of music for a long time [28]. Genre and emotion provide complementary descriptions of music content and often correlate with each other. For example, a rock song is often aggressive, and a rhythm and blues (R&B) song is more likely to be sentimental. Chapter 12 describes a computational framework that utilized genre metadata to improve MER.

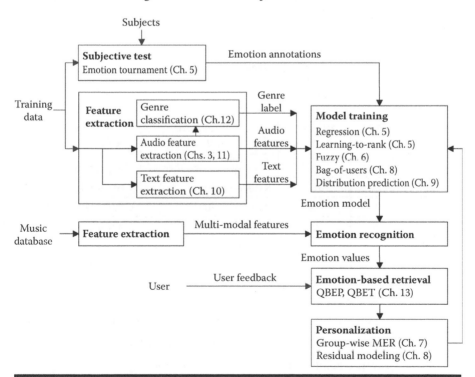

Figure 1.4   Overview of the book.

1.4 Summary

So far, we have described the key motivations of the research on music emotion recognition. We have also described four main challenges of MER: the ambiguity and granularity issues of emotion description, the heavy cognitive load of emotion annotation, the subjective nature of emotion perception, and the semantic gap between low-level features and high-level perception. The remainder of the book is structured to introduce methods that have been developed to address these issues.

Figure 1.4 illustrates the overall organization of this book. We first describe the low-level features that are often extracted to model music emotion in Chapter 3. Chapter 4 describes a regression approach for predicting the valence and arousal values of a music piece. Chapter 5 describes a ranking-based annotation method that reduces the effort of collecting annotations for numerical emotion values. Chapters 10–12 describe the use of mid-level features extracted from lyrics, chord sequence, and genre metadata to improve the accuracy of MER. We also describe several computational models that address the subjectivity issues of MER in Chapters 6–9. Based on the emotion models, emotion-based retrieval systems can be easily realized to help users manage and retrieve music with a 2D interface, as described in Chapter 13.

Table 1.4   The Data Sets Utilized in This Book

	Number of Songs	*Average Number of Subjects per Song*	*Annotation Method*	*Related Chapter(s)*
1a	195	7	**Classify** to 4 emotions	Chapters 6, 11
1b	195	10+	**Rate** VA values	Chapter 4
2	60	40	**Rate** VA values	Chapters 5, 7–9
3a	1240	4.3	**Rank** valence	Chapter 5
3b	1240	1	**Classify** to 4 emotions	Chapter 10
4	1535	N/A	**Classify** to 12 emotions	Chapter 12

1b: http://mpac.ee.ntu.edu.tw/~ yihsuan/MER/taslp08/

2: http://mpac.ee.ntu.edu.tw/~ yihsuan/MER/NTUMIR-60/

3a: http://mpac.ee.ntu.edu.tw/~ yihsuan/MER/NTUMIR-1240/

4: http://mpac.ee.ntu.edu.tw/~ vagante/genreEmo/

This book includes several empirical evaluations of MER systems. Table 1.4 summarizes the data sets that are utilized in this book. Many of them can be freely downloaded from the Internet. With these data sets and the techniques introduced in this book, the readers should be able to construct their own music emotion recognition systems.

2

Overview of Emotion Description and Recognition

It has been claimed that music is one of the finest languages of emotion [252]. The relationship between music and emotion has been studied by researchers from several disciplines. Many researchers have suggested that music is an excellent medium for studying emotion, because people tend to make judgments about music and their affective responses to music [102, 159]. The purpose of this chapter is to provide an overview of the techniques developed for emotion description and emotion recognition. Specifically, this chapter is divided into two parts. The first part discusses the emotion models that have been proposed by psychologists, so that the readers can get a sense of how emotions are usually conceptualized. The second part describes some well-known work on MER and provides the details of the basic components of an MER system. The concepts introduced in this chapter are important to the understanding of the remaining chapters of the book.

2.1 Emotion Description

The relationship between music and emotion has been well studied by psychologists for decades. The research problems faced by psychologists include whether the everyday emotions are the same as emotions that are perceived in music, whether music *represents* emotions (that are perceived by the listener) or *induces* emotions (that are felt by the listener), how the musical, personal, and situational factors affect emotion perception, and how we should conceptualize music emotion [159].

As there has been rich literature on these research topics, below we focus on emotion conceptualization alone, for it is closely related to MER.

In the study of emotion conceptualization, psychologists often utilize people's verbal reports of emotion responses [159]. For example, the celebrated paper of Hevner [126] studied the relationship between music and emotion through experiments in which subjects are asked to report the adjectives that came to their minds as the most representative part of a music piece played. From these empirical studies, a great variety of emotion models have been proposed, most of which belong to one of the following two approaches to emotion conceptualization: the categorical approach and the dimensional approach.

2.1.1 Categorical Approach

The categorical approach to emotion conceptualization considers that people experience emotions as categories that are distinct from each other. Essential to this approach is the concept of basic emotions, that is, the idea that there are a limited number of innate and universal emotion categories, such as happiness, sadness, anger, fear, disgust, and surprise, from which all other emotion classes can be derived [22, 82, 154, 166, 186, 192, 253, 288]. Each "basic" emotion can be defined functionally in terms of a key appraisal of goal-relevant events that have occurred frequently during evolution. The basic emotions can be found in all cultures, and they are often associated with distinct patterns of physiological changes or emotional expressions. The notion of basic emotions is diversified; different researchers have come up with different sets of basic emotions [299].

Another famous categorical approach to emotion conceptualization is Hevner's adjective checklist [126, 127]. Through experiments, eight clusters of affective adjectives are discovered and laid out in a circle, as shown in Figure 2.1. The adjectives within each cluster are similar, whereas the meaning of neighboring clusters varies in a cumulative way until reaching a contrast in the opposite position. Hevner's adjective checklist (proposed in 1935) was later refined and regrouped into ten groups by Farnsworth in 1954 [87, 88] and into nine groups in 2003 by Schubert [285]. For example, in [285], 46 affective adjectives are grouped according to their positions on a two-dimensional emotion space. The resulting nine clusters and the associated affective adjectives are shown in Table 2.1.

The major drawback of the categorical approach is that the number of primary emotion classes is too small in comparison with the richness of music emotion perceived by humans. Using a finer granularity, on other hand, does not necessarily solve the problem because the language for describing emotions is inherently ambiguous and varies from person to person [158]. Moreover, using a large number of emotion classes could overwhelm the subjects and is impractical for psychological studies [299].

1
spiritual
lofty
awe-inspiring
dignified
sacred
solemn sober
serious

8
vigorous
robust
emphatic
martial
ponderous
majestic
exalting

2
pathetic
doleful
sad
mournful
tragic
melancholy
frustrated
depressing
gloomy
heavy
dark

7
exhilarated
soaring
triumphant
dramatic
passionate
sensational
agitated
exciting
impetuous
restless

3
dreamy
yielding
tender
sentimental
longing
yearning
pleading
plaintive

6
merry
joyous
gay
happy
cheerful
bright

4
lyrical
leisurely
satisfying
serene
tranquil
quiet
soothing

5
humorous
playful
whimsical
fanciful
quaint
sprightly
delicate
light
graceful

Figure 2.1 Hevner's eight clusters of affective terms [126, 127].

Table 2.1 The Nine Emotion Clusters Proposed by E. Schubert in 2003 [285]

Cluster	Emotions in Each Cluster
1	Bright, cheerful, happy, joyous
2	Humorous, light, lyrical, merry, playful
3	Calm, delicate, graceful, quiet, relaxed, serene, soothing, tender, tranquil
4	Dreamy, sentimental
5	Dark, depressing, gloomy, melancholy, mournful, sad, solemn
6	Heavy, majestic, sacred, serious, spiritual, vigorous
7	Tragic, yearning
8	Agitated, angry, restless, tense
9	Dramatic, exciting, exhilarated, passionate, sensational, soaring, triumphant

2.1.2 Dimensional Approach

While the categorical approach focuses mainly on the characteristics that distinguish emotions from one another, the dimensional approach to emotion conceptualization focuses on identifying emotions based on their positions on a small number of emotion "dimensions" with named axes, which are intended to correspond to internal human representations of emotion. These internal emotion dimensions are found by analyzing the correlation between affective terms. This is often done by asking human subjects to use a large number of rating scales of affective terms to describe the emotion of music stimulus and then employing factor analysis techniques to obtain a small number of fundamental factors (dimensions) from the correlations between the scales. Although the names differ, past researchers gave very similar interpretations of the resulting factors: tension/energy, gaiety-gloom, and solemnity-triviality; intensity-softness, pleasantness-unpleasantness, and solemnity-triviality; tension-relaxation, gaiety-gloom, and attraction-repulsion; to name a few [243, 256, 265, 272, 310, 337]. It has been found that most of these factors correspond to the following three dimensions of emotion: *valence* (or pleasantness; positive and negative affective states), *arousal* (or activation; energy and stimulation level), and *dominance* (or potency; a sense of control or freedom to act) [278].

In his seminal work, Russell proposed a circumplex model of emotion [272]. This model consists of a two-dimensional, circular structure involving the dimensions of valence and arousal. Within this structure, emotions that are inversely correlated are placed across the circle from one another. Supportive evidence was obtained by scaling 28 affective adjectives in four different ways: a circular ordering of variables by Ross's technique [270], a multidimensional scaling procedure [78] based on perceived similarity among the terms, a unidimensional scaling on hypothesized pleasure-displeasure and degree-of-arousal dimensions, and a principal component analysis [319] of 343 subjects' self-reports of their current affective states [272].*
As shown in Figure 2.2, all these methods result in a valence-arousal and circular-structure arrangement of the 28 affective terms (the horizontal axis corresponds to valence, whereas the vertical axis corresponds to arousal). Interestingly, it can be found that emotions that are reliably perceived, such as happiness and sadness, appear to have distinctive valence and arousal values. Emotions that are easy to be confused, such as calm and sadness, appear to have similar valence and arousal values. This result implies that valence and arousal may be the most fundamental and most clearly communicated emotion dimensions among others.

Among the strengths of the circumplex model is that it suggests a simple yet powerful way of organizing different emotions in terms of their affect appraisals (valence) and physiological reactions (arousal), and it allows direct comparison of

---

* The 28 terms are *happy, delighted, excited, astonished, aroused, tense, alarmed, angry, afraid, annoyed, distressed, frustrated, miserable, sad, gloomy, depressed, bored, droopy, tired, sleepy, calm, relaxed, satisfied, at ease, content, serene, glad and pleased.*

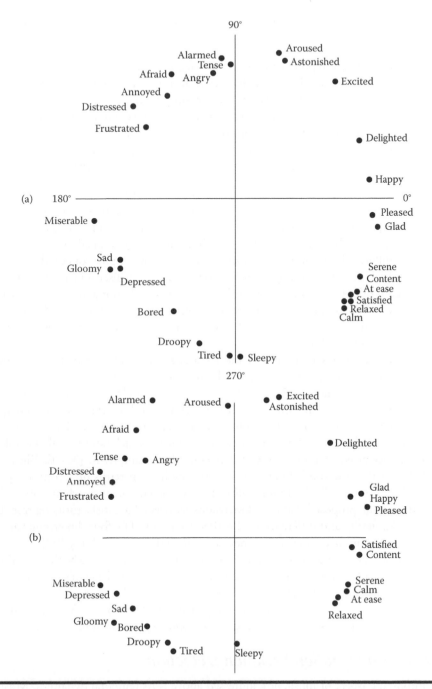

Figure 2.2 The Russell's circumplex model of affect; the result of scaling 28 affective terms using (a) circular ordering and (b) multidimensional scaling (Data from J.A. Russell. *J. Personality & Social Psychology* **39(6): 1161–1178, 1980).**

different emotions on two standard and important dimensions. In [159] it is noted that

> from a theoretical point of view one can argue that activation or arousal variation is one of the major distinctive features of emotion, and the valence dimension, the pervasive pleasant-unpleasant quality of experience, maps directly into the classic approach-avoidance action tendencies that have direct relevance for behavior. Recently, Russell even went as far as claiming that valence and arousal are the "core processes" of affect, constituting the raw material or primitive of emotional experience [273].

The dimensional approach, however, is not free of criticism. It is argued that the dimensional approach blurs important psychological distinctions and consequently obscures important aspects of the emotion process [191]. For example, anger and fear are placed close in the valence-arousal plane (both in the second quadrant), but they have very different implications for the organism. The same applies for boredom and melancholy. Using the two-dimensional model would not discriminate the music pieces that produce one emotion from the other and would not allow a theoretical examination of the origin and mechanisms of such affective effects [299]. Moreover, it has been argued that using only a few emotion dimensions cannot describe all emotions without residuum [67].

In response to this deficiency, some researchers have advocated the addition of a third dimension, such as potency (dominant–submissive), to obtain a more complete picture of emotion [33,67,80]. However, this would increase the cognitive load on the subjects at the same time. It requires a careful interface design to help subjects annotate emotion in three-dimensional space. In addition, what the third dimension will be and whether a three-dimensional model captures all possible emotions perceived in music are still debatable. For example, in [33] E. Bigand et al. found that the third dimension is better defined in terms of a continuity–discontinuity or melodic–harmonic contrast rather than dominance, whereas in [92] J. Fontaine et al. proposed that four dimensions are needed to satisfactorily represent semantic similarity and difference of the affective terms. The four dimensions are, in order of importance, valence, potency, arousal, and unpredictability [92].

The general consensus in the research community so far appears to be that two dimensions provide a good balance between a parsimonious definition of emotion and the complexity of the study [159]. This two-dimensional valence-arousal conceptualization of emotion is also adopted in many chapters of this book. We sometimes refer to the two-dimensional emotion space as *emotion plane* or simply 2DES.

2.1.3 *Music Emotion Variation Detection*

An important aspect of music not addressed above is its temporal dynamics. Most research has focused on music pieces that are homogeneous with respect to emotional expression. However, as many styles of music (e.g., classical music) express different emotions as time unfolds, it is important to investigate the time-varying relationship between music and emotion. Techniques for *continuous* recording, sometimes combined with nonverbal responses, have been used to study the dynamic process of emotion perception since the seminal work of F. V. Nielsen [237]. According to E. Schubert [282],

> Continuous response tools measure self-reported affective responses during the listening process and help researchers to better understand the moment-to-moment fluctuations in responses. The approach means that the music does not need to be broken into small portions to enable lucid response, nor does the listener have to compress their response by giving an overall impression at the end of the excerpt. A more realistic listening experience is possible. This realism [118] contributes to the ecological validity of experimental design at the expense of experimental control.

Because categorical responses require the subjects to constantly choose an emotion term, the dimensional approach to emotion conceptualization, in contrast, is found more useful for capturing the continuous changes of emotional expression [100, 283]. Usually subjects are asked to rate the valence and arousal values (typically by clicking a point in the emotion plane) every one second in response to the stimulus [70, 181, 274]. Psychologists then analyze the continuous recording to investigate the relationship between music and emotion [81, 284, 312]. Readers are referred to [282] for a comprehensive overview of psychological studies of music emotion variation.

2.2 Emotion Recognition

A great many efforts have been made by MIR researchers to automate MER, and the type of music under study has gradually shifted over the past few years from symbolic music [164, 214, 336, 367] to raw audio signals and from Western classical music [173, 203, 214, 217, 336] to popular music. Western classical music is often chosen in the early studies partly because of the rich literature in musicology and psychology on classical music, and partly because it seems to be easier to gain agreement on the perceived emotion of a classical music selection. However, since the purpose of MER is to facilitate music retrieval and management in everyday music listening, and since it is the popular music that dominates the everyday music listening, analyzing the affective content of popular music has gained increasing attention lately.

The machine learning technique used for training an automatic recognition model typically consists of the following steps: A number of features are extracted to represent the music signal, the ground truth emotion labels or emotion values are collected from human annotators (subjects), and a learning algorithm is applied to learn the relationships between music features and emotion labels/values. The resulting computational model is then applied to predict the emotion of an input song.

Table 2.2 Comparison of Research on Automatic Prediction of Music Emotion

Methodology	Conceptualization of Emotion	Description
Categorical MER	Categorical	Predicting the *discrete* class labels of music pieces [140, 217, 288]
Dimensional MER	Dimensional	Predicting the *numerical* emotion values of music pieces [80, 220, 364]
MEVD	Dimensional	Predicting the *continuous* emotion variation within each music piece [173, 282]

A central issue of MER is the conceptualization of emotion and the associated emotion taxonomy. Different viewpoints on this issue have led to different ways of emotion annotation, model training, and data visualization. As shown in Table 2.2, research work on MER can be classified into three approaches. The *categorical* approach categorizes emotions into a number of discrete classes and applies machine learning techniques to train a classifier. The predicted emotion labels can be incorporated into a text-based or metadata-based music retrieval system. The *dimensional* approach to MER defines emotions as numerical values over a number of emotion dimensions (e.g., valence and arousal). A regression model is trained to predict the emotion values that represent the affective content of a song, thereby representing the song as a point in an emotion space. Users can then organize, browse, and retrieve music pieces in the emotion space, which provides a simple means for user interface. Finally, instead of predicting an emotion label or value that represents a song, *music emotion variation detection* (MEVD) focuses on the dynamic process of music emotion recognition and makes emotion predictions for every short-time segment of a song, resulting in a series of emotion predictions. Users can then track the emotion variation of a song as time unfolds. Below we discuss the three methodologies separately.

2.2.1 Categorical Approach

The major advantage of the categorical approach to MER, or categorical MER, is that it is easy to be incorporated into a text-based or metadata-based retrieval system. Similar to other music metadata for genres and instrumentations, emotion labels provide an atomic description of music that allows users to retrieve music through a few keywords. Much work followed this direction and trained classifiers that assign a single emotion label to each music segment [79, 140, 211, 217]. Some key issues of MER have also been identified, such as the granularity and ambiguity issues, the subjectivity of emotion perception, the semantic gap between the object feature level and the human cognitive level of emotion perception, and the lack of a standard taxonomy [217, 278, 308, 325, 364]. Many of these issues have been discussed in Chapter 1.

Below we describe the commonly adopted methods and corresponding data preparation, subjective test, and model training for categorical MER.

2.2.1.1 Data Collection

For lack of a common database, most researchers have to compile their own [3, 352]. A large-scale database covering all sorts of music types and genres is desirable. It is often suggested that one should get rid of the so-called *album effect* or *artist effect* and collect music pieces from a variety of albums and artists [169]. Because manual annotation is labor intensive, the size of the database of the early work on MER is usually less than one thousand.

There are many factors that impede the construction of a common database. First, there is still no consensus on which emotion model or how many emotion categories should be used. As Table 2.3 shows, the numbers of emotion classes adopted in past work include 3 classes [314], 4 classes [90, 183, 217, 341, 365], 5 classes [137, 140], 6 classes [316, 336], 8 classes [343], 13 classes [203, 340], and 18 classes [142], to name a few. The adopted emotion taxonomy is based on the basic emotions proposed by psychologists or derived from the clustering of affective terms or emotion tags (e.g., [137, 189]). Comparing systems that use different emotion categories and different data sets is virtually impossible. Second, due to the copyright issues, the audio files cannot be distributed as freely as other multimedia data such as text documents or images [109, 227]. Although the emotion annotations can be made publicly available, the audio files cannot. The audio files are needed if one wants to extract new music features relevant to emotion expression.

In response to this need, the audio mood classification (AMC) task of the annual music information retrieval evaluation exchange (MIREX) has been held since 2007, aiming at promoting MER research and providing benchmark comparisons [140]. The audio files are available to the participants of the task, who have agreed not to distribute the files for commercial purpose. Being the only benchmark in the field of MER so far, this contest draws many participants every year. For example, six teams participated in the AMC 2007 and 16 teams in the AMC 2009. However, MIREX uses an emotion taxonomy that consists of five emotion clusters (see Table 2.4) [137],* which have not been frequently used in past MER work (cf. Table 2.3). A more popular emotion taxonomy is to categorize emotions to the four emotion classes: *happy, angry, sad,* and *relaxing,* partly because they are related to the basic emotions studied in psychology and partly because they cover the four quadrants of the two-dimensional valence-arousal plane [183]. Moreover, it has been pointed

---

* The five-emotion taxonomy is determined via a statistical examination of the emotion tags obtained from AMG [1]. See [137] for more details.

Table 2.3   Comparison of Some Well-Known Work on MER

Approach	# Emotion	# Song	Genre	# Subject per Song	Learning Algorithm
Feng 03 [90]	4	223	Pop	N/A	Neural network
Li 03 [203]	13	499	Pop	1	Multilabel SVC
Li 04 [204]	3	235	Jazz	2	Multilabel SVC
Wang 04 [336]	6	N/A	Classical	20	SVC [69]
Wieczorkowska 04 [338]	13	303	Pop	1	k-NN [78]
Leman 05 [196, 197]	15	60	Pop	40	MLR [291]
Tolos 05 [314]	3	30	Pop	10	Max. likelihood
Wieczorkowska 06 [340]	13	875	Pop	1	k-NN
Yang 06 [365]	4	195	Pop	>10	Fuzzy k-NN [165]
Lu 06 [217]	4	250	Classical	3	SVC
Wu 06 [341]	4	75	Pop	60	SVC
Skowronek 07 [298]	12	1059	Pop	6	
Hu 08 [140]	5	1250	Pop	<8	
Laurier 08 [183]	4	1000	Pop	from Last.fm	SVC
Wu 08 [344]	8	1200	Pop	28.2	SVC
Trohidis 08 [316]	6	593	Pop	3	MLkNN [369]
Lin 09 [207]	12	1535	Pop	from AMG	Multilabel SVC
Han 09 [114]	11	165	Pop	from AMG	SVR [301]
Hu 09 [142]	18	4578	Pop	from Last.fm	SVC
Korhonen 06 [173]	2DES	6	Classical	35	System ID [215]
MacDorman 07 [163]	2DES	100	Pop	85	NN
Yang 07 [354, 361, 366]	2DES	60	Pop	40	SVR [301]
Yang 08 [364]	2DES	195	Pop	>10	SVR
Yang 09 [355]	2DES	1240	Pop	4.3	Listnet [49]
Schmidt 09 [279]	2DES	120	Pop	>20	MLR
Eerola 09 [80]	3DES	110	Soundtrack	116	MLR

Table 2.4   The Emotion Taxonomy Adopted in MIREX [140]

Cluster	Description
1	Passionate, rousing, confident, boisterous, rowdy
2	Rollicking, cheerful, fun, sweet, amiable/good-natured
3	Literate, poignant, wistful, bittersweet, autumnal, brooding
4	Humorous, silly, campy, quirky, whimsical, witty, wry
5	Aggressive, fiery, tense/anxious, intense, volatile, visceral

out that there is a semantic overlap (ambiguity) between clusters 2 and 4, and an acoustic overlap between clusters 1 and 5 [184]. The issues concerning how many and which emotion classes should be used seem to remain open.

2.2.1.2 Data Preprocessing

To compare the music pieces fairly, the music pieces are normally converted to a standard format (e.g., 22,050 Hz sampling frequency, 16 bits precision, and mono channel). Moreover, since complete music pieces can contain sections with different emotions (cf. Sections 2.1.3 and 2.2.3), a 20- to 30-second segment that is representative of the whole song is often selected to reduce the emotion variation within the segment and to lessen the burden of emotion annotation on the subjects [140, 217]. This segment/selection process is typically done by one of the following methods: manually selecting the most representative part [197, 297, 364], conducting music structure analysis to extract the chorus section [59, 221, 306], or simply selecting the middle 30-second segment [140] or the 30-second segment starting from the 30th second of a song [276, 355, 366]. Few studies, if any, have been conducted to investigate the influence of music segmentation on emotion recognition.

Regarding the length of the music segment, a good remark can be found in [163]:

> In principle, we would like the segment to be as short as possible so that our analysis of the song's dynamics can likewise be as fine grained as possible. The expression of a shorter segment will also tend to be more homogeneous, resulting in higher consistency in an individual listener's ratings. Unfortunately, if the segment is too short, the listener cannot hear enough of it to make an accurate determination of its emotional content. In addition, ratings of very short segments lack ecological validity because the segment is stripped off its surrounding context.

One may find from the literature that a 30-second segment is a common choice, perhaps because it is the typical length of a chorus section of popular music. As for classical music, Z.-Z. Xiao et al. have empirically studied which length of music segment best presents the stable mood states of classical music and found that 6-second or 8-second segments seem to be good [348].

It is also a common practice to normalize the volume of music pieces to a standard value to mitigate the *production effect* (i.e., some songs are recorded with a higher volume, while others are recorded with a lower volume). A possible approach of volume normalization is to look for the loudest volume of the audio waveform and then amplify or attenuate the entire waveform until the loudest volume reaches a particular value. This approach is implemented in Cool Edit Pro, a famous music editing tool [2].*

Another approach is to normalize with respect to the root-mean-square (rms) energy or the sound pressure level (SPL) of music signal. The former is defined as

$$p_{\mathrm{rms}} = \sqrt{\frac{x_1^2 + x_2^2 + \cdots + x_i^2 + \cdots + x_n^2}{n}}, \tag{2.1}$$

where x_i^2 is the energy of the i-th sample of the music signal and n is the length of the music signal, whereas the latter is defined as

$$L_p = 10 \log_{10} \left(\frac{p_{\mathrm{rms}}}{p_{\mathrm{ref}}} \right)^2 = 20 \log_{10} \left(\frac{p_{\mathrm{rms}}}{p_{\mathrm{ref}}} \right), \tag{2.2}$$

where p_{ref} is the referenced sound pressure [43]. This approach is implemented in, for example, the MIR toolbox [182]. Regardless of the approach taken, the original dynamics of the music signal would not be distorted, because every point in the waveform is amplified equally.

2.2.1.3 Subjective Test

Because emotion is a subjective matter, the collection of the ground truth data should be conducted carefully. Annotation methods can be grouped into two categories: expert based or subject based. The *expert-based* method employs only a few musical experts (often less than five) to annotate emotion (e.g., [203, 217, 316, 338]). Music pieces whose emotions cannot gain consensus among experts are often simply abandoned. The *subject-based* method conducts a subjective test and employs a large number of untrained subjects to annotate emotion. The ground truth is often set by averaging the opinions of all subjects. Typically a song is annotated by more than ten subjects [163, 173, 341, 365].

As the annotation process can be very time consuming and labor costly, one needs to pay attention to the experimental design to reduce human fatigue. Some common practices include the following:

■ Reducing the length of the music pieces [297, 364].
■ Providing synonyms to reduce the ambiguity of the affective terms [297].

---

* Adobe Systems Incorporated acquired Cool Edit Pro from Syntrillium Software in May 2003 and introduced Adobe Audition software (a rebranded release of Cool Edit Pro) in August 2003 [online] http://www.adobe.com/special/products/audition/syntrillium.html.

- Using exemplar songs (or mini-training) to better articulate what each emotion class means [140]. These exemplar songs are often selected as the songs whose emotion assignments are unanimously judged by a number of people.
- Allowing the user to skip songs when none of the candidate emotion classes is appropriate to describe the affective content of the song [140].
- Designing a user-friendly annotation interface [356, 366].

Moreover, to enhance the reliability of the emotion annotations, the subjective test is rarely longer than an hour. The number of songs a subject is asked to annotate is accordingly limited. For example, in [364] a subject is asked to annotate 15 songs.

Some lectures may also be needed to ensure the quality of the annotations, as MER may be new to the subjects. For example, in [366] instructions regarding the purpose of MER, the meaning of valence and arousal, and the difference between perceived emotion and felt emotion are given to the subjects before annotation. It is also found that subjects are prone to misinterpret positive/negative valence as preferred/not preferred. A clear set of instructions is indeed important.

Because the perception of music emotion is multidimensional, the following questions may also deserve attention: Should we ask the subjects to deliberatively ignore the lyrics? Should we use songs of a language foreign to the subjects to eliminate the influence of lyrics? Should we ask the subjects to annotate songs with which they are familiar or unfamiliar? Should we ask the subjects to annotate songs of their favorite genre? Should we invite subjects from a variety of backgrounds to the subjective test? Should the number of female annotators and the number of male annotators be roughly the same? It seems no consensus has been reached regarding these issues so far.

To mitigate the cognitive load of subjective test, a recent trend is to obtain emotion tags directed from music websites such as AMG and Last.fm. Typically, this can be done by a simple script-based URL lookup. The advantage of this approach is that it is easy to obtain the annotation of a great many songs (e.g., [34, 142, 189, 207]). However, the weakness is that the quality of such annotations is relatively lower than those collected through subjective test. For example, in AMG the emotion labels are applied to artists and albums, not tracks. In Last.fm the tags may be incorrect because they are typically assigned by nonexperts for their own personal use. An extensive study on social tagging of music pieces can be found in [178].

The other trend is to harness the so-called human computation to turn annotation into an entertaining task. More specifically, the idea is to make users contribute emotion annotations as a by-product of playing Web-based games [26, 168, 190, 224, 322]. Such games are often designed as a collaborative game; that is, multiple users are playing the game at the same time to compete with each other. This practice could usually ensure the quality of the annotations. A famous example of such online, multiplayer games is D. Turnbull's *Listen Game* [322]. When playing the game, a player sees a list of semantically related words (e.g., instruments, emotions, usages, genres) and picks both the best and worst word to describe a song. Each player's score is determined by the amount of agreement between the player's choices and the choices of all other players and shown to each user immediately. Such games require little administration effort and typically obtain high-quality (and free) annotations.

2.2.1.4 Feature Extraction

A number of musical features are extracted from the music signal to represent the different perceptual dimensions of music listening, such as melody, timbre, and rhythm. The incorporation of text features extracted from the lyrics has also been studied [139, 183, 219, 288, 326, 363]. A detailed discussion of features that are often utilized for MER is presented in Chapter 3.

After feature extraction, feature normalization is usually applied to make the range of each feature comparable. Popular normalization methods include the one that linearly normalizes the range of each feature to [0, 1] (*linear normalization*) and the one that normalizes each feature to zero mean and unit standard deviation (*z-score normalization*). It should be noted that, to avoid "cheating" on the test accuracy, the normalization parameters (e.g., the minimum and maximum values of a feature) should be obtained from the training data and then applied to both the training and test data.

2.2.1.5 Model Training

After obtaining the ground truth labels and the musical features, the next step is to train a machine learning model to learn the relationship between emotion and music. As described in Section 1.2, music emotion classification is often carried out by well-established classification algorithms, such as neural network, k-nearest neighbor (k-NN), maximum likelihood, decision tree, or support vector machine [69, 184]. For example, the best-performing systems of MIREX AMC 2007–2009 are based on support vector classification (SVC) [54, 140, 323], Gaussian mixture models (GMM) [250], and the combination of SVC and GMM [47, 48], respectively. Many MER studies also report that SVC tends to give superior performance [114, 184, 186, 364]. The most popular implementation of SVC is based on the LIBSVM library [54]. More details about SVC are described in Section 4.3.3.

It is noted, however, that most submitted systems to MIREX are "general purpose." That is, the same classification architecture, as well as the music feature set, is used for other music classification tasks such as genre classification or instrument classification as well. The distinct characteristics of emotion perception, such as its subjectivity nature and the likelihood that a song expresses more than one emotion, is not considered in the contest so far [140].

Efforts have been made to address specific issues of MER. Considering the fact that a song may express more than one emotion, multilabel classification algorithms such as multilabel SVC [202] and MLkNN [369] have been applied to assign multiple emotion labels to a song [203, 316, 340]. Motivated by the fact that emotion perception is influenced by personal factors such as cultural background, generation, sex, and personality [147], Y.-H. Yang et al. proposed a fuzzy approach that measures the strength of each emotion in association with the song under classification and provides a more objective measurement of emotion [365] (cf. Chapter 6). T.-L. Wu et al. also proposed a probabilistic approach that predicts the probability distribution of a music piece over the Hevner's eight emotion classes [344], using the probabilistic estimate of SVC [254].

2.2.2 Dimensional Approach

The attractive features of the dimensional approach, on the other hand, are the two-dimensional user interface and the associated emotion-based retrieval methods that can be created for mobile devices. In addition, because the emotion plane implicitly offers an infinite number of emotion descriptions, the granularity and ambiguity issues are alleviated. Instead of providing merely the class labels, "a dimension with more discrete values or a continuous range of values is preferable, because it at least has the potential to make finer distinctions," according to Karl F. MacDorman [163]. The dimensional approach to MER, or dimensional MER, has received increasing attention from both academia and industry [145].

As described in Section 2.1.3, the dimensional perspective is first adopted to track the emotion variation of a classical song [173,279,280,282], with particular focus on the dynamic process of music and emotional response. The idea of representing the overall emotion of a popular song as a point in the emotion plane for music retrieval is studied in [364] and [220], under the assumption that the dominant emotion of a popular song undergoes less changes than that of a classical song (this assumption is also made in the MIREX AMC contest [140]). MER is formulated as a regression problem [291] and two independent regression models (regressors) are trained to predict the VA values. This regression approach has a sound theoretical foundation and exhibits promising prediction accuracy. Based on this computational model, several emotion-based music retrieval methods have been developed (see Figure 2.3 for an illustration) [362]. The regression approach has been extended to describe the emotions of movie soundtracks in the 3DES, using the third dimension "potency" to better differentiate emotions that are close neighbors in the 2DES, such as anger and fear [80].

Unlike its categorical counterpart, the dimensional MER requires the subjects to annotate the numerical VA values (using either the standard rating scale [163] or the graphic rating scale [70, 282, 364, 366]). This requirement imposes a high cognitive load on the subjects. To address this issue, a ranking-based approach has been developed to simplify the annotation process of MER and enhance the quality of the ground truth [355, 356]. Subjects are asked to rank (by making pairwise comparisons) rather than rate the emotion of songs. More details of the ranking approach to MER are provided in Chapter 5. Many efforts have also been made to address the subjectivity issue of the dimensional approach to MER [155, 354, 361, 366], most of which are described in the following chapters of this book.

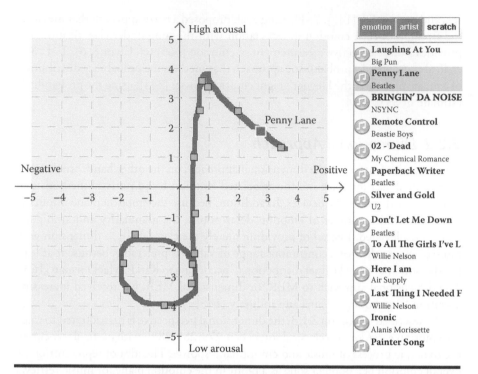

Figure 2.3 **The dimensional approach to MER represents each song as a point in the 2D valence-arousal emotion plane [272]. A user can retrieve music of a certain emotion by simply specifying a point or a path in the plane [362]. See Chapter 13 for more details.**

Note that the use of valence and arousal as the two emotion dimensions, though largely inspired from the psychology domain, has also been empirically validated by MIR researchers. M. Levy et al. [200] and C. Laurier et al. [189] have independently investigated the semantic mood/emotion space spanned from social music tags and found that the derived semantic space conforms to the valence-arousal emotion space. In another study, by applying factor analysis on emotion annotations of 15 bipolar affective terms, M. Leman et al. [197] also found that the underlying three-dimensional space corresponds to valence (gay-sad), activity (tender-bold), and interest (exciting-boring), which are very close to the valence-arousal-potency model.

Whether the emotions should be modeled as categories or continua has been a long debate in psychology, and either perspective has its pros and cons [67, 82, 126, 310]. In fact, many researchers consider categorical and dimensional approaches to emotion as complementary to each other, and both receive some support from neurophysiological data [72, 240]. From an engineering perspective, the categorical approach and the dimensional approach also show different strengths in emotion-based music retrieval. We can imagine a mobile device that employs both approaches to facilitate music retrieval in the future.

Based on the techniques described in [80], O. Lartillot et al. have incorporated the function of predicting both the numerical emotion values and class labels from audio features in the MIR toolbox (version 1.3) [182]. Given a music piece, the toolbox extracts music features from it and then applies multiple linear regression [291] (cf. Section 4.3.3.1) to predict its emotion values in the 3DES (namely, arousal, valence, and potency) and to classify its emotion to one of the following five basic emotion classes: happy, sad, tender, angry, and fear. The toolbox is publicly available and very useful for music emotion research.

2.2.3 Music Emotion Variation Detection

As described in Section 2.1.3, it is also important to model the time-varying relationship between music and emotion. Attempts have been made to automatically detect the emotion variation within a music piece, or music emotion variation detection (MEVD). Two approaches can be found in the literature. The first one exploits the temporal information of the music segments while computing the VA values, such as the time series analysis method [282] and the system identification method [173]. For example, M. D. Korhonen et al. employed system identification [215] to model music emotion as a function of 18 musical features. The ground truth data were collected for every one second of the music pieces, so the music pieces are also segmented every second for feature extraction. The data set consists of six Western classical music pieces of various emotions. Experimental results show that it is possible to detect the emotion variation of classical music [173]. See Section 4.2.3 for more details.

The second approach neglects the temporal information underlying the music signal and makes a prediction for each music segment independently [217,365]. For example, in [365] a sliding window of 10 second and 1/3 overlap is used to segment a music piece, whereas in [217] the potential emotion change boundaries are identified first and then utilized to segment the music piece. More specifically, the approach described in [217] uses an intensity outline to coarsely detect potential boundaries and then uses timbre and rhythm features to detect possible emotion changes in each contour of the intensity outline. In addition, because a musical paragraph is often composed of 16 bars according to music theory [160], the minimum length of a segment containing a constant emotion is set to 16 seconds. After segmentation of the music piece, the emotion of each segment is then recognized sequentially.

Besides music, the dimensional approach has been adopted to track the emotion variation within video sequences [23, 75, 117, 335, 372] and speech signals [105]. For example, A. Hanjalic et al. proposed to detect the emotion variation in movie sequences by the weighted sums of some component functions computed along the timeline [116, 117]. The component functions used for arousal are the motion vectors between consecutive video frames, the changes in shot lengths, and the energy of sound, whereas the component function used for valence is the sound pitch. The resulting valence and arousal curves are then combined to form an *affective curve*,

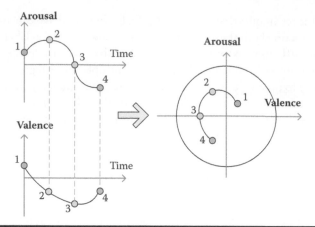

Figure 2.4 With emotion variation detection, one can combine the valence and arousal curves (left) to form the affective curve (right), which represents the dynamic changes of the affective content of a video sequence or a music piece (Data from A. Hanjalic and L.-Q. Xu. *IEEE Trans. Multimedia,* 7(1): 143–154, 2005).

which makes it easy to track the emotion variation of the video sequence and to identify the segments with strong affective content. See Figure 2.4 for an illustration. This work was later extended by S.-L. Zhang et al. [370–372], who modeled the emotion of music videos (MVs) and movies using 22 audio features (e.g., intensity, timbre, rhythm) and five visual features (motion intensity, shot switch rate, frame brightness, frame saturation, and color energy) and proposed an interface for affective visualization on time axis. The emotion prediction for each short-time video clip is conducted independently. In their system, a movie sequence is segmented every 14 seconds, with an overlap of two seconds between consecutive segments [371].

Although both MEVD and dimensional MER view emotions from the dimensional perspective, they are different in the way the computational problem is formulated and approached. MEVD computes the VA values of each short-time segment and represents a song as a series of VA values (points), whereas the dimensional MER computes the VA values of a representative segment (often 30 seconds) of a song and represents the song as a single point in the emotion plane. However, it should be noted that an MER system can also be applied to MEVD, if we neglect the temporal information and compute the VA values of each segment independently. An example is presented in Section 4.6.5.

2.3 Summary

In this chapter, we have provided an overview of emotion description and recognition. It can be found that MIR researchers tend to adopt the emotion models proposed by psychologists to build MER systems. Some researchers take the categorical approach, some take the dimensional approach, and some others focus on the emotion variation of music pieces. We have also described the ways MIR researchers conduct data preparation, emotion annotation, model training, and data visualization. Most of them are basic techniques that would be used throughout the whole book.

Table 2.2 summarizes the research on automatic prediction of music emotion, including a brief description of some recommended papers. It can be found that the three methodologies target at predicting *discrete emotion labels*, *numerical emotion values*, and *continuous emotion variation*, respectively. Because these methodologies share the same goal of emotion prediction, the techniques developed for dimensional MER may also be applied to categorical MER and MEVD. The former can be approached by partitioning the emotion plane into several regions and considering each region as an emotion class [114, 345], whereas the latter can be approached by computing the emotion values for each short-time segment independently [365].

3

Music Features

The experience of music listening is multidimensional. Different emotion perceptions of music are usually associated with different patterns of acoustic cues [126, 157, 175]. For example, while arousal is related to tempo (fast/slow), pitch (high/low), loudness (high/low), and timbre (bright/soft), valence is related to mode (major/minor) and harmony (consonant/dissonant) [101]. It is also noted that emotion perception is rarely dependent on a single music factor but a combination of them [126, 268]. For example, loud chords and high-pitched chords may suggest more positive valence than soft chords and low-pitched chords, irrespective of mode. See [101] for an overview of the empirical research concerning the influence of different music factors on emotion perception.

As summarized in Table 3.1, several features are extracted to represent the following five perceptual dimensions of music listening: energy, rhythm, temporal, spectrum, and melody. Many of these features have been used for MER. This chapter describes the semantic meanings of these features, how they are extracted, and their relationship to music emotion. To better illustrate the relationship between these features and emotion perception, we show the features of the following four songs as running examples:

(a) *Smells Like Teen Spirit* by **Nirvana** Negative valence and high arousal (quadrant II of 2DES).
(b) *Are We the Waiting* by **Green Day** Positive valence and high arousal (quadrant I of 2DES).
(c) *Mad World* by **Gary Jules** Negative valence and low arousal (quadrant III of 2DES).
(d) *White Christmas* by **Lisa One** Positive valence and low arousal (quadrant IV of 2DES).

These songs are randomly selected from the data set #2 of Table 1.4.

Table 3.1 Extracted Feature Sets

Feature Set	Extractor	Features
Energy	PsySound [44]	Dynamic loudness
	SDT [31]	Audio power, total loudness, and specific loudness sensation coefficients
Rhythm	Marsyas [324]	Beat histogram
	MA toolbox [246], RP extractor [206]	Rhythm pattern, rhythm histogram, and tempo
	MIR toolbox [182]	Rhythm strength, rhythm regularity, rhythm clarity, average onset frequency, and average tempo [217]
Temporal	SDT	Zero-crossings, temporal centroid, and log attack time
Spectrum	Marsyas, SDT	Spectral centroid, spectral rolloff, spectral flux, spectral flatness measures, and spectral crest factors
	MA toolbox, Marsyas, SDT	Mel-frequency cepstral coefficients
	MATLAB	Spectral contrast [152], Daubechies wavelets coefficient histogram [205], tristimulus, even-harm, and odd-harm [338]
	MIR toolbox	Roughness, irregularity, and inharmonicity
Harmony	MIR toolbox	Salient pitch, chromagram centroid, key clarity, musical mode, and harmonic change
	Marsyas	Pitch histogram
	PsySound	Sawtooth waveform inspired pitch estimate [46]

3.1 Energy Features

The energy of a song is often highly correlated with the perception of arousal [101]. We can measure **perceived loudness** by the dynamic loudness model of Chalupper and Fastl [53] implemented in PsySound [44, 267], a computer program that models parameters of auditory sensation based on some psychoacoustic models, such as the Bark critical band [374] for modeling auditory filters in our ears, an auditory temporal integration model, and Zwicker and Fastl's model for modeling sharpness, a subjective measure of sound on a scale extending from dull to sharp [375]. As a full understanding of these psychoacoustic models is beyond the scope of this book, interested readers are referred to [44] and the references therein for more details.

The sound description toolbox (SDT) extracts a number of MPEG-7 standard descriptors and others from raw audio signals [31]. We can also use it to extract 40 energy-related features including **audio power** (AP), **total loudness** (TL), and **specific loudness sensation coefficients** (SONE). AP is simply the power of the audio signal. The extraction of TL and SONE is based on the perceptual models implemented in the MA (music analysis) toolbox [246], including an outer-ear model, the Bark critical-band rate scale (psychoacoustically motivated critical-bands), and spectral masking (by applying spreading functions). The resulting power spectrum, which better reflects human loudness sensation, is called the sonogram. See [247] for more details of the computation of the sonogram. SONE is the coefficients computed from the sonogram, which consists of up to 24 Bark critical bands (the actual number of critical bands depends on the sampling frequency of the audio signal). TL is computed as an aggregation of SONE based on Stevens's method [121], which takes the sum of the largest SONE coefficient and a 0.15 ratio of the sum of the remainder coefficients. By default, all these features are extracted for each short time frame (23 ms, 50% overlapping) and then aggregated by taking the mean and standard deviation for temporal integration [228].

Figures 3.1 and 3.2 show the audio power and total loudness for each frame of the four example songs, whose volume level has been normalized by fixing the maximal volume of the audio waveform (cf. Section 2.2.1). It can be observed that these two features are fairly related to the arousal perception of music pieces. Songs (a) and (b) have higher audio power and total loudness than songs (c) and (d). For example, the average values of the total loudness across frames of the four songs are 22.5, 18.2, 12.4, and 9.19, respectively. Song (a) has the highest total loudness. However, we find that song (b) has a higher audio power than song (a), possibly because audio power does not take perceptual models into account.

Figure 3.3 shows the SONE coefficients of the four example songs. It can be observed that the energy of song (a) is particularly high in high frequency, whereas that of song (c) is particularly high in low frequency. The energy distributions of songs (b) and (d) are relatively uniform across the frequency bands. This result shows that the SONE coefficients of songs of different emotions may have different characteristics.

3.2 Rhythm Features

Rhythm is the pattern of pulses/notes of varying strength. It is often described in terms of tempo, meter, or phrasing. A song with fast tempo is often perceived as having high arousal. Besides, flowing/fluent rhythm is usually associated with positive valence, whereas firm rhythm is associated with negative valence [101].

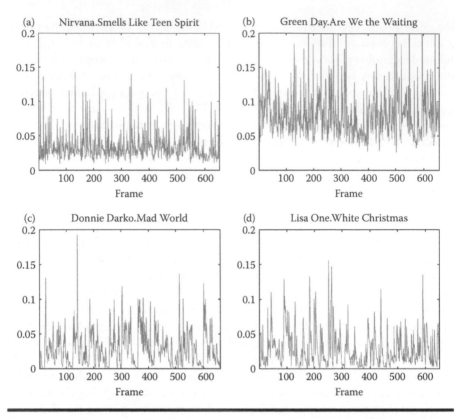

Figure 3.1 The values of audio power [31, 246] of the four sample songs (Data from E. Benetos, et al. *Proc. Int. Conf. Music Information Retrieval*, 2007 and E. Pampalk. *Proc. Int. Conf. Music Information Retrieval*. 2004).

Because of their importance, many toolboxes can be utilized to extract rhythm features. Marsyas is a free software framework for rapid development and evaluation of computer audition applications [324]. We can use Marsyas (version 0.1) to compute the **beat histogram** of music and generate six features from it, including beat strength, amplitude and period of the first and second peaks of the beat histogram, and the ratio of the strength of the two peaks in terms of bpm (beats per minute). The beat histogram is constructed by computing the autocorrelation of the signal envelope in each octave frequency band. The dominant peaks of the autocorrelation function correspond to various periodicities of the signal's envelope. See [324] for more details.

The MA toolbox [246] can also be utilized to extract **rhythm pattern** (or fluctuation pattern), which contains information on how strong and fast beats are played within the respective frequency bands [247]. The MA toolbox applies short-time Fourier transform (STFT) to obtain the amplitude modulation of SONE of each 6-second segment of a music piece. Reoccurring patterns in the individual

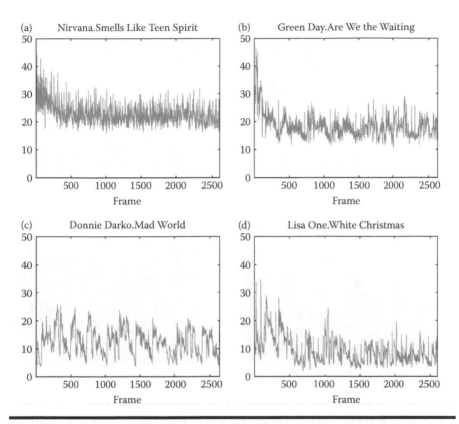

Figure 3.2 The values of total loudness [31, 246] of the four example songs. It can be observed that arousal perception is related to total loudness. (Data from E. Benetos, et al. *Proc. Int. Conf. Music Information Retrieval*, 2007 and E. Pampalk. *Proc. Int. Conf. Music Information Retrieval*. 2004).

modulation frequency resemble rhythm. Specifically, 60 values of amplitude modulation for modulation frequencies between 1/6 and 10 Hz (i.e., from 10 bpm to 600 bpm) per critical-band are computed. The amplitude modulation coefficients are then weighted based on a psychoacoustic model of fluctuation strength [89]. Amplitude modulation coefficients corresponding to modulation frequency around 4 Hz are assigned with more weights, because the sensation of fluctuation strength is most intense around 4 Hz [247]. Gradient and Gaussian filters are also applied to emphasize distinctive beats and to reduce irrelevant information. The rhythm pattern of the overall music piece is computed as the median of the rhythm patterns of its 6-second non-overlapping segments. Figure 3.4 shows the rhythm patterns of the four example songs. It can be observed that songs of high arousal are associated with strong and fast beats. For example, song (a) has strong beats in the modulation frequency around 8 Hz in low-frequency critical bands (probably created by

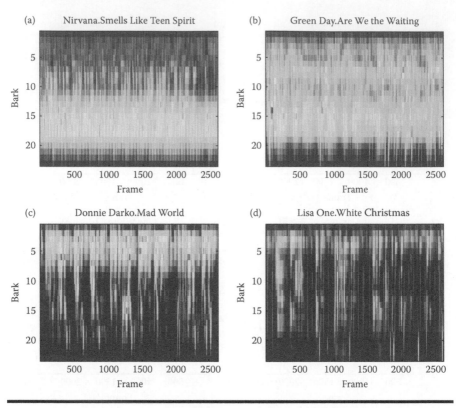

Figure 3.3 Specific loudness sensation coefficients in 23 Bark critical bands [31, 246] of the four example songs. Larger index of the Bark scale corresponds to higher frequency band. (Data from E. Benetos, et al. *Proc. Int. Conf. Music Information Retrieval,* **2007 and E. Pampalk.** *Proc. Int. Conf. Music Information Retrieval.* **2004).**

percussion), whereas songs (c) and (d) have no strong beats above the modulation frequency of 4 Hz, which interestingly corresponds to the modulation frequency of most intense sensation of fluctuation strength [89].

A rhythm pattern can be integrated into a 60-bin **rhythm histogram** by summing the amplitude modulation coefficients across critical bands. The mean of the rhythm histogram can be also regarded as an estimate of the average tempo. These features can also be extracted by the rhythm pattern (RP) extractor [206].

Finally, the following five rhythm features proposed in [217] have also been shown relevant to both valence and arousal perception: rhythm strength, rhythm regularity, rhythm clarity, average onset frequency, and average tempo. All of them can be extracted using the utility functions in the MIR toolbox [182]. **Rhythm strength** is calculated as the average onset strength of the onset detection curve,

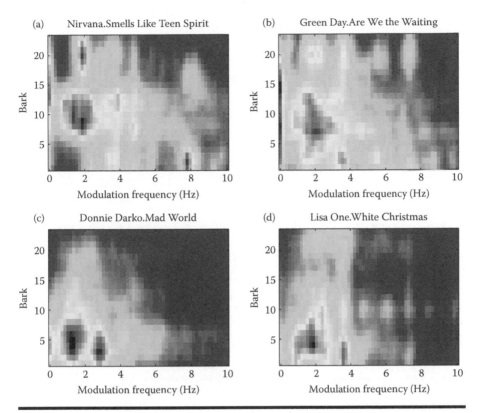

(a) Nirvana.Smells Like Teen Spirit

(b) Green Day.Are We the Waiting

(c) Donnie Darko.Mad World

(d) Lisa One.White Christmas

Figure 3.4 Rhythm (fluctuation) patterns [246] of the four example songs. A total of 60 values of amplitude modulation for modulation frequencies between 1/6 and 10 Hz (that is, from 10 bpm to 600 bpm) per critical-band are computed. It can be observed that songs of high arousal are associated with strong and fast beats. (Data from E. Pampalk *Proc. Int. Cont. Music Information Retrieval,* 2004)

which is computed based on the algorithm described by Klapuri [171]. Here the term *onset* refers to the starting time of each musical event (note). See [29] for a tutorial on onset detection in music signals. **Rhythm regularity** and **rhythm clarity** are computed by performing autocorrelation on the onset detection curve. If a music segment has an obvious and regular rhythm, the peaks of the corresponding autocorrelation curve will be obvious and strong as well. **Onset frequency**, or event density, is calculated as the number of note onsets per second, while **tempo** is estimated by detecting periodicity from the onset detection curve.

We show the onset detection curves of the four example songs in Figure 3.5 and the values of the five features in Table 3.3. It can be observed that these features are fairly relevant to both valence and arousal perception. Both rhythm strength and average tempo are particular high for song (a) and particularly low for song (c), both rhythm regularity and rhythm clarity are highly relevant to arousal perception, and

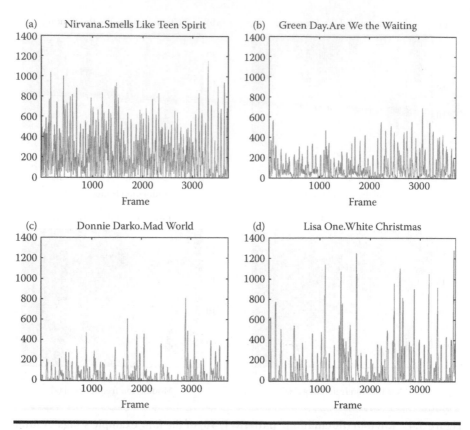

Figure 3.5 Onset detection curves of [182] the four sample songs (Data from O. Lartillot and P. Toiviainen. *Proc. Int. Cont. Music Information Retrieval*, 127–130, 2007).

average onset frequency is particularly high for song (c). This example illustrates the importance of rhythm features.

3.3 Temporal Features

We use the sound description toolbox [31] to extract zero-crossing rate, temporal centroid, and log attack time to capture the temporal quality of music. **Zero-crossing rate**, a measure of the signal noisiness, is computed by taking the mean and standard deviation of the number of signal values that cross the zero axis in each time window (i.e., sign changes).

$$\text{zero-crossing rate} = \frac{1}{T} \sum_{t=m-T+1}^{m} \frac{|\text{sgn}(s_t) - \text{sgn}(s_{t-1})|}{2} w(m-t), \qquad (3.1)$$

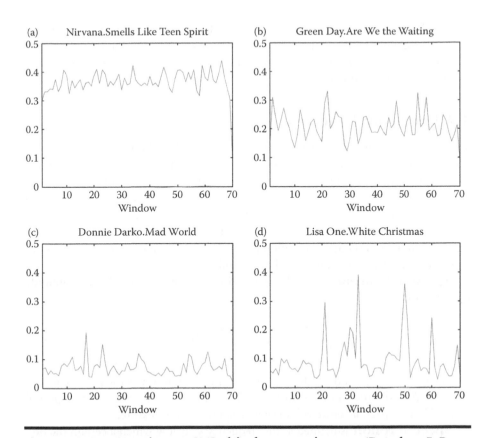

Figure 3.6   Zero-crossing rate [31] of the four example songs. (Data form E. Benetos et al., *Proc. Int. Conf. Music Information retrieval,* 2007).

where T is the length of the time window, s_t is the magnitude of the t-th time-domain sample, and $w(\cdot)$ is a rectangular window. The default length of the time window is 1.6% of the total length of the input signal, with 10% overlapping. Zero-crossing rate is often utilized to discriminate noise, speech, and music [218,275,349]. Its value is typically high for noise and speech, modest for music with vocals, and low for instrumental music. **Temporal centroid** and **log attack time**, on the other hand, are two MPEG-7 harmonic instrument timbre descriptors that describe the energy envelope [21]. The former is simply the time average over the energy envelope, whereas the latter is the logarithm of the duration between the time the signal starts and the time the signal reaches its maximum energy value. By default the start time is defined as the time the signal reaches 50% of the maximum energy value. Both temporal centroid and log attack time are often utilized in music instrument classification [124, 249, 296].

Figure 3.6 shows the values of zero-crossing rate of the four example songs. It can be found that song (a) has the highest average zero-crossing rate, and song (b) is second to it. From this result it seems that the zero-crossing rate is helpful. In addition, we find that the variance of zero-crossing rate for song (c) is much smaller than that of song (d). Therefore, the standard deviation of zero-crossing rate may be useful for valence prediction.

3.4 Spectrum Features

Spectrum features are features computed from the STFT of an audio signal [249]. One can use Marsyas (version 0.2) to extract the timbral texture features including spectral centroid, spectral rolloff, spectral flux, spectral flatness measures (SFM), and spectral crest factors (SCF).* These features are extracted for each frame and then by taking the mean and standard deviation for each second. The sequence of feature vectors is then collapsed into a single vector representing the entire signal by taking again the mean and standard deviation [324]. Note that many of these features can also be extracted by the sound description toolbox [31].

Spectral centroid means the centroid (center of gravity) of the magnitude spectrum of STFT,

$$\text{spectral centroid} = \frac{\sum_{n=1}^{N} n A_t^n}{\sum_{n=1}^{N} A_t^n}, \tag{3.2}$$

where A_t^n is the magnitude of the spectrum at the t-th frame and the n-th frequency bin, and N is the total number of bins. The centroid is a measure of the spectral shape. Higher spectral centroid indicates "brighter" audio texture.

Spectral rolloff is defined as the frequency κ_t below which a certain fraction of the total energy is contained. In [324] this ratio is fixed by default to 0.85 (another common practice sets the ratio to 0.95 [257]).

$$\sum_{n=1}^{\kappa_t} A_t^n = 0.85 * \sum_{n=1}^{N} A_t^n. \tag{3.3}$$

Spectral rolloff estimates the amount of high frequency in the signal. It is another measure of the spectral shape.

Spectral flux is defined as the square of the difference between the normalized magnitudes of successive frames [324],

$$\text{spectral flux} = \sum_{n=1}^{N} \left(a_t^n - a_{t-1}^n \right)^2, \tag{3.4}$$

---

* When the software Marsyas was first introduced [324], it could extract only 19 timbral texture features, 6 rhythmic content features, and 5 pitch content features. More features have been incorporated into Marsyas since then. We refer to the early system described in [324] as version 0.1 and the up-to-date one as version 0.2 (the specific version we refer to here is version 0.2.18).

where *a* denotes the normalized magnitude of the spectrum (normalized for each frame). Spectral flux estimates the amount of local spectral change. Moreover, as noted in [217], because spectral flux represents the spectrum variations between adjacent frames, it might be roughly correlated to *articulation*, an important factor of emotional perception that is difficult to compute from polyphonic music [101, 217, 266].

Spectral flatness measures and **spectral crest factors** are both related to the *tonalness* of audio signal [21]. Tonalness is often related to the valence perception; joyful and peaceful melodies are tonal (tone-like), while angry melodies are atonal (noise-like) [311]. SFM is the ratio between the geometric mean of the power spectrum and its arithmetic mean, whereas SCF is the ratio between the peak amplitude and the root-mean-square amplitude.

$$\text{spectral flatness measure} = \frac{\left(\Pi_{n \in B^k} A_t^n\right)^{1/N_k}}{\frac{1}{N_k}\sum_{n \in B^k} A_t^n},\tag{3.5}$$

$$\text{spectral crest factor} = \frac{\max_{n \in B^k} A_t^n}{\frac{1}{N_k}\sum_{n=1}^{N} A_t^n},\tag{3.6}$$

where B^k denotes the k-th frequency subband, and N_k is the number of bins in B^k. A total number of 24 subbands are used in Marsyas [324].

One can also use the MA toolbox [246] to extract **Mel-frequency cepstral coefficients** (MFCCs), the coefficients of the discrete cosine transform (DCT) of each short-term log power spectrum expressed on a nonlinear perceptual-related Mel-frequency scale [73], to represent the formant peaks of the spectrum. Typically, the mean and standard deviation of the first 13 or 20 MFCCs of each frame are taken. MFCC has been widely used in speech signal processing and MIR research [50]. See Table 3.2 for an example MATLAB® code for extracting MFCCs using the MA toolbox.

Figures 3.7, 3.8, and 3.9 show the MFCCs, values of spectral centroid, and values of spectral rolloff of the four example songs. It can be found that the average spectral centroid is highly related to arousal perception; song (a) has the highest spectral centroid, and song (b) has the second highest. This is not amazing since high arousal values are usually associated with bright timbre, whereas low arousal values are associated with soft timbre [101]. It can also be found that the standard deviation of spectral rolloff seems to be correlated with arousal. Song (c) has the smallest standard deviation of spectral rolloff among the four songs.

A criticism of MFCC, however, is that it averages the spectral distribution in each subband and thus loses the relative spectral information [217]. To compensate for this disadvantage, octave-based **spectral contrast** was proposed in [152] to capture the relative energy distribution of the harmonic components in the spectrum. This feature considers the spectral peak, spectral valley, and their

Table 3.2 An Example MATLAB Code for Extracting Mel-Frequency Cepstral Coefficients (MFCCs) of a Song Using the MA Toolbox

```
function X = ma_feat_extract(songname);
% input: songname - the song from which MFCCs are extracted
% output: X - 1 by 80 feature vector
%          1-20 mean of mfccs (the first 20 coefficients)
%          1-20 std of mfccs
%          1-20 mean of dmfccs (delta mfccs)
%          1-20 std of mfccs

% read the song (assuming a wav file)
[data p.fs] = wavread( songname );
      % using mp3read for mp3 files (available on Dan Ellis's
      % Web page, http://www.ee.columbia.edu/~dpwe/resources/)

% parameter setting
p.fft_size = 512;
p.hopsize = p.fft_size/2;
p.num_ceps_coeffs = 20;
p.use_first_coeff = 1;
p.visu = 0;
p.hist_res = 30;

% extract MFCCs
[mfcc DCT] = ma_mfcc(data, p);

X = zeros(1,p.num_ceps_coeffs*4);
X = [mean(mfcc') std(mfcc') mean(diff(mfcc'))
      std(diff(mfcc'))];
```

Source: Data from E. Pampalk. *Proc. Int. Conf. Music Information Retrieval,* 2004.

Table 3.3 The Values of Rhythm Features Proposed for the Example Four Songs

	Rhythm Strength	Rhythm Regularity	Rhythm Clarity	Avg. Onset Frequency	Average Tempo
(a) *Smells Like Teen Spirit*	234	0.376	0.614	108	240
(b) *Are We the Waiting*	99	0.376	0.517	96	169
(c) *Mad World*	51	0.175	0.295	130	96
(d) *White Christmas*	105	0.136	0.246	95	125

Source: Data from L. Lu, et al. *IEEE Trans. Audio, Speech & Language Processing,* 14(1): 5–18, 2006.

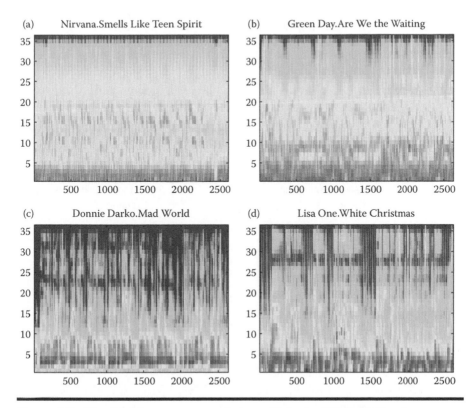

Figure 3.7 The Mel-frequency cepstral coefficients [246] of the four example songs. Source: Data from E. Pamplk. *Proc. Int. Conf. Music Information Ritrieval,* **2004.**

dynamics in each subband and roughly reflects the relative distribution of the harmonic and nonharmonic components in the spectrum. It has been shown that the spectral contrast features perform better than MFCC for music genre classification [152].

Another spectrum feature that is often used in existing MER work is the **DWCH**, or the Daubechies wavelets coefficient histogram [203–205]. It is computed from the histograms of Daubechies wavelet coefficients at different frequency subbands with different resolutions. As [205] states, due to the use of wavelet technique, DWCH features have better ability in representing both the local and global information of the spectrum than traditional features. Both spectral contrast and DWCH can be easily implemented in MATLAB, which contains a complete wavelet package [10].

Besides, we also use the MIR toolbox [182] (version 1.2) to generate the following three sensory dissonance features: roughness, irregularity, inharmonicity.

Roughness, or spectral dissonance, measures the noisiness of the spectrum; any note that does not fall within the prevailing harmony is considered dissonant.

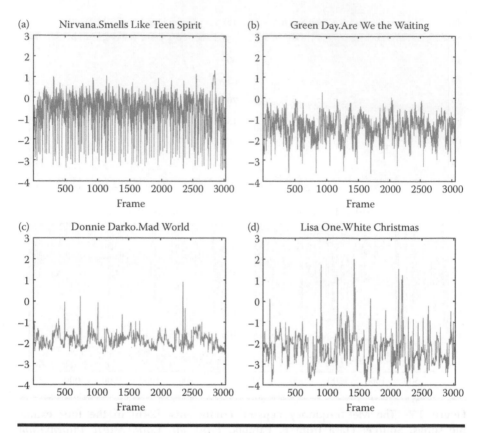

Figure 3.8 **The values of spectral centroid [31] of the four example songs. (Data from E. Benetos et al.** *Proc. Int. Conf. Music Information Retrieval,* **2007.)**

It is estimated by computing the peaks of the spectrum and taking the average of all the dissonance between all possible pairs of peaks [292].

Irregularity measures the degree of variation of the successive peaks of the spectrum [99]. It is computed by summing the square of the difference in amplitude between adjoining partials [151],

$$\text{irregularity} = \frac{\sum_{n=1}^{N} \left(A_t^n - A_t^{n+1} \right)^2}{\sum_{n=1}^{N} A_t^n * A_t^n}. \tag{3.7}$$

Another method of measuring irregularity is based on the Krimphoff's method [174], which defines irregularity as the sum of amplitude minus the mean of the preceding, current, and next amplitude,

$$\text{irregularity} = \sum_{n=2}^{N-1} |A_t^n - \frac{A_t^{n-1} + A_t^n + A_t^{n+1}}{3}|, \tag{3.8}$$

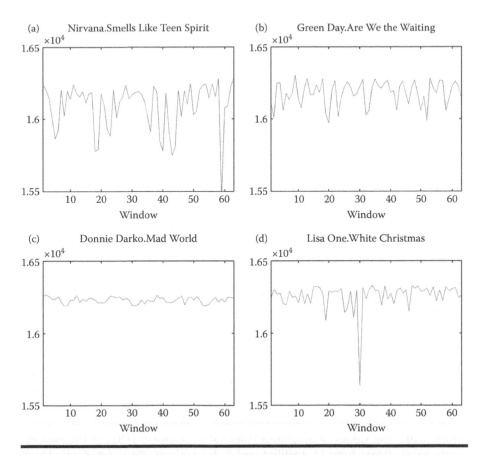

Figure 3.9 **The values of spectral rolloff [31] of the four example songs. (Data from E. Benetos et al.** *Proc. Int. Conf. Music Information Retrieval,* **2007)**

Inharmonicity estimates the amount of partials that departs from multiples of the fundamental frequency. It is computed as an energy weighted divergence of the spectral components from the multiple of the fundamental frequency [249].

$$\text{inharmonicity} = \frac{2}{f_0} \frac{\sum_{n=1}^{N} |f_n - n f_0| \left(A_t^n\right)^2}{\sum_{n=1}^{N} \left(A_t^n\right)^2}, \tag{3.9}$$

where f_n is the n-th harmonic of the fundamental frequency f_0. The inharmonicity represents the divergence of the signal spectral components from a purely harmonic signal. Its value ranges from 0 (purely harmonic) to 1 (inharmonic).

Figure 3.10 shows the values of roughness of the four example songs. Interestingly, this feature seems to be correlated with our valence perception. We see that songs of negative valence seem to have higher roughness values and that song (b) has very small roughness values. This result is consistent with previous psychology

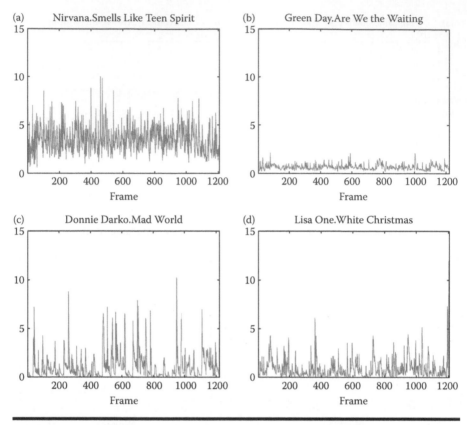

Figure 3.10 The values of roughness (spectral dissonance) [182] of the four example songs. (Data from O. Lartillot and P. Toivianinen. *Proc. Int. Conf. Music Information Retrieval.* 127–130, 2007).

studies [101], which indicated that valence perception is associated with the harmony content (consonant/dissonant) of music signals.

Other spectrum features that are used in previous MER work include tristimulus, even-harm, and odd-harm [338–340]. **Tristimulus** parameter are calculated as follows [258]:

$$\text{tristimulus1} = \frac{\left(A_t^1\right)^2}{\sum_{n=1}^{N}\left(A_t^n\right)^2}, \tag{3.10}$$

$$\text{tristimulus2} = \frac{\sum_{n=2,3,4}\left(A_t^n\right)^2}{\sum_{n=1}^{N}\left(A_t^n\right)^2}, \tag{3.11}$$

$$\text{tristimulus3} = \frac{\sum_{n=5}^{N}\left(A_t^1\right)^2}{\sum_{n=1}^{N}\left(A_t^n\right)^2}. \tag{3.12}$$

Even-harm and **odd-harm** represent the even and odd harmonics of the spectrum. They can be calculated as follows:

$$\text{even-harm} = \sqrt{\frac{\sum_{n=1}^{\lfloor N/2 \rfloor} \left(A_t^{2n} \right)^2}{\sum_{n=1}^{N} \left(A_t^n \right)^2}}, \tag{3.13}$$

$$\text{odd-harm} = \sqrt{\frac{\sum_{n=1}^{\lfloor N/2+1 \rfloor} \left(A_t^{2n-1} \right)^2}{\sum_{n=1}^{N} \left(A_t^n \right)^2}}. \tag{3.14}$$

Spectrum and temporal features summarize the timbre content of music.

3.5 Harmony Features

Harmony features are features computed from the sinusoidal harmonic modeling of the signal [249]. A lot of natural sounds, especially musical ones, are harmonic — each sound consists of a series of frequencies at a multiple ratio of the lowest frequency, called the fundamental frequency f_0.

We can use the MIR toolbox [182] to generate two pitch features (salient pitch and chromagram center) and three tonality features (key clarity, mode, harmonic change). The MIR toolbox estimates the pitch, or the perceived fundamental frequency, of each short time frame (50 ms, 1/2 overlapping) based on the multi-pitch detection algorithm described by Tolonen and Karjalainen [313]. The algorithm decomposes an audio waveform into two frequency bands (below and above 1 kHz), computes the autocorrelation function of the envelope in each subband, and finally produces pitch estimates by picking the peaks from the sum of the two autocorrelation functions. The pitch estimate corresponding to the highest peak is returned as the **salient pitch**. The MIR toolbox also computes the wrapped chromagram, or the pitch class profile, for each frame (100 ms, 1/8 overlapping) and uses the centroid of the chromagram as another estimate of the fundamental frequency. This feature is called the **chromagram centroid**. A wrapped chromagram projects the frequency spectrum onto 12 bins representing the 12 distinct semitones (or chroma) of the musical octave. For example, frequency bins of the spectrum around 440 Hz (C4) and 880 Hz (C5) are all mapped to the chroma C. Therefore, the chromagram centroid may be regarded as a pitch estimate that does not consider absolute frequency.

Figures 3.11 and 3.12 show the values of salient pitch and chromagram centroid of the four example songs. It can be found that the resulting two pitch estimates are fairly close, but the result of salient pitch seems to be spikier. Both results show that high arousal values are usually associated with high average pitch. Moreover, positive valence values seem to be associated with higher standard deviation of pitch values.

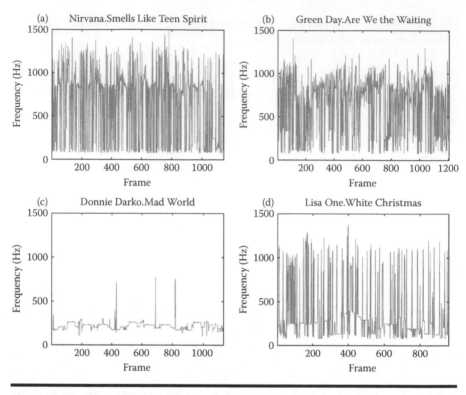

Figure 3.11 The values of salient pitch [182] of the four example songs. (Data from O. Lartillot and P. Toivianinen. *Proc. Int. Conf. Music Information Retrieval.* 127–130, 2007).

Each bin of the chromagram corresponds to one of the twelve semitone classes in the Western twelve-tone equal temperament scale. By comparing a chromagram to the 24 major and minor key profiles [107], we can perform key detection and estimate the strength of the frame in association with each key (e.g., C major). The strength associated with the best key, that is, the one with the highest strength, is returned as the **key clarity**. The difference between the best major key and the best minor key in key strength is returned as the estimate of the **musical mode**, which describes a certain fixed arrangement of the diatonic tones of an octave [241]. It is returned as a numerical value: The higher its value, the more major the given piece is supposed to be. Mode is often related to the valence perception of music [101, 242]. However, from Figure 3.13 it is difficult to tell whether the values of musical mode are correlated with valence. The average values of musical mode of the four songs are 0.060, 0.0689, 0.0095, and −0.0513, respectively. The result shows that it is still challenging to extract musical mode directly from polyphonic music signals, as indicated in [217].

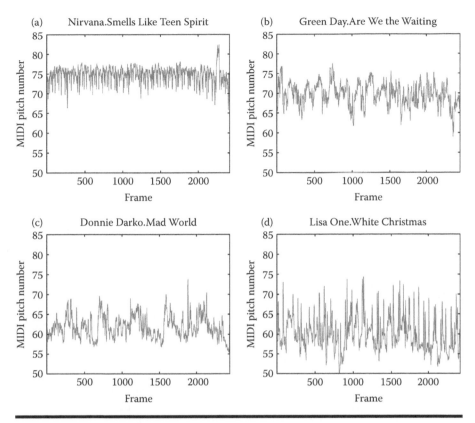

Figure 3.12 **The values of chromagram centroid [182] of the four example songs. (Data from O. Lartillot and P. Toivianinen. *Proc. Int. Conf. Music Information Retrieval.* 127–130, 2007).**

The MIR toolbox also utilizes the algorithm described in [120] to compute a 6-dimensional feature vector called tonal centroid from the chromagram and use it to detect the **harmonic changes** (e.g., chord change) in musical audio. High harmonic change indicates large difference in harmonic content between consecutive frames. The short-term features are aggregated by taking mean and standard deviation [228].

We can also use the Marsyas toolbox (version 0.1) to compute the pitch histogram and generate five features from it, including tonic, main pitch class, octave range of the dominant pitch, main tonal interval relation, and the overall pitch strength [324]. In addition, one can use PsySound to compare 16 pitch-related features including the mean, standard deviation, skewness, and kurtosis of the pitch and pitch strength time series estimated by SWIPE (sawtooth waveform inspired pitch estimator) and SWIPE'. The latter restricts the analysis to first and prime harmonics [44, 46].

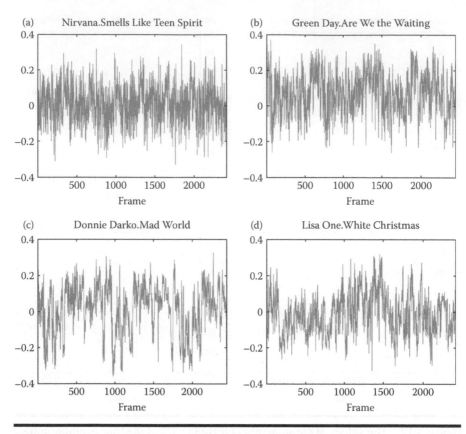

Figure 3.13 **The values of musical mode [182] of the four example songs (Data from O. Lartillot and P. Toivianinen.** *Proc. Int. Conf. Music Information Retrieval.* **127–130, 2007).**

3.6 Summary

In this chapter, we have described the music features that have been utilized for MER, including features that represent the following five perceptual dimensions of music listening: energy, rhythm, temporal, spectrum, and harmony. We have also described the toolboxes that are all publicly available for extracting these features. The relationship between these features and the perception of valence and arousal has also been discussed. Many of these features are used in the following chapters.

4

Dimensional MER by Regression

This chapter introduces the regression approach to MER, which is one of the earliest and most widely adopted techniques for dimensional MER. The regression approach is also applicable to music emotion variation detection (MEVD) and categorical MER. In fact, it is the root of many other computational models for dimensional MER, including those described in the subsequent chapters. Therefore, a thorough understanding of the regression approach is a prerequisite to the study of advanced dimensional MER systems.

4.1 Adopting the Dimensional Conceptualization of Emotion

One may categorize emotions into a number of classes and train a classifier (could be a standard pattern recognition procedure) to learn the relationship between music and emotion. A straightforward and perhaps the simplest classification of emotion adopts the basic emotions (e.g., happy, angry, sad, and fear) as the emotion classes [90, 204]. On the other hand, the emotion classes can be defined in terms of valence (how positive or negative) and arousal (how exciting or calming) [217, 336, 342, 352, 365]. For example, in the classification shown in Figure 4.1, the emotion classes are classified as the four quadrants in the emotion plane [272, 310].

However, even with the emotion plane as a convenient way to visualize the emotion classification, the categorical taxonomy of emotion classes is still inherently ambiguous. Each emotion class represents an area in the emotion plane, and the emotion states within each area may vary a lot. For example, the first quadrant of

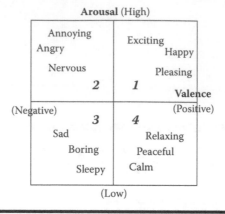

Arousal (High)

Annoying Angry Nervous **2**	Exciting Happy Pleasing **1**

Valence

(Negative)   (Positive)

3 Sad Boring Sleepy	**4** Relaxing Peaceful Calm

(Low)

Figure 4.1   The 2D valence-arousal emotion plane. (Data from J. A. Russell. J. *Personality & Social Pychology.* **39(6): 1161–1178. 1980 and R. E. Thayer.** *The Biopsychology of Mood and Arousal,* **Oxford University Press, New York, 1989)**

the emotion plane contains emotions such as exciting, happy, and pleasing, which are different in nature. More importantly, as we have discussed in Section 1.3.1, this categorical approach faces a granularity issue that the number of emotion classes is too small in comparison with the richness of emotion perceived by humans. Using a finer granularity for emotion description does not necessarily address the issue since language is ambiguous, and the description for the same emotion varies from person to person [159].

Unlike other approaches, the regression approach to MER developed in [364] and [163] adopts the dimensional conceptualization of emotion (cf. Section 2.1.2) and views the emotion plane as a continuous space. Each point of the plane is considered an emotion state. In this way, the ambiguity associated with the emotion classes or the affective terms is avoided since no categorical class is needed. The regression approach is also free of the granularity issue, since the emotion plane implicitly offers an infinite number of emotion descriptions.

The regression approach applies a computational model that predicts the valence and arousal (VA) values of a music piece, which determine the placement of the music piece in the emotion plane. The placement of a music piece in the emotion plane directly indicates the affective content of the music piece. A user can then retrieve music by specifying a point in the emotion plane according to his/her emotion state, and the system would return the music pieces whose locations are closest to the specified point. Because the 2D emotion plane provides a simple means for user interface, novel emotion-based music organization, browsing, and retrieval can be easily created for mobile devices. Such a user interface is of great use in managing large-scale music databases. Chapter 13 has more details about this aspect of the approach.

Clearly, the viability of the regression approach to MER heavily relies on the accuracy of predicting the valence and arousal values, or *VA prediction*. As its name implies, the regression approach formulates VA prediction as a regression problem and applies regression techniques to directly predict the VA values of music pieces from the extracted features. Before going into details of the regression approach, we introduce some earlier methods for VA prediction.

4.2 VA Prediction

Some methods that were in fact developed for categorical MER or MEVD can also be applied to compute the VA values, though this was not their original purpose. This section introduces three such methods, including weighted-sum of component functions, the fuzzy approach, and the system identification approach. As shown in rows 1–3 of Table 4.1, all these early approaches either lack the mechanism for quantitative evaluation or require information that is inexact or absent. As shown in row 4 of Table 4.1, the computational model for regression analysis adopted by the regression approach is free of such drawbacks.

4.2.1 Weighted Sum of Component Functions

As described Section 2.1.3, the dimensional conceptualization of emotion is often adopted for MEVD. Therefore, systems developed for MEVD also require the prediction of VA values. For example, to detect the emotion variation in video sequences, A. Hanjalic et al. proposed to utilize the weighted combination of a number of component functions to compute the VA values along the timeline [116, 117]. The component functions used for arousal are the motion vectors between consecutive video frames, the changes in shot lengths, and the energy of sound, whereas the component function used for valence is the sound pitch. More specifically, this method computes the arousal value of a short-time music segment simply as the weighted sum of the values of three component functions of the music segment. The magnitude of the valence value of a short-time music segment is simply set according to the arousal value; only the sign of the valence value is determined by the sound pitch. After convolving with a sufficiently long smoothing window to

Table 4.1 Comparison of the Methods for VA Prediction

Method	Field	Quantitative Evaluation	Not Rely on Temporal Info	Not Involve Geometric Operation
Hanjalic's method [117]	Video	X	O	O
Fuzzy approach [365]	Music	X	O	X
System ID [173]	Music	O	X	O
Regression approach [364]	Music	O	O	O

merge neighboring local maxima into one peak or to eliminate jumps due to the sign change, the resulting valence and arousal curves are then combined to form a single affective curve, making it easy to trace the emotion variation of the video sequence and to identify the segments with strong affective content (cf. Section 2.2.3).

Although this method is based on some psychological understandings and the extracted features are intuitively related to emotion perception, it is difficult to evaluate the performance quantitatively due to the lack of ground truth data. Moreover, the combination of the component functions seems to be somewhat ad hoc. It can be found that *no* model training is involved in the computational process of this method. A more rigorous approach that allows performance study would be more favorable.

4.2.2 Fuzzy Approach

In [365], emotion classes are defined according to the four quadrants of the emotion plane (see Figure 4.1) and each music piece is associated with a fuzzy vector that indicates the relative strength of each class by fuzzy classifiers [165, 315]. The fuzzy vector μ can be expressed as

$$\mu = [\mu_1, \mu_2, \mu_3, \mu_4]^\top, \quad \sum_{i=1}^{4} \mu_i = 1, \tag{4.1}$$

where μ_i is the relative strength of class i, and $\top$ denotes vector/matrix transposition. The final decision of classification is the class with the maximal strength (i.e., majority vote). More details of the fuzzy approach are described in Chapter 6.

Given a fuzzy vector, the fuzzy approach exploits the geometric relationship of the four emotion classes and computes the VA values by the following transformation:

$$v = \mu_1 + \mu_4 - \mu_2 - \mu_3, \tag{4.2}$$

$$a = \mu_1 + \mu_2 - \mu_3 - \mu_4, \tag{4.3}$$

where v denotes valence, and a denotes arousal. However, the transformation involves emotion classes that are not necessarily independent of and orthogonal to each other. Since the geometric relationship between valence and arousal is inexact, it could be improper to perform arithmetic operations on the VA values. In addition, the fuzzy approach is also short of an evaluation mechanism that quantifies the accuracy of VA prediction.

4.2.3 System Identification Approach (System ID)

In the system identification approach to MEVD [173], a system identification technique [215] is employed to model music emotion as a function of 18 music features.

The ground truth data are collected every second, so the music pieces are also segmented every second before feature extraction is performed. Six Western classical music pieces of various moods form the data set. This approach provides a means to the generalization of the emotional content for a genre of music (Western classical music), and the reported average R^2 statistics [291] is 78.4% for arousal and 21.9% for valence (cf. Section 2.2.3). More details of the R^2 statistics are described in Section 4.6.

The system ID approach, however, computes the VA values by exploiting the temporal relationship between music segments, which is absent for MER. Therefore, it cannot be applied to MER. The time series analysis approach proposed earlier by Schubert [282] also suffers from this drawback.

To sum up, a robust VA prediction algorithm should have a sound theoretical foundation and allows quantitative performance study. Among the three methods described above, only the system ID approach embeds a theoretical structure, yet it utilizes the temporal information that is not available for dimensional MER. In addition, the computation of VA values should not involve any geometric operation of the VA values due to the inexact relationship between valence and arousal. It is also desirable to directly predict the numerical emotion values from music features.

4.3 The Regression Approach

In this section, we first describe the essence of regression, then show how to formulate MER as a regression problem, and finally introduce three popular regression algorithms.

4.3.1 Regression Theory

The well-studied regression theory aims at predicting a real value from observed variables (i.e., music features). It has a sound theoretical foundation, allows easy performance analysis and optimization, and generally provides reliable prediction [291]. Besides, the VA values are predicted directly from music features, without any involvement of temporal information or geometric operations. Therefore, formulating MER as a regression problem is a promising approach.

Given N inputs $(\mathbf{x}_i, y_i)$, $i \in \{1, \ldots, N\}$, where $\mathbf{x}_i$ is the feature vector of an object (i.e., music piece) d_i and y_i is the real value (i.e., valence or arousal) to be predicted, a regressor $r(\cdot)$ is created by minimizing the mean squared error (MSE) ϵ,

$$\epsilon = \frac{1}{N} \sum_{i=1}^{N} (y_i - r(\mathbf{x}_i))^2, \tag{4.4}$$

where $r(\mathbf{x}_i)$ is the prediction result for d_i. Note that we use bold font to represent vectors and matrices in this book.

4.3.2 Problem Formulation

Since the VA values are viewed as real values from the dimensional perspective, the regression theory can be well applied to directly predict valence and arousal. To formulate MER as a regression problem, the following points are taken into account:

- Domain of valence and arousal: The emotion plane is viewed as a coordinate space spanned by valence and arousal, where each value is confined within $[-1, 1]$.
- Ground truth: The ground truth is obtained via a subjective test by averaging the subjects' opinions of the VA values of each music piece (see Section 4.5.3).
- Feature extraction: The extracted features need to be relevant to emotion perception for the regressor to be accurate (see Sections 4.5.2 and 4.6.3).
- Regression algorithm: Although regression theory has been well studied and many good regressors are readily available [291], the performance of a regressor is case dependent. A number of regressors should be adopted and compared to find the best one (see Sections 4.3.3 and 4.6.4).
- Number of regressors: Since we need to predict both the valence and arousal values, a typical approach is to train two regressors *independently* for valence and arousal. We refer to these two regressors as r_V and r_A hereafter. However, because there might be a certain degree of dependency between valence and arousal, apart from training r_V and r_A, we need to study whether the prediction accuracy is improved if the correlation between valence and arousal is considered (see Section 4.6.2).

4.3.3 Regression Algorithms

4.3.3.1 Multiple Linear Regression

MLR is a standard regression algorithm that assumes a linear relationship between variables and estimates the linear relationship by a least squares estimator [291]. More specifically, the relationship between the input variable $\mathbf{x}_i$ and estimate is modeled as*

$$r(\mathbf{X}) = \mathbf{X}\beta + \xi, \qquad (4.5)$$

where $\mathbf{X} = [\mathbf{x}_1, \mathbf{x}_2, \ldots, \mathbf{x}_N]^\top$ is an $N \times M$ data matrix, β is an $M \times 1$ vector of weights, or regression coefficients, ξ is an $N \times 1$ vector of error terms, or noise, and $\mathbf{X}\beta$ is the matrix-vector product. The regression coefficients β can be obtained by

---

* The constant b in regression analysis can be neglected here since the input variables have been normalized.

minimizing the MSE between $r(\mathbf{X})$ and $\mathbf{y}$,

$$\epsilon = \frac{1}{N}(\mathbf{y} - \mathbf{X}\beta)^\top(\mathbf{y} - \mathbf{X}\beta). \tag{4.6}$$

Taking the derivative of the above equation with respect to β and setting it to zero, we have the following set of equations (also called the *normal equations*):

$$\frac{\partial\epsilon}{\partial\beta} = \frac{2}{N}\mathbf{X}^\top(\mathbf{y} - \mathbf{X}\beta) \triangleq 0, \tag{4.7}$$

$$\mathbf{X}^\top\mathbf{y} = \mathbf{X}^\top\mathbf{X}\beta, \tag{4.8}$$

$$\beta = (\mathbf{X}^\top\mathbf{X})^{-1}\mathbf{X}^\top\mathbf{y} = \mathbf{X}^\dagger\mathbf{y}, \tag{4.9}$$

where $\mathbf{X}^\dagger$ is the pseudo-inverse of $\mathbf{X}$. For a new input $\mathbf{x}_*$, the estimate is therefore

$$r(\mathbf{x}_*) = \mathbf{x}_*\beta = \mathbf{x}_*\mathbf{X}^\dagger\mathbf{y}. \tag{4.10}$$

For simplicity, the MLR is often adopted as the baseline method in many regression systems. Sometimes its performance is as good as that of other complicated methods. For example, T. Eerola et al. have employed MLR to train their regressors and obtained promising accuracy of predicting the emotion values [80].

4.3.3.2 ϵ-Support Vector Regression

Support vector machines (SVMs) refer to a set of learning algorithms that *nonlinearly* map input feature vectors $\mathbf{x}$ to a higher dimensional feature space $\phi(\mathbf{x})$ by the so-called 'kernel trick' and learn a nonlinear function by a linear learning machine in the kernel-induced feature space, where data are more separable [69, 301]. The SVMs for classification are usually called support vector classification (SVC), whereas those for regression are called support vector regression (SVR) [69].* The SVC has been adopted for categorical MER and achieved great classification performance [184, 204, 288, 336, 352].

For classification, we look for the optimal separating hyperplane that has the largest distance to the nearest training data points of any class. For regression, we look for a function $f(\mathbf{x}_s) = \mathbf{m}^\top\phi(\mathbf{x}_s) + b$ that has at most ε deviation from the ground truth y_s for all the training data and meanwhile is as flat as possible (i.e., $\mathbf{m}^\top\mathbf{m}$ is small) [301]. In other words, we do not care about errors as long as they

---

* Note that sometimes SVM is used to refer to SVC.

are less than ε. But we do not accept any deviation larger than ε. Moreover, under the soft margin principle [40], we introduce slack variables ξ_s and ξ_s^* to allow for errors greater than ε. Consequently, we have the following optimization problem:

$$\underset{\mathbf{m},b,\xi,\xi^*,\varepsilon}{\arg\min} \quad \frac{1}{2}\mathbf{m}^\top\mathbf{m} + C\sum_{s=1}^{N}(\xi_s + \xi_s^*),$$

$$\text{subject to} \quad (\mathbf{m}^\top\phi(\mathbf{x}_s) + b) - y_s \le \varepsilon + \xi_s, \tag{4.11}$$

$$y_s - (\mathbf{m}^\top\phi(\mathbf{x}_s) + b) \le \varepsilon + \xi_s^*,$$

$$\xi_s, \xi_s^* \ge 0, s = 1, \dots, N, \ \varepsilon \ge 0,$$

where the parameter C controls the trade-off between the flatness of $f(\cdot)$ and the amount up to which deviations larger than ε are tolerated [301]. A common kernel function is the radial basis function (RBF),

$$K(\mathbf{x}_p, \mathbf{x}_q) \equiv \phi(\mathbf{x}_p)^\top\phi(\mathbf{x}_q) = \exp(-\gamma||\mathbf{x}_p - \mathbf{x}_q||^2), \tag{4.12}$$

where γ is a scale parameter [69]. Typically the parameters of SVR are determined empirically by performing a grid search. The above quadratic optimization problem can be efficiently solved by known techniques [40].

4.3.3.3 AdaBoost Regression Tree (AdaBoost.RT)

AdaBoost.RT is another nonlinear regression algorithm in which a number of regression trees are trained iteratively and weighted according to the prediction accuracy on the validation data [303]. After the iterative process, the prediction result of each regression tree is combined using the weighted mean to form the final hypothesis. The basic underlining concept of the boosting process is based on the observation that finding a number of weak predicting rules is much easier than finding a single, highly accurate one [303]. Boosting algorithms have been successfully applied to many pattern recognition problems, such as face detection [330].

4.4 System Overview

Figure 4.2 shows a system diagram of the regression approach, which consists of data preprocessing, subjective test, feature extraction, regressor training, and emotion visualization. Unlike its categorical counterpart, dimensional MER requires subjects to annotate the numerical VA values in the subjective test. Given the numerical ground truth emotion values and feature representations of music, regression algorithms are

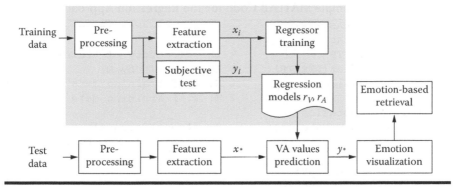

Figure 4.2 Schematic diagram of the regression approach. In the (upper) train-ing phase, regression models (regressor) are trained by learning the relationship between music features x and ground truth emotion values y. We use r_V and r_A to denote the regressor for valence and arousal, respectively. In the (lower) test phase, given the features x_* of an input song, the regressors r_V and r_A can be applied to predict its emotion values $y_* = [v_*, a_*]^\top = [r_V(x_*), r_A(x_*)]^\top$.

applied to train the regressors before they can be applied to predict the VA values of unseen music pieces without further labeling. Associated with the VA values, each music piece is visualized as a point in the emotion plane, and the similarity between music pieces can be estimated by computing the Euclidean distance in the emotion plane. A user interface that supports music retrieval/recommendation by specifying a point in the emotion plane can thus be realized.

Table 4.2 shows an example MATLAB® code for the regression approach to MER. Here the feature normalization is done via z-score normalization, and model training is done by employing the support vector regression implemented in the free library LIBSVM [54].

4.5 Implementation

To demonstrate how an MER system is built and to evaluate the regression ap-proach, we describe the details of an implementation of the regression approach in this section. Each component of the MER system (cf. Figure 4.2) is discussed. An extensive performance evaluation of the resulting MER system can be found in the next section.

4.5.1 Data Collection

The music database is made up of 195 popular songs selected from a number of Western, Chinese, and Japanese albums [365] according to the following two criteria: (1) The emotions of these songs should be uniformly distributed in the four quadrants

Table 4.2 An Example MATLAB Code for the Regression Approach to MER

```
%% TRAINING PHASE----------------------------------------------
% feature extraction
DIR_TR = 'DIR_TR';              % the directory of training song
X = extract_feat(DIR_TR);       % features (N by M)
[N M] = size(X);                % N: # of training data
                                % M: # of training data
% emotion annotation
[Y_v Y_a] = annotate_emotion;   % valence, arousal
Y = [Y_v Y_a];                  % ground truth (N by 2)

% feature normalization
[X p_mu p_std] = zscore(X);
                % p_mu and p_std are normalization parameters,
                % keep them to normalize the test data

% model training
models = cell(2,1);
for va = 1:2
    models{va} = svmtrain( Y(:,va), X, '-s 3');
                % INPUT: ground truth, features, LIBSVM
                  parameters
                %       -s svm_type : type of SVM
                %            3 -- epsilon-SVR
                % OUTPUT: trained regression model
end

%% TEST PHASE----------------------------------------------
DIR_TE = 'DIR_TE';              % the directory of test songs
Xtest = extract_feat(DIR_TE);   % features (Ntest by M)
Ntest = size(Xtest,1);
Ypred = zeros(Ntest,2);         % to be predicted

% feature normalization
for j=1:M
    Xtest(:,j) = (Xtest(:,j)-p_mu(j))/p_std(j);
end

% prediction
for va = 1:2
    Ypred(:,va) = svmpredict( zeros(Ntest,1),
    Xtest, models{va});
end
```

Note: Here feature normalization is done via z-score normalization, and model training is done by employing the support vector regression implemented in LIBSVM.

Source: Data from C.-C. Chang and C.-J. Lin. *LIBSVM: A library for support vector machines,* 2001.

of the emotion plane; and (2) each music piece should express a certain dominant emotion. The former is to balance the emotion distribution of the music pieces, whereas the latter is to reduce the emotion variation within each music piece.

Note that the genre of this database is popular music of different countries rather than the Western classical music, which is commonly adopted in other work [173, 204, 217, 282, 336, 341]. Western classical music is often chosen because it is much easier to gain agreement on perceived emotion and thus involves less subjectivity [204]. However, since the purpose of MER is to facilitate music retrieval and management in everyday music listening, and since it is the popular music that dominates everyday music listening, we should not shy away from the subjectivity issue by using only Western classical music. More discussions on the subjectivity issue are provided in Chapters 6–9.

To compare the segments fairly, the music pieces are converted to a uniform format (22,050 Hz, 16 bits, and mono channel PCM WAV) and normalized to the same volume level. Besides, since the emotion within a music piece may vary over time [117,173,217,282], for each song we manually selected a 25-second segment (mostly the chorus part) that is representative of the song and expresses a certain dominant emotion. Accordingly, we predict the emotion of a music segment and consider the prediction result as the emotion of the entire song. Note that we trim music manually because building a robust structure analysis algorithms is difficult [59, 221].

4.5.2 Feature Extraction

After preprocessing, the spectral contrast algorithm [152], DWCH algorithm [204], and two computer programs PsySound (version 2) [44] and Marsyas (version 0.1) [324] are employed to extract music features that construct a 114-dimension feature space, which is referred to as ALL hereafter. The extracted features, which are described in detail below, have been used for MER in earlier work. See Table 4.3 for denotations and brief descriptions.

PsySound extracts four types of measures: loudness, level, dissonance, and pitch. Loudness measures include loudness, sharpness (sound brightness), and timbral width (sound flatness). Level measures include sound pressure level, background noise level, and so forth. Dissonance measures are related to the perception of short irregularities in a sound. Pitch measures are related to the perceived fundamental frequency of a sound. Because of this psychoacoustical foundation, the features extracted by PsySound, especially 15 of them [365], are closely related to emotion perception. These 15 features form a second feature space called Psy15. See Table 4.4 for the description of Psy15.

Marsyas generates 19 spectrum features (spectral centroid, spectral rolloff, spectral flux, time domain zero-crossing and MFCC), six rhythm features (by beat and tempo detection) and five pitch features (by multi-pitch detection). In addition, 12 spectral contrast features and 28 DWCH features are also extracted. These features are described in Chapter 3.

Table 4.3   The Adopted Feature Extraction Algorithms

Method	#	Description
PsySound (P)	44	Extracts features including loudness, level, pitch multiplicity, and dissonance based on psychoacoustic models [44].
Marsyas (M)	30	Extracts timbral texture, rhythmic content, and pitch content features [324]
Spectral contrast (S)	12	Represents the relative characteristics of each spectral subband and reflects the distribution of harmonic components [152]
DWCH (D)	28	Daubechies wavelets coefficient histogram, which has better ability in representing both local and global information [204]
Total (ALL)	144	

Default values of the parameters used in these feature extraction algorithms/ toolkits are adopted. Specifically, the analysis window for frame-level features is set to 23 ms (512 samples at 22,050 Hz sampling rate), and the frame-level features are integrated to clip-level features by the MeanVar model [228], which models each frame-level feature as a Gaussian distribution and represents the feature by mean

Table 4.4   The 15 PsySound Features (Psy15) Recommended in

	Feature	Description
1	Spectral centroid	The centroid of spectral density function
2	Loudness	Human perception of sound intensity
3, 4*	Sharpness	A pitch-like (low-high) aspect of timbre
5	Timbral width	The flatness of a loudness function
6	Volume	Human perception of the size of sound
7, 8*	Spectral dissonance	Roughness of all spectrum components
9, 10*	Tonal dissonance	Roughness of just the tonal components
11	Pure tonal	The audibility of the spectral pitches
12	Complex tonal	The audibility of the virtual pitches
13	Multiplicity	The number of pitches heard
14	Tonality	Major-minor tonality, e.g., C major
15	Chord	Musical pitches sounded simultaneously

* Two algorithms are used to extract the feature.

Source: Data from Y.-H. Yang, C. C. Liu, and H. H. Chen, *Proc. ACM. Int. Conf. Multimedia*, 81–84, 2006.

and variance. This is a common practice for temporal integration. All features are linearly normalized to [0, 1].

4.5.3 Subjective Test

The purpose of the subjective test is to obtain the ground truth of the VA values. The subjective test described here involves a total of 253 volunteers recruited from the campus of National Taiwan University. Each of them is asked to listen to 12 randomly selected music pieces and to label the VA values from −1.0 to 1.0 in 11 ordinal levels (visualized as a set of radio buttons). The subjects are asked to annotate the perceived emotion. The ground truth is then set by averaging the opinions of all subjects. On the average, each music piece is labeled by at least 10 subjects.

No limitations on the background (e.g., psychology expertise, musicianship) are imposed when recruiting subjects since the MER system is expected to be applicable to all people. However, because the concept of MER may be new to the subjects, we need to inform them of the essence of the emotion model, the purpose of the experiment, and the following rules of the subjective test:

- Label the perceived emotion rather than the felt emotion (cf. Section 1.2).
- Express the general feelings in response to melody, lyrics, and singing (vocal) of the song. We do not attempt to ignore the influences of the lyrics and singing even though the related features have not been considered so far.
- No limitation is given to the total duration of the labeling process. The subjects are allowed to listen to the music pieces more than once to ensure that the labels can truly reflect their feelings. Typically the total duration of the labeling process is less than 15 minutes.
- Music emotion perception is in nature subjective. The subjects are free to annotate personal feeling.

The quality of the ground truth is central to the system performance. An evaluation of the consistency of the ground truth data is described in Section 4.6.1.

4.5.4 Regressor Training

The 195 $(\mathbf{x}_i, y_i)$ inputs from feature extraction and subjective test are then used to train the regressors using one of the algorithms described in Section 4.3.3: MLR, SVR, or AdaBoost.RT. The implementation of SVR is based on the library LIBSVM [54], along with a grid parameter search to find the best parameters. AdaBoost.RT is implemented in the Java language. For AdaBoost.RT, the maximal number of iterations is empirically set (via a cross-validation procedure [78]) to 30 and the threshold φ for demarcating correct and incorrect predictions is set to 0.1. MLR can be easily implemented in MATLAB.

4.6 Performance Evaluation

We run a series of experiments to evaluate the performance of the regression approach with various ground truth data spaces, feature spaces, and regression algorithms. The R^2 statistics, which is a standard way for measuring the goodness of fit of regression models, is calculated as follows [291]:

$$R^2(\mathbf{y}, r(\mathbf{X})) = 1 - \frac{N\epsilon}{\sum_{i=1}^{N}(y_i - \bar{y}))^2} = 1 - \frac{\sum_{i=1}^{N}(y_i - r(\mathbf{x}_i))^2}{\sum_{i=1}^{N}(y_i - \bar{y})^2}, \quad (4.13)$$

where $\bar{y}$ is the mean of the ground truth. Unlike MSE, R^2 is comparable between experiments because of the normalization of the total squared error ($N\epsilon$) by the energy of the ground truth. R^2 is often interpreted as the proportion of underlying data variation that is accounted for by the fitted regression model [232]. The value of R^2 lies in $[-\infty, 1]$; an R^2 of 1.0 means the model perfectly fits the data, while a negative R^2 means the model is even worse than simply taking the sample mean.

Note that sometimes R^2 is calculated as the square of the Pearson correlation coefficient between the ground truth and the estimate,

$$R^2(\mathbf{y}, r(\mathbf{X})) = \frac{\text{cov}(\mathbf{y}, r(\mathbf{X}))^2}{\text{var}(\mathbf{y})\text{var}(r(\mathbf{X}))}. \quad (4.14)$$

In this case, the value of R^2 lies in $[0, 1]$; $R^2 = 1$ means the model perfectly fits the data, whereas $R^2 = 0$ indicates no linear relationship between the ground truth and the estimate. This definition of R^2 is adopted in LIBSVM [54]. Though the R^2 values computed by Eqs. 4.13 and 4.14 are not always equivalent, a higher value of R^2 does indicate that the prediction accuracy of a regressor is higher. One should clearly specify which definition of R^2 is used in an evaluation, though. We use Eq. 4.13 in this chapter and we use Eq. 4.13 in this chapter and Chapters 7 but Eq. 4.14 in Chapter 8 and 9.

We evaluate the performance of regression by the 10-fold cross-validation technique [78], in which the whole data set is randomly divided into 10 parts, 9 of them for training and the remaining one for testing. The above process is repeated 20 times to get the average result. The R^2 for each data dimension (say, valence and arousal) is computed separately.

4.6.1 Consistency Evaluation of the Ground Truth

The consistency of the ground truth is evaluated in two ways. First, the consistency of annotations given by different subjects for the same song is evaluated by the standard deviation of annotations. Since the ground truth is obtained by averaging subjects' annotations, the larger the standard deviation is, the less representative the ground truth can be.

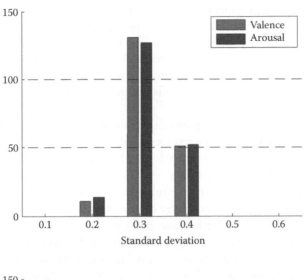

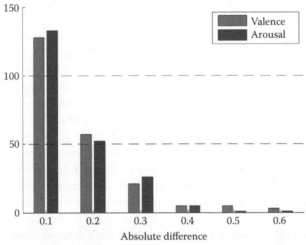

Figure 4.3 **(a) Histogram of standard deviations for valence and arousal of 195 songs in the first course of subjective test. (b) Histogram of absolute difference for valence and arousal of 220 data pairs in the test-retest stability study.**

Figure 4.3(a) shows the histogram of standard deviations for arousal and valence of (the first course of) the subjective test. We see that most standard deviations of music pieces are about 0.3, which give rise to a 95% confidence interval [232] of roughly ±0.2 (sample size is 10 since each music piece is labeled by more than 10 subjects). On a range of −1.0 to 1.0, a range of 0.4 is not that big, yet it reflects the subjectivity issue described in Section 1.3.3.

Second, we evaluate whether the annotations given by the same subject are similar after a span of time by conducting a test-retest reliability study [65] to find the absolute difference between corresponding annotations for the same song. The larger the absolute difference is, the less repeatable the subjective test could be. The second course of subjective test is separated from the first one by two months, with 22 subjects reinvited to annotate the music pieces they have annotated in the first course.

Figure 4.3(b) shows the histogram of absolute difference for arousal and valence of 220 (22 × 10) data pairs in the test-retest stability study. We see that more than one half of the absolute differences fall below 0.1, showing that the annotations given by the same person are quite consistent.

While Figure 4.3(b) shows that the subjective test by the same person is repeatable, Figure 4.3(a) shows a certain degree of inconsistency in the ground truth data. The inconsistency is reasonable because music perception is subjective in nature. However, it should be noted that the consistency can be improved if we personalize the MER system, or, in a similar sense, reduce the individual differences of the subjects by grouping them according to personal factors. See Chapters 6–9 for more details.

Using the absolute difference of test-retest reliability, we can compute an upper bound of R^2 for the regression approach: 58.6% for valence and 80.5% for arousal. This approximated upper bound defines both the viability of the regression approach and the kind of R^2 that is reasonable for the regression approach. The low upper bound for valence is not surprising since, as it has been pointed out in [282] and many previous work on MER, arousal is generally much easier to model than valence. There are two main reasons, which are actually related to each other, for this phenomenon. First, while there are a number of features relevant to arousal such as loudness (loud/soft), tempo (fast/slow), and pitch (high/low), there are few salient features for valence. Second, the perception of valence is more subjective than that of arousal; there is a good chance that people perceive opposite valence for the same song.

After evaluating the consistency of the ground truth data, we move on to evaluate the performance of the regression approach using different data spaces and different feature spaces.

4.6.2 Data Transformation

A major issue of the dimensional approach to MER is the dependency between the two dimensions in the valence-arousal (denoted as VA) data space, as evident from the high coefficient value (0.3368) of Pearson's correlation [232] between valence and arousal in the data set. Therefore, it is interesting to examine the influence of the data correlation on the accuracy of MER.

A popular method for reducing the correlation between variables is the principal component analysis (PCA) [78], which entails the computation of a loading matrix

L to transform original data Y to principal components U such that

$$U = L(Y - mean(Y)), \tag{4.15}$$

$$Y = L^{-1}U + mean(Y), \tag{4.16}$$

where U is the representation of Y in the principal component space. By PCA, we are able to transform the original data space VA to the principal component space (denoted by PC) where the resulting two dimensions are almost uncorrelated. Therefore, besides training r_V and r_A, we train another two regressors r_p and r_q in the PC space (where p and q denote the two dimensions of PC). In testing, we would apply r_p and r_q first and then transform the data space of the estimate from PC back to VA using Eq. 4.16. Note that although r_p and r_q are also trained independently, the underlying dimensions p and q are almost uncorrelated (the Pearson's correlation coefficient is close to zero).

4.6.3 Feature Selection

Besides considering the data space, we also consider feature selection to improve the prediction accuracy. We begin with a brief introduction of feature selection.

From the machine learning point of view, features are not necessarily of equal importance or quality, and irrelevant or redundant features may lead to inaccurate conclusion. Although domain knowledge helps identify good features, there is only limited understanding of how music evokes emotion. One solution for addressing this problem is to extract a number of music features and then use a feature selection algorithm to identify good features [112, 230].

The purpose of feature selection is to find the optimal feature subset that gives the maximal prediction accuracy and keeps the feature dimension minimal. For simplicity and effectiveness, RReliefF [333] is adopted here. It evaluates the features to the prediction task one by one and assigns a real number to each feature to indicate its importance. Because it takes feature interrelationship into account, RReliefF is better than other statistical measures such as correlation coefficient, information gain, and signal-to-noise ratio [333].

RReliefF is an extension of the ReliefF algorithm, which is a feature selection algorithm for classification problems. The key idea of ReliefF is to estimate the importance of each feature according to how well its value distinguishes between instances that are near to each other. That is,

$$\omega_m = P(\text{difference in the } m\text{-th feature value} \mid \text{nearest instances from difference classes})$$
$$- P(\text{difference in the } m\text{-th feature value} \mid \text{nearest instances from same class}), \tag{4.17}$$

where ω_m is the estimated importance of the m-th feature. For RReliefF, since the output variables are numerical values instead of classes, a kind of probability that the predicted values of two instances are different is introduced,

$$P_{\text{diffC}} = P(\text{different predicted values} \mid \text{nearest instance}). \qquad (4.18)$$

$$P_{\text{diffM}} = P(\text{different value of feature } m \mid \text{nearest instance}). \qquad (4.19)$$

Therefore, Eq. 4.17 can be rewritten as

$$\omega_m = P(\text{difference in feature } m \mid \text{nearest instances, different predicted values})$$

$$- P(\text{difference in feature } m \mid \text{nearest instances, similar predicted values})$$

$$= P_{\text{diffM} \mid \text{diffC}} - P_{\text{diffM} \mid \overline{\text{diffC}}}$$

$$= \frac{P_{\text{diffC} \mid \text{diffM}} P_{\text{diffM}}}{P_{\text{diffC}}} - \frac{(1 - P_{\text{diffC} \mid \text{diffM}}) P_{\text{diffM}}}{1 - P_{\text{diffC}}}.$$

$$(4.20)$$

The above values are estimated by randomly sampling n instances from the database and computing the P_{diffC} and P_{diffA} for k nearest neighbors of each sampled instance,

$$P_{\text{diffC}} \propto \text{diff}(y_i, y_j) \cdot d(i, j),$$

$$P_{\text{diffM}} \propto \text{diff}(x_{im}, x_{jm}) \cdot d(i, j), \qquad (4.21)$$

where i and j are the indices of two instances, x_{im} is the m-th feature of $\mathbf{x}_i$, diff$(\cdot, \cdot)$ takes the absolute difference between two values (which may have been normalized), and $d(i, j)$ takes into account the distance between the two instances. In [333], $d(i, j)$ is defined as follows:

$$d(i, j) = \frac{d_1(i, j)}{\sum_{l=1}^{k} d_1(i, l)},$$

$$d_1(i, j) = \exp(-\frac{1}{\sigma} \text{rank}(i, j)^2), \qquad (4.22)$$

where rank(i, j) is the rank of j in a sequence of instances ordered in ascending order of the distance from i, and σ is a parameter controlling the influence of the distance. See Table 4.5 for a pseudo code of RReliefF [333].

We ran RReliefF for each data space and ranked the features by importance.* Then we ran SVR with the top-m and top-n selected features for the two dimensions

---

* The parameters k and σ are empirically set to 10 and $k/3$, respectively.

Table 4.5   Pseudo Code of the RReliefF Feature Selection Algorithm

INPUT: training data $\{\mathbf{x}_i\}_{i=1}^{N}$, $\{y_i\}_{i=1}^{N}$, parameters K, σ, n
OUTPUT: vector W of estimations of the importance of features
  set N_{dC}, $N_{dM}[m]$, $N_{dC\&dM}[m]$, $W[m]$ to 0
  for $t = 1$ to n
    randomly select an instance i
    select k instances nearest to i
    for each neighbor j
      $N_{dC} = N_{dC} + \text{diff}(y_i, y_j) \cdot d(i, j)$
      for $m = 1$ to M
        $N_{dM}[m] = N_{dM}[m] + \text{diff}(x_{im}, x_{jm}) \cdot d(i, j)$
        $N_{dC\&dM}[m] = N_{dC\&dM}[m] + \text{diff}(y_i, y_j) \cdot \text{diff}(x_{im}, x_{jm}) \cdot d(i, j)$
      end
    end
  end
  for $m = 1$ to M
    $W[m] = N_{dC\&dM}[m]/N_{dC} - (N_{dM}[m] - N_{dC\&dM}[m])/(n - N_{dC})$
  end

Source: M. R. Šikonja and I. Kononenko. *Machine Learning.* 2003.

in each data space to decide the best combination of m and n that lead to minimal ϵ. The top-m and top-n selected features form the third feature space RRF$_{m,n}$. The best feature dimensions m and n of RRF, along with the adopted feature spaces, are summarized in Table 4.6. We show the comparison of ϵ using different feature dimensions for VA and PC in Figure 4.4 and list the top five RRF features for VA in Table 4.7, from which we see that the top features for arousal are related to spectral shape and pitch, whereas the top features for valence are more related to rhythmic (beat and tempo) and pitch properties of sound. Note the combination of the first

Table 4.6   The Three Features Spaces Used in the Performance Evaluation

Name	Dimension	Description
ALL	114 / 114	Use the features in Table 4.3.
Psy15	15 / 15	Use the features in Table 4.4.
RRF$_{m,n}$	VA: 3 / 8 PC: 15 / 18	Features selected from ALL by the algorithm RReliefF [333], the number of selected features is determined by minimizing the ϵ of a validation set.

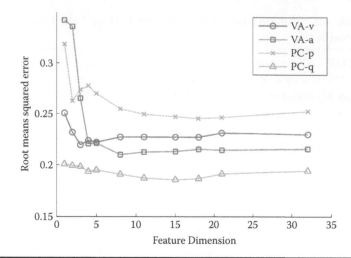

Figure 4.4 Comparison of the root mean squared error using different feature dimensions for VA and PC. The features are the top ones selected by RReliefF. (Data form M. R. Šikonja and I. Kononenko. *Machine Learning*. 2003.)

three features for valence gives rise to the minimal ϵ. Among them, the spectral dissonance (computed using Sethares' algorithm [44]) is related to the noisiness of the spectrum, the tonality is related to pitch, and the overall sum of beat histogram is related to tempo. It is also observed that energy-related features are not much relevant to arousal, a phenomenon that may result from the normalization of sound volume.

4.6.4 Accuracy of Emotion Recognition

We first evaluate the accuracy of emotion recognition using different regression algorithms. The feature space is fixed to Psy15. From the first three rows of

Table 4.7 Top Five Selected Features by RReliefF for VA and PC Spaces

Valence			Arousal		
Name	*Extractor*	*Weight*	*Name*	*Extractor*	*Weight*
spectral diss(S)	P*	0.0223	stdFlux	M	0.0123
tonality	P*	0.0210	tonality	P*	0.0115
sum of beat hist	M	0.0167	multiplicity	P*	0.0095
chord	P*	0.0129	meanFlux	M	0.0093
sum of pitch hist	M	0.0108	meanRolloff	M	0.0092

Note: The symbol * denotes the Psy15 features.

Table 4.8 The R^2 Statistics for Different Combinations of Different Regression Algorithms, Data Spaces, and Feature Spaces

			R^2 Statistics	
Method	*Data Space*	*Feature Space*	*v*	*a*
MLR	VA	Psy15	10.9%	56.8%
AdaBoost.RT	VA	Psy15	11.7%	55.3%
SVR	VA	Psy15	22.2%	57.0%
SVR	PC	RRF$_{15,18}$	28.1%	58.3%
Test-retest#	N/A	N/A	58.6%	80.5%

Note: The entry denoted # is the method for estimating the upper bound performance; see Section 4.6.1.

Table 4.8, it can be found that the R^2 of SVR reaches 22.2% for valence and 57.0% for arousal, representing the most prominent prediction accuracy among the three. Consequently, we employ SVR as the regressor hereafter. Also note that AdaBoost.RT does not outperform the baseline method MLR much, showing that a simple method may work just as well.

Next, we compare the R^2 of various combinations of data spaces and feature spaces using SVR as the regressor. Table 4.9 shows the following:

■ The best combination of data and feature space by summing the R^2 of valence and arousal directly is PC+RRF$_{15,18}$, and the resulting R^2 reaches 28.1% for valence and 58.3% for arousal.

■ Transforming the data to PC does not significantly affect to the prediction accuracy. This is interesting, since reducing the correlation between valence and arousal seems to have little influence. One possible reason for this phenomenon is that subjects can independently annotate valence and arousal to a certain extent, but more experiments are needed to validate this argument.

Table 4.9 The R^2 Statistics of SVR with Different Data and Feature Spaces

		Valence	*Arousal*
Data Space	*Feature Space*	*Prediction (v)*	*Prediction (a)*
VA	ALL	14.6%	58.6%
	Psy15	22.2%	57.0%
	RRF	25.4%	60.9%
PC	ALL	16.2%	60.2%
	Psy15	18.1%	58.5%
	RRF	28.1%	58.3%

- Selecting features by RReliefF greatly improves the accuracy (especially for valence), which shows the importance of feature selection. Generally the performance of adopted feature spaces is RRF > Psy15 > ALL.
- Using Psy15 as the feature space rather than ALL does not exhibit evident accuracy improvement for PC, which may be reasonable because the psychoacoustic meaning of the Psy15 features might be lost in the principal space.
- Recall that when we use VA+RRF, only three features are used to predict valence (see Table 4.6); however, the reported R^2 of 25.4% is high enough compared to the best one, 28.1%. This finding implies that most of the 114 extracted features may not be so relevant to valence.

We also show the distributions of ground truth and prediction result for PC+RRF$_{15,18}$+SVR in Figure 4.5. It can be found that the aggregated distributions are fairly similar. Figure 4.6 is obtained from Figure 4.5 by connecting predicted values to the corresponding ground truth values with arrows.

In summary, the best performance of the regression approach reaches 28.1% for valence and 58.3% for arousal by using PC+RRF$_{15,18}$+SVR. This performance is considered satisfactory since it meets over half the upper bound estimated from the test-retest reliability study with less than 20 features for both valence and arousal (see the last two rows of Table 4.8).

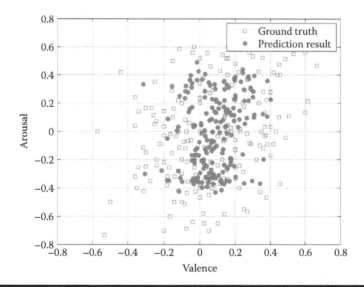

Figure 4.5   Distributions of songs according to the ground truth (squares) and the prediction result (filled circles) of PC+RRF$_{15,18}$+SVR. It can be observed that the distributions are similar. For a closer look, see Figure 4.6.

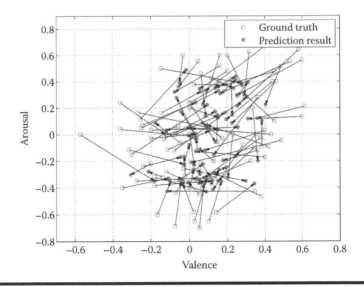

Figure 4.6 Distributions of songs according to the ground truth values (blue stars), with lines connecting to the corresponding predicted values (red circles) by PC+RRF$_{15,18}$+SVR. For space limitation, only 100 songs are shown.

4.6.5 Performance Evaluation for Music Emotion Variation Detection

We also apply the regression approach to detect the emotion variation of (cf., Section 4.23) music pieces and compare the performance against the system ID approach [173], which has a quantitative performance analysis and a publicly accessible data set. To have a fair comparison, we train SVR using the same ground truth data and music features described in [173], where six classical music pieces are segmented every second, and 18 music features are extracted (17 of them are extracted by PsySound and Marsyas). The R^2 reported in [173] is 21.9% for valence and 78.4% for arousal. We use SVR to predict the VA values for each one-second segment and compute the average R^2 statistics. The result (52.9% for valence and 64.8% for arousal) shown in Table 4.10 indicates that the regression approach outperforms the system

Table 4.10 The R^2 Statistics for MEVD Using the Data Set of [173]

			R^2 Statistics	
Method	*Data Space*	*Feature Space*	v	a
System ID	6 classical music annotated in the VA space	11 PsySound features + 6 Marsyas features + average tempo	21.9%	78.4%
SVR	As above	As above	52.9%	64.8%

ID approach by a great margin for valence prediction and achieves comparable results for arousal prediction. This performance is satisfying since the regression approach does not exploit any temporal information embedded in the time sequence. This experiment demonstrates the effectiveness of the regression approach for VA prediction and shows the regression approach can be applied to MEVD as well.

4.6.6 Performance Evaluation for Emotion Classification

Since it is easy to convert the regression results to discrete ones when a categorical taxonomy is required, we also evaluate the performance of the regression approach for categorical MER. Defining the emotion categories as the four quadrants in the emotion plane, we determine the emotion label of a music piece according to whether its predicted valence or arousal value is larger than zero. The performance is evaluated in terms of the classification accuracy. The following observations are made from Table 4.11:

- The system performs better in classifying class 1 and class 4 samples, perhaps because the emotion perception of negative emotions is more subjective than that of positive emotions [93].
- Class 2 samples are often misclassified as class 1 samples, whereas class 3 samples are often misclassified as class 4 samples. This result shows again the difficulty of modeling our valence perception.
- The overall classification accuracy reaches 60.5% even though the regressors are trained without distinguishing positive and negative values (e.g., predicting 0.1 as –0.1 or 0.3 brings about the same prediction error). Therefore, it is fair to say that the performance is satisfactory.

This study shows that the regression approach can be applied not only to dimensional MER but also to MEVD and categorical MER. The use of SVR allows us to obtain promising accuracy for emotion prediction and classification.

Table 4.11   Confusion Matrix of the Regression Approach for Emotion Classification

	Class 1	Class 2	Class 3	Class 4
Class 1	**74.2%**	9.7%	1.6%	14.5%
Class 2	41.7%	**45.8%**	8.3%	4.2%
Class 3	21.3%	10.6%	**36.2%**	31.9%
Class 4	12.3%	1.8%	14.0%	**71.9%**
Overall	60.5%			

4.7 Summary

In this chapter, we have described a computational model that represents each music piece as a point in the emotion plane. This regression approach is free of the ambiguity and granularity issues from which the conventional categorical approaches suffer. In addition, because there is more freedom in describing a song, the subjectivity issue is also alleviated. Besides the quadrant to which the song belongs, one can further know the emotion intensity ($\sqrt{v^2 + a^2}$) by inspecting the VA values.

The accuracy of the VA prediction determines the viability of the dimensional MER system. We formulate MER as a regression problem and adopt the support vector regression for direct estimation of the VA values. Compared with other VA prediction algorithms, the regression approach has a sound theoretical basis, allows thorough performance study, and generally exhibits reliable prediction. Moreover, the regression approach does not require temporal information or geometric operations.

We have also presented an extensive performance evaluation of the regression approach by using different combinations of data spaces, feature spaces, and regression algorithms. Support vector regression [301] is found to produce better prediction accuracy than multiple linear regression (MLR) [291] and AdaBoost.RT [303], another two popular regression algorithms. The R^2 statistic reaches 58.3% for arousal and 28.1% for valence. This performance is considered satisfactory since it reaches half the upper bound estimated from the test-retest reliability study. We have investigated the use of principal component analysis (PCA) to decorrelate valence and arousal and the use of RReliefF to remove irrelevant features and found that the latter process improves the prediction accuracy. Besides dimension SVR, our evaluation also shows the effectiveness of the regression approach to categorical MER and MEVD.

The regression approach to MER, however, is not free of issues. First, the regression approach suffers from the subjectivity issue of emotion perception as it assigns the valence and arousal values to a music piece in a deterministic way. It is likely that different users perceive different emotion values in the music piece. Second, the regression approach requires numerical emotion ground truth to train the computational model, but performing such an emotion rating is a heavy cognitive load to the subjects. These issues are addressed in the following chapters.

5

Ranking-Based Emotion Annotation and Model Training

Dimensional MER involves an emotion annotation process that is more labor costly than that of its categorical counterpart. Subjects need to determine the numerical valence and arousal (VA) values of music pieces rather than assign emotion labels to them. The heavy cognitive load of emotion annotation impedes the collection of large-scale ground truth annotations and also harms the reliability of the annotations. Because the generality of the training instances (which is related to the size of the training data set) and the quality of ground truth annotations are essential to the performance of a machine learning model, reducing the effort of emotion annotation plays a key role in the progress of dimensional MER. This chapter provides the details of a ranking approach that resolves this issue.

5.1 Motivation

To collect the ground truth data for dimensional MER, the subjects are often asked to *rate* the emotion values of music pieces in a continuum [234, 282, 364, 366]. Performing such an emotion rating, however, is a heavy cognitive load to the subjects [352]. Low-motivated subjects may give largely uniform ratings and thereby understate the differences of emotion values among songs [269]. Moreover, it is unclear whether the distance between two values rated 0.7 and 0.9 is the same as the distance between two other values rated 0.2 and 0.4 in a subject's mind [244]. Consequently, the quality of the ground truth data can vary a lot, which in turn deteriorates the accuracy of emotion recognition.

To overcome this difficulty, the ranking approach to MER developed in [355] determines the coordinates of a music piece in the 2D emotion plane by the *relative* emotion of the song with respect to other songs instead of directly computing the *exact* emotion values of the song. Specifically, this approach utilizes a machine learning algorithm called *learning-to-rank* algorithm to train two computational models that rank a collection of music pieces by their valence or arousal values. Two computational models are trained for valence and arousal, respectively. The ranking order of music pieces is then mapped to the valence or arousal values. The music pieces that are ranked topmost are assigned with the maximal valence or arousal values, and vice versa. In this way, a dimensional visualization of the music pieces in the emotion plane can also be generated.

The advantage of this approach is twofold. First, because the model training process of this approach requires ranking music pieces only by emotion, the annotation process of MER is greatly simplified. The subjects only have to *rank* (e.g., by making pairwise comparisons) the music pieces, which intuitively is a much easier task than the one that requires the determination of exact emotion values. It has been found that the ranking approach works remarkably better than the conventional rating approach in practice. By relieving the cognitive load on the subjects, the reliability of the ground truth is also enhanced.

Second, due to the semantic gap between the object feature level and the human cognitive level of emotion perception, it is difficult to accurately compute the emotion values [364]. Because machine learning algorithms that minimize the mean squared error (MSE) between the ground truth and the estimates tend to make conservative estimates when the computational model is inaccurate, the regression approach described in the previous chapter suffers a reduction of the coverage of the emotion plane. For example, it can be observed from Figure 4.5 that the range of the estimates is smaller than that of the ground truth. The ranking approach is free of this issue because songs associated with topmost/lowermost rankings are assigned with the highest/lowest emotion values, producing a full coverage of the emotion plane.

Below we first describe the ranking-based annotation method that is employed to replace conventional rating-based methods and then the learning-to-rank algorithms that better exploit the ranking-based annotations.

5.2 Ranking-Based Emotion Annotation

The basic idea of ranking-based emotion annotation is to ask the subjects to *rank* music pieces by emotion rather than *rate* the exact emotion values. This approach greatly reduces the cognitive load of emotion annotation because ranking is generally easier to perform than rating. Intuitively, emotion ranking can be accomplished by asking subjects to determine the straight order of a number of music pieces. However, this would be a lengthy process since determining the straight order of n music pieces requires $n(n-1)/2$ comparisons.

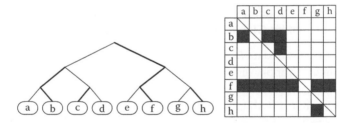

Figure 5.1 Left: the music emotion tournament, which groups eight randomly chosen music pieces in a tournament of seven matches. We use a bold line to indicate the winner of each match. Right: the corresponding preference matrix, with the entry (*i*, *j*) painted black to indicate that the object d_i is ranked higher than the object d_j. The global order f>b>c=h>a=d=e=g can be estimated by the greedy algorithm described in Table 5.1.

Figure 5.1 illustrates a ranking-based annotation method called *music emotion tournament* that resolves this issue. Instead of making exhaustive pairwise comparisons, the *n* music pieces are organized into *n* − 1 matches, which form a hierarchy of $\log_2 n$ levels. A subject compares the emotion values of two music pieces in a match and determines which one has the larger emotion value (e.g., more positive valence value or higher arousal value). In this way, the number of comparisons is greatly reduced from $n(n-1)/2$ (quadratic) to *n* − 1 (linear). The results of the pairwise comparisons are then incorporated into an *N* × *N* binary *preference matrix* **P** (one for valence and one for arousal), with each entry $P_{i,j}$ representing whether object d_i is ranked higher than object d_j, as exemplified in the right-hand side of Figure 5.1. Here *N* denotes the total number of music pieces of the database and *n* denotes the number of music pieces to be annotated by a subject; usually $N \gg n$.

To approximate a *global order* π from the preference matrix, the greedy algorithm described in [66] can be utilized. The intuition is simple: The more objects an object d_i dominates (ranked higher), or the fewer objects that d_i is dominated by, the greater global order d_i would have. Specifically, each object is assigned a *potential* value defined as

$$\rho_i = \sum_{j \in V} \left(P_{i,j} - P_{j,i} \right), \tag{5.1}$$

where *V* denotes the set of objects whose global order has not been determined. The greedy algorithm picks an object d_t that has maximum potential and assigns it a rank $\pi_t = N - |V| + 1$, which effectively places it ahead of all the remaining objects. For example, the object that is picked in the first place is assigned with the highest rank $\pi_t - 1$. The object d_t is then removed from *V*, and the potential values of the remaining objects are updated by

$$\rho_i = \rho_i + P_{t,i} - P_{i,t}. \tag{5.2}$$

Table 5.1   Pseudo Code of the Greedy Algorithm for Approximating Global Order from Pairwise Comparisons

Input: a list of data D and the associated preference matrix **P**
Output: an approximated optimal global order π
let $N = |D|, V = D$
for each $d_i \in V$, **do**
$\rho_i = \sum_{j \in V} \left(P_{i,j} - P_{j,i} \right)$
while V is non-empty **do**
  let $T = \arg\max_{i \in V} \rho_i$
  for each $d_t \in T$ **do**
    $\pi_t = N - |V| + 1$
  $V = V - T$
  for each $d_i \in V$ and $d_t \in T$ **do**
    $\rho_i = \rho_i + P_{t,i} - P_{i,t}$
end while

Note: The greedy algorithm has been modified to handle ties.

Source: W. W. Cohen et al. *J. Artificial Intelligence Research*, 1999.

This algorithm is guaranteed to find a good approximation [66]. However, the original algorithm described in [66] does not deal with ties, which may present when the preference matrix is sparse. This issue can be resolved by using a set of objects T instead of a single object d_t. Table 5.1 shows a pseudo code of the modified greedy algorithm.

Since the top-ranked objects are associated with larger emotion values, the *ranking score* s_i of an object d_i can be defined as

$$s_i = N - \pi_i, \tag{5.3}$$

and can train a regression model to automatically predict the ranking scores. However, since the emotion values have been obtained in a ranking-based way, one can also use a learning-to-rank algorithm to directly optimize a ranking-based objective function for better accuracy.

5.3 Computational Model for Ranking Music by Emotion

Learning-to-rank is another type of supervised machine learning problem other than classification and regression [213]. Its goal is to produce a permutation of items in such a way that certain semantic meaning is embedded in the ranking order. This section briefly introduces the learning-to-rank problem and describes three popular algorithms for learning-to-rank.

5.3.1 Learning-to-Rank

Any system that presents ordered results to a user is performing a ranking. A common example is the ranking of search results from a search engine (e.g., Google). A *ranking algorithm* assigns a ranking score to each object and ranks the object by the score. In the literature, the task of training a ranking model to accurately estimate the ranking scores of test data is commonly referred to as *learning-to-rank* [123, 153, 213, 347]. Given a list of objects with ground truth ranking scores $\mathbf{s} = \{s_1, s_2, \ldots, s_N\}$ and feature vectors $\mathbf{x} = \{\mathbf{x}_1, \mathbf{x}_2, \ldots, \mathbf{x}_N\}$, a ranking model $f(\cdot)$ is trained by minimizing $L(\mathbf{s}, f(\mathbf{x}))$, where $L(\cdot, \cdot)$ is a loss function for ranking. The estimate for d_i is denoted as $f(\mathbf{x}_i)$, where $\mathbf{x}_i = [x_{i1}, x_{i2}, \ldots, x_{iM}]^\top$, M is the number of features.

5.3.2 Ranking Algorithms

5.3.2.1 RankSVM

The state-of-the-art ranking algorithms fall into two categories: pairwise and listwise. The *pairwise* approach takes object pairs as learning instances, formulates the problem as the classification of object pairs into two categories (correctly and incorrectly ranked), and trains classification models for ranking. The use of support vector machine (SVM), boosting, or neural network as the classification model leads to the methods RankSVM [123], RankBoost [96], and RankNet [42]. For example, RankSVM adapts the support vector machines to classify object pairs in consideration of large margin rank boundaries [123, 153]. Specifically, the ranking problem is considered as the classification of object pairs into two categories (correctly ranked and incorrectly ranked) and a SVM model is trained by minimizing the classification error $\sum_{i,j}^{N} (f(\mathbf{x}_i) - f(\mathbf{x}_j))(y_i - y_j)$. Though the pairwise approach offers advantages, it ignores the fact that ranking is essentially an estimation task applied to a list of objects. Moreover, taking every possible pair is of complexity $O(N^2 M)$, which is exceedingly time-consuming when N is large.

5.3.2.2 ListNet

The *listwise* approach conquers the shortcomings of the pairwise approach by using score lists directly as learning instances and minimizing the listwise loss between the ground truth ranking list and the estimated one [49, 180, 262, 332, 347]. In this way, the optimization is performed directly on the list and the computational cost is reduced to $O(NM)$. For example, to define a listwise loss function, the List-Net algorithm described in [347] uses the top-one probability to transform a list of ranking scores into a probability distribution. The top-one probability $P(s_i)$ of object d_i, defined as follows, represents the probability of the object being ranked on the top,

$$P(s_i) = \frac{\Phi(s_i)}{\sum_{j=1}^{N} \Phi(s_j)} = \frac{\exp(s_i)}{\sum_{j=1}^{N} \exp(s_j)}, \qquad (5.4)$$

where i and j are object indices, and $\Phi(\cdot)$ is an increasing and strictly positive function such as the exponential function. Modeling the list of scores as a probabilistic distribution, a metric such as the cross entropy can be used to measure the distance (listwise loss) between the ground truth list and the estimated one,

$$L(\mathbf{s}, f(\mathbf{x})) = -\sum_{i=1}^{N} P(s_i) \log P(f(\mathbf{x}_i)). \qquad (5.5)$$

Because this cost function is differentiable, it can be minimized by the gradient descent procedure [40]. (The Gamma statistic [304] used later in the performance evaluation, however, is nondifferentiable and thus not suitable here.) In [347], the authors adopted the linear neural network model as the ranking model [122], with the constant b omitted,

$$f(\mathbf{x}_i) = \mathbf{w}^\top \mathbf{x}_i, \qquad (5.6)$$

and updated the weights $\mathbf{w}$ at a learning rate η as follows:

$$\mathbf{w} \leftarrow \mathbf{w} - \eta \cdot \Delta \mathbf{w},$$

$$\Delta \mathbf{w} = \frac{\partial L(\mathbf{s}, f(\mathbf{x}))}{\partial \mathbf{w}} = \sum_{i=1}^{N} (P(f(\mathbf{x}_i)) - P(s_i)) \mathbf{x}_i, \qquad (5.7)$$

where $\Delta \mathbf{w}$ is derived by computing the gradient of Eq. 5.5 with respect to $\mathbf{w}$. Specifically,

$$
\begin{aligned}
\Delta w_m &= \frac{\partial L(\mathbf{s}, f(\mathbf{x}))}{\partial w_m} \\
&= -\sum_{i=1}^{N} P(s_i) \frac{\partial \log P(\mathbf{w}^\top \mathbf{x}_i)}{\partial w_m} \\
&= -\sum_{i=1}^{N} P(s_i) \frac{\partial}{\partial w_m} \log \frac{e^{\mathbf{w}^\top \mathbf{x}_i}}{\sum_{k=1}^{N} e^{\mathbf{w}^\top \mathbf{x}_k}} \\
&= -\sum_{i=1}^{N} P(s_i) \frac{\partial}{\partial w_m} \left(\mathbf{w}^\top \mathbf{x}_i - \log \sum_{k=1}^{N} e^{\mathbf{w}^\top \mathbf{x}_k} \right) \\
&= -\sum_{i=1}^{N} P(s_i) \left(x_{im} - \frac{1}{\sum_{k=1}^{N} e^{\mathbf{w}^\top \mathbf{x}_k}} \sum_{k=1}^{N} \frac{\partial e^{\mathbf{w}^\top \mathbf{x}_k}}{\partial w_m} \right) \\
&= -\sum_{i=1}^{N} P(s_i) x_{im} + \frac{1}{\sum_{k=1}^{N} e^{\mathbf{w}^\top \mathbf{x}_k}} \sum_{k=1}^{N} x_{km} e^{\mathbf{w}^\top \mathbf{x}_k}.
\end{aligned} \qquad (5.8)
$$

The last equation can be rewritten as

$$\Delta w_m = \sum_{i=1}^{N} \left(-P(s_i) + P(\mathbf{w}^\top \mathbf{x}_i) \right) x_{im}$$

$$= \sum_{i=1}^{N} \delta(f(\mathbf{x}_i), s_i) \nabla_{w_m} f(\mathbf{x}_i),$$

(5.9)

where $\delta(f(\mathbf{x}_i), s_i) = P(f(\mathbf{x}_i)) - P(s_i)$ is the normalized error for the i-th object.

5.3.2.3 RBF-ListNet

Despite that ListNet has been found effective and efficient (e.g., see [358, 359]), its performance is sometimes limited by the oversimplified assumption that considers a linear relationship between the ranking scores and the features. Moreover, it has been shown that the characteristics of music are better modeled with a nonlinear function such as radial basis function (RBF) [245, 364]. Due to these concerns, Yang et al. replaced the linear neural network model of ListNet by the RBF neural network model [122, 162] and developed a new ranking algorithm called RBF-ListNet in [355].

Figure 5.2 shows the architecture of an RBF neural network. Under certain mild conditions on the radial basis functions, the RBF neural networks can approximate well any function [57]. The performance of an RBF neural network depends on the number and the centers of the RBFs, their shapes, and the method used for learning the input-output mapping. For its superiority over the conventional Gaussian radial basis function [162], the cosine radial basis function is employed here. The estimate

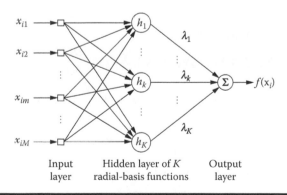

Figure 5.2 Architecture of a radial-basis neural network model [122], which is used as the ranking model in the algorithm RBF-ListNet.

for an object d_i is expressed as

$$f(\mathbf{x}_i) = \sum_{k=1}^{K} \lambda_k h_k(\mathbf{x}_i),$$

$$h_k(\mathbf{x}_i) = \frac{\alpha_k}{\left(||\mathbf{x}_i - \mathbf{v}_k||^2 + \alpha_k^2\right)^{1/2}}, \tag{5.10}$$

where λ_k is the weight of the k-th function $h_k(\cdot)$, $h_k(\mathbf{x}_i)$ is the response of the function located at the k-th prototype $\mathbf{v}_k$ to an input vector $\mathbf{x}_i$, α_k is the reference distance for $h_k(\cdot)$, and K is the number of RBFs. Note that $h_k(\mathbf{x}_i)$ approaches zero as $||\mathbf{x}_i - \mathbf{v}_k||^2$ approaches infinity and it becomes 1 if $\mathbf{x}_i$ coincides with $\mathbf{v}_k$. On the other hand, as α_k approaches zero, $h_k(\mathbf{x}_i)$ also approaches zero. Also, as α_k increases and approaches infinity, $h_k(\mathbf{x}_i)$ increases and approaches 1 regardless of the value of $||\mathbf{x}_i - \mathbf{v}_k||^2$.

To minimize the listwise loss function defined in Eq. 5.5, one can derive the gradients of λ_k, $\mathbf{v}_k$, α_k and update them by gradient descent [40]. The gradients are derived as follows:

$$\Delta\lambda_k = \sum_{i=1}^{N} \delta(f(\mathbf{x}_i), s_i)\nabla_{\lambda_k} f(\mathbf{x}_i),$$

$$\Delta\mathbf{v}_k = \sum_{i=1}^{N} \delta(f(\mathbf{x}_i), s_i)\nabla_{\mathbf{v}_k} f(\mathbf{x}_i), \tag{5.11}$$

$$\Delta\alpha_k = \sum_{i=1}^{N} \delta(f(\mathbf{x}_i), s_i)\nabla_{\alpha_k} f(\mathbf{x}_i),$$

and

$$\nabla_{\lambda_k} f(\mathbf{x}_i) = h_k(\mathbf{x}_i),$$

$$\nabla_{\mathbf{v}_k} f(\mathbf{x}_i) = \lambda_k \nabla_{\mathbf{v}_k} h_k(\mathbf{x}_i) = \lambda_k \nabla_{\mathbf{v}_k} \frac{\alpha_k}{b_{ki}}$$

$$= \lambda_k \frac{-\alpha_k}{b_{ki}^2} \nabla_{\mathbf{v}_k} b_{ki} = \lambda_k \frac{\alpha_k}{b_{ki}^3}(\mathbf{x}_i - \mathbf{v}_k)$$

$$= \lambda_k \frac{h_k(\mathbf{x}_i)^3}{\alpha_k^2}(\mathbf{x}_i - \mathbf{v}_k), \tag{5.12}$$

$$\nabla_{\alpha_k} f(\mathbf{x}_i) = \lambda_k \nabla_{\alpha_k} h_k(\mathbf{x}_i)$$

$$= \lambda_k \frac{b_{ki} - \alpha_k \nabla_{\alpha_k} b_{ki}}{b_{ki}^2} = \lambda_k \frac{b_{ki}^2 - \alpha_k^2}{b_{ki}^3}$$

$$= \lambda_k \frac{h_k(\mathbf{x}_i)}{\alpha_k}(1 - h_k(\mathbf{x}_i)^2),$$

where $b_{ki} = (||\mathbf{x}_i - \mathbf{v}_k||^2 + \alpha_k^2)^{1/2}$, $h_k(\mathbf{x}_i) = \frac{\alpha_k}{b_{ki}}$, and

$$
\begin{aligned}
\nabla_{\mathbf{v}_k} b_{ki} &= -(\mathbf{x}_i - \mathbf{v}_k) b_{ki}^{-1}, \\
\nabla_{\alpha_k} b_{ki} &= \alpha_k b_{ki}^{-1}.
\end{aligned}
\tag{5.13}
$$

Accordingly, the values of λ_k, $\mathbf{v}_k$, α_k are updated as follows:

$$
\lambda_k \leftarrow \lambda_k - \eta \cdot \Delta\lambda_k = \lambda_k - \eta \sum_{i=1}^{N} \delta(f(\mathbf{x}_i), s_i) h_k(\mathbf{x}_i),
$$

$$
\begin{aligned}
\mathbf{v}_k &\leftarrow \mathbf{v}_k - \eta \cdot \Delta\mathbf{v}_k \\
&= \mathbf{v}_k - \eta \sum_{i=1}^{N} \delta(f(\mathbf{x}_i), s_i) \lambda_k \frac{h_k(\mathbf{x}_i)^3}{\alpha_k^2} (\mathbf{x}_i - \mathbf{v}_k),
\end{aligned}
\tag{5.14}
$$

$$
\begin{aligned}
\alpha_k &\leftarrow \alpha_k - \eta_2 \cdot \Delta\alpha_k \\
&= \alpha_k - \eta_2 \sum_{i=1}^{N} \delta(f(\mathbf{x}_i), s_i) \lambda_k \frac{h_k(\mathbf{x}_i)}{\alpha_k} (1 - h_k(\mathbf{x}_i)^2),
\end{aligned}
$$

where η_2 is a learning rate that is set one order of magnitude lower than η according to [162]. As for initialization, the output weights λ are set to zero, the prototypes $\mathbf{v}_k$ are determined by K-means clustering [162], and the reference distances α are computed according to the nearest prototype heuristic described in [161], that is, $\alpha_k = \min_{1 \le p \le K, p \ne k} ||\mathbf{v}_k - \mathbf{v}_p||$. The time complexity of RBF-ListNet is $O(NKM)$.

Table 5.2 shows the pseudo code of RBF-ListNet. The learning process terminates when the change of loss is smaller than a convergent threshold δ. The values of K, η, and δ are usually determined empirically by a grid search.

Table 5.2 Pseudo Code of the Learning-to-Rank Algorithm RBF-ListNet

Input: training data $(\mathbf{x}_i, s_i)$, $i \in \{1,\ldots,N\}$
Output: RBF neural network model parameters λ, $\mathbf{v}$, α
Parameter: number of radial basis functions K, learning rates η, η_2, and convergent threshold δ.
Initialize parameters λ, $\mathbf{v}$, α
while true **do**
  Compute $f(\mathbf{x}_i)$ according to Eq. 5.10.
  Transform the ranking scores to probabilities using Eq. 5.4.
  Compute the loss l between s_i and $f(\mathbf{x}_i)$ according to Eq. 5.5.
  if change in l is smaller than δ
    break
  end if
  Update the parameters at rates η and η_2 according to Eq. 5.14.
end while

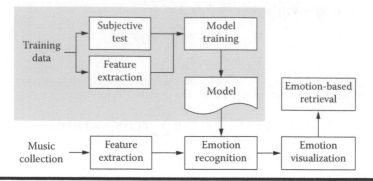

Figure 5.3 Schematic diagram of the ranking approach. Note that this diagram is a generalization of the diagram depicted in Figure 4.2. Since the learning algorithm used for model training is not restricted to regression algorithms, we have replaced regressor training by model training.

5.4 System Overview

Figure 5.3 shows a system diagram of the ranking approach. The music emotion tournament scheme described in Section 5.2 is used in the subjective test to collect emotion annotation. The ground truth needed by this algorithm is obtained by approximating the global order and then computing the ranking scores using Eq. 5.3. The ranking algorithms described in Section 5.3.2 are then employed to train a ranking model by minimizing a ranking-based cost function. After training, the ranking model takes the features of a new song as input and outputs the estimated ranking score of the song. The ranking scores of a music collection are mapped to the emotion plane to generate a dimensional representation. The songs that are ranked topmost (bottommost) are assigned with the maximal (minimal) valence or arousal values; then for simplicity the remaining ones are mapped in a linear fashion.

Table 5.3 shows an example MATLAB code for the ranking approach to MER, using ListNet for model training and prediction. Note that the code also includes the optional feature selection step. See Sections 4.6.3 and 5.6.2.1 for more details of feature selection.

5.5 Implementation

This section describes an implementation of the ranking approach. An extensive performance evaluation of the resulting MER system can be found in the next section.

Table 5.3   An Example MATLAB® Code for the Ranking Approach to MER, Using ListNet for Model Training and Prediction

```
%% TRAINING PHASE---------------------------------------
% feature extraction
DIR_TR = 'DIR_TR';          % the directory of training songs
X = extract_feat(DIR_TR);   % features (N by M)
[N M] = size(X);
[X p_mu p_std] = zscore(X); % feature normalization

% emotion annotation
R = emotion_tournament;
            % rankings of songs in terms of valence or
            % arousal value, estimated by the greedy method
S = (max(R)-R+1)/max(R);
            % convert rankings to scores (in [0, 1])

% feature selection using RReliefF (optional step)
do_fs = true;
if do_fs,
    W = RReliefF(S, X);     % W: importance of each feature
    [W_sorted idx] = sort(W,'descend');
    Nfeat = 70;             % number of features to use
    feat_idx = idx(1:Nfeat); % select the top Nfeat most
                            % important features
else
    feat_idx = 1:M;         % use all features
end

% model training
model = listNet_train( S, X(:,feat_idx));

% convert (linearly maps) scores to emotion values
  (in [-1, 1])
Strain = listNet_predict( X(:,feat_idx), model);
Ytrain = (Strain - min(Strain))/range(Strain)*2 - 1;

%% TEST PHASE------------------------------------------
DIR_TE = 'DIR_TE';          % the directory of test songs
Xtest = extract_feat(DIR_TE);
for j=1:M                    % feature normalization
    Xtest(:,j) = (Xtest(:,j)-p_mu(j))/p_std(j);
end

% prediction
Stest = listNet_predict( Xtest(:,feat_idx), model);

% convert scores to emotion values
Ytest = (Stest-min(Strain))/range(Strain)*2 - 1;
```

Table 5.4   Statistics of the Two Data Sets Utilized in the Implemented System

Data Set	# of Songs	Annotation Method(s)	Annotated Emotion(s)	# of Annotators per Song
db1	60	Rating	Valence, arousal	40
db2	1240	Rating, ranking	Valence	4.3

5.5.1 Data Collection

As summarized in Table 5.4, two data sets are utilized in this implementation. The first data set, db1, consists of 60 famous pop songs collected from English albums. For fair comparison, the songs are converted to a standard format (22,050 Hz sampling frequency, 16 bits precision, and mono channel). Besides, to lessen the burden of emotion annotation on the subjects, each song is represented by a 30-second segment manually trimmed from the chorus part of the song. A total of 99 subjects (46 male, 53 female) are recruited from the campus of National Taiwan University to rate both the valence and arousal values with a graphic interface called "AnnoEmo" [366] in a silent computer lab. We partition the data set into four subsets, each with 15 music pieces whose emotions are roughly uniformly distributed in the emotion plane, and randomly select one of the subsets for a subject to annotate. A subject annotates the emotion of a music piece by clicking on the emotion plane displayed by computer. A rectangle is then formed on the specified point, making it easy for the subject to compare the annotations of different music pieces. The subject can click on the rectangle to listen to the music piece again, or drag and drop the rectangle to modify the annotation [366]. Many subjects find the annotation pleasant and volunteer to annotate more. In that case, we remove the rectangles and present him/her another subset of music to annotate. Six subjects annotate the entire data set. In the end, each music piece is annotated by 40 subjects. The ground truth annotation of each music piece is set by taking the average. See Table 5.5 for the titles of the 60 songs and Chapter 7 for more details of the data set. This data set is used in many chapters of this book, including Chapters 7–9.

To evaluate the ranking approach on a larger data set, we compile another data set, db2, using 1240 Chinese pop songs. Each song is represented by a 30-second segment starting from the initial 30th second of the song, a common practice in music classification [276]. An online subjective test is conducted to collect the emotion annotations. Each subject is invited to annotate eight ($n = 8$) randomly selected music pieces using both rating- and ranking-based measures. We use a scroll bar between 0 and 100 for the rating measure and use the music emotion tournament scheme described in Section 5.2 for the ranking measure. In addition, since the prediction of arousal has been shown relatively easier [93, 173, 217, 364], only the valence values are annotated for this data set. The song titles and artist names are shown during annotation. A total of 666 subjects (289 male, 377 female; mostly

Table 5.5   The Titles of the 60 Songs Used in Chapters 5, 7–9

1. "Smells Like Teen Spirit" by *Nirvana*	30. "White Christmas" by *Lisa One*
2. "Are We the Waiting" by *Green Day*	31. "I Want to Hold Your Hand" by
3. "Sweet Child O' Mine" by *Guns N'*	*Beatles*
Roses	32. "Take a Bow" by *Muse*
4. "Oh Happy Day"	33. "Imagine" by *John Lennon*
5. "The Drugs Don't Work" by *Verve*	34. "Your Song" by *Elton John*
6. "Dancing Queen" by *ABBA*	35. "Zombie" by *Cranberries*
7. "As Time Goes By" by *Lisa Ono*	36. "We Wish You the Merriest"
8. "Dying in the Sun" by *Cranberries*	37. "A Whole New World"
9. "Barriers" by *Aereogramme*	38. "Highway to Hell" by *ACDC*
10. "I Feel Good" by *James Brown*	39. "Gloomy Sunday" by *Billie Holiday*
11. "Diamonds and Rust" by *Joan Baez*	40. "She" by *Elvis Costello*
12. "Anticonformity" by *Krystal Meyers*	41. "Jingle Bells" by *Frank Sinatra*
13. "Sweet Dreams" by *Marilyn*	42. "Suzanne" by *Leonard Cohen*
Manson	43. "Champagne Supernova" by
14. "Into the Woods" by *My Morning*	*Oasis*
Jacket	44. "Tell Laura I Love Her" by *Ritchie*
15. "The Sound of Silence" by *Paul*	*Valens*
Simon	45. "All I Have to Do Is Dream"
16. "Oh Pretty Woman" by *Roy*	46. "Like a Virgin" by *Madonna*
Orbison	47. "With or without You" by *U2*
17. "I Will Always Love You" by	48. "I Want It that Way" by
W. Houston	*Backstreet Boys*
18. "American Idiot" by *Green Day*	49. "Just the Way You Are" by *Billy Joel*
19. "Copycat" by *Cranberries*	50. "C'est La Vie" by *Shania Twain*
20. "Hells Bells" by *ACDC*	51. "C'est La Vie" by *Bwitched*
21. "Castles In the Air" by *Don McLean*	52. "Mad World" by *Gary Jules*
22. "Hallelujah" by *Happy Mondays*	53. "Civil War" by *Guns N' Roses*
23. "The Rose" by *Janis Joplin*	54. "Our Lips Are Sealed" by *Hilary*
24. "Perfect Day" by *Lou Reed*	*Duff*
25. "What a Wonderful World" by	55. "Louie Louie" by *Iggy Pop*
Armstrong	56. "Hallelujah" by *Jeff Buckley*
26. "Stay" by *U2*	57. "When a Man Loves a Woman"
27. "The Christmas Song" by *N. K. Cole*	58. "Day Is Done" by *Norah Jones*
28. "A Thousand Miles" by *Vanessa*	59. "Where Have All the Flowers
Carlton	Gone"
29. "Where the Streets Have No Name"	60. "Labita" by *Lisa One*
by *U2*	

under the age of 30) participated in the subjective test, making each music piece annotated by 4.3 subjects on the average. The number of annotators per music piece ranges from 1 to 10.

The subjects are asked to annotate the perceived emotion. Since the MER system is expected to work for ordinary people, no limitations on the background (e.g., psychology expertise, musicianship) are imposed when recruiting subjects for annotating the two data sets. However, because MER may be new to the subjects, instructions regarding the purpose of MER, the meaning of valence and arousal, and the difference between perceived emotion and felt emotion are given to the subjects before the annotation process begins.

To investigate what factors may also influence emotion perception, the subjects are also asked to answer the following five questions after annotating emotion:

■ How much does the acoustic property of music (harmony, rhythm, and timbre) influence your emotion perception? (five-point scale, weak to strong)
■ How much do the lyrics of music influence your emotion perception? (five-point scale, weak to strong)
■ What factors of music, besides the above two, influence your emotion perception? (free text; optional problem)
■ Would you like to search/retrieve/organize music by emotion? (three-point scale, weak to strong)
■ What accuracy do you expect for an automatic emotion recognition system? (five-point scale, 60%, 70%, 80%, 90%, 100%)

The average ratings of the 622 subjects that answer the first two questions are 4.46 and 3.33, respectively. Both the acoustic property and the lyrics are considered important for emotion perception, but clearly the former exerts a stronger effect than the latter. This is reasonable since the power of music is universal; we can perceive emotion from songs that are purely instrumental or in an unfamiliar language [175]. According to this result, we focus on the extraction of audio features for modeling emotion in this implementation.

Many observations can be made from the 179 responses to the third question, which are shown in Table 5.6. First, vocal timbre also influences the emotion perception of music and therefore the use of speech features such as formants and prosody contours [289, 329] may improve the prediction accuracy.* Second, emotion perception is indeed subjective and is under the influence of listening context, mood, familiarity, memory, and preference. Finally, subjects report that song titles should not be shown during the annotation and that a proper segment selection should have been done to capture the most representative part of a song. These comments could be considered by future MER systems.

---

* However, robust techniques of melodic source separation need to be developed to extract such features from music. See Section 14.1 for more discussions.

Table 5.6 The Factors of Music Listening, Other than Harmony, Rhythm, Timbre, and Lyrics, that Are Considered Important for Emotion Perception

Factor	Frequency
Vocal timbre/singing skill	41
Song title	18
Segment Selection	16
Volume	7
Genre	6
Instrumentation	5
Recording quality	4
Ordering of the songs	1
Listening mood/context	25
Familiarity/associated memory	24
Preference of the singer/performer	17
Preference of the song	15

As for the fourth question, 68% of subjects report a high interest in adopting emotion-based music retrieval and organization, while only 5% of subjects report no interest. This result validates the research on music emotion recognition. As for the last question, 37% of subjects ask for accuracy of 80%, while only 10% of subjects ask for accuracy up to 100%. In terms of the percentage of subjects who are satisfied with a particular level of accuracy, the result is 15%, 30%, 67%, 90%, and 100% for prediction accuracy of 60%, 70%, 80%, 90%, and 100%, respectively. Therefore, to satisfy 90% of users, prediction accuracy up to 90% may be needed. Moreover, the correlation between the last two questions is only 0.165, which is not high. Even if we only consider subjects who report a high interest in emotion-based retrieval, it still requires an accuracy of about 90% to satisfy 90% of users. This level of accuracy, however, is fairly difficult to achieve by current MER systems, including the one implemented here (cf. Section 5.6.2).

5.5.2 Feature Extraction

As summarized in Table 5.7, a number of features are extracted to represent the following three perceptual dimensions of music listening: harmony, timbre, and rhythm, which are all closely related to emotion perception. The details of all these features are described in Chapter 3.

Harmony. We use the MIR toolbox [182] to generate two pitch features (salient pitch and chromagram center) and three tonality features (key clarity, mode,

Table 5.7   **Extracted Feature Sets**

Set	#	Features
Harmony	10	Salient pitch, chromagram center, key clarity, mode, and harmonic change [182]. Take mean and standard deviation for temporal integration [228].
Timbre	142	48 spectral flatness measures, 48 spectral crest factors [324], 40 Mel-scale frequency cepstral coefficients [246], the mean and standard deviation of roughness, irregularity, and inharmonicity [182].
Rhythm	5	Rhythm strength, rhythm regularity, rhythm clarity, average onset frequency, and average tempo [217].

harmonic change). We take the mean and standard deviation of these short-time features for temporal aggregation.

Timbre. We use the Marsyas [324] to extract 48 spectral flatness measures (SFM) and 48 spectral crest factors (SCF), both related to the tonalness of audio signal [21]. Moreover, we use the MIR toolbox [182] to extract the mean and standard deviation of the following three dissonance features: roughness, irregularity, inharmonicity. We also use the MA toolbox [246] to extract Mel-frequency cepstral coefficients (MFCC), the most widely used feature representation for audio signal processing [324]. We compute it by taking the mean and standard deviation of the first 20 coefficients of the cosine transform of each short-term log power spectrum expressed on a nonlinear perceptual-related Mel-frequency scale, and then taking the mean and standard deviation to collapse the feature values. A total of 142 timbre features are extracted for each music piece.

Rhythm. To describe the rhythmic property of music, we employ the MIR toolbox again to extract the following five features described in [217]: rhythm strength, rhythm regularity, rhythm clarity, average onset frequency, and average tempo.

The features and annotations of the two data sets are publicly available. [Online] http://mpac.ee.ntu.edu.tw/~yihsuan/MER/NTUMIR-1240/. Note that db1 and db2 correspond to data sets #2 and #3a in Table 1.4.

5.6 Performance Evaluation

We run a series of experiments to study the performance of the ranking approach. First, we compare the cognitive load of emotion annotation of the conventional rating measure and that of the music emotion tournament. Second, we compare the accuracy of emotion prediction using different feature sets, learning algorithms, and parameter settings. Feature selection is also conducted to obtain the best feature representation. Finally, we evaluate the subjective satisfaction of the prediction result of the resulting MER system.

5.6.1 Cognitive Load of Annotation

A questionnaire is presented at the end of the annotation process of db2 with the following three evaluation inquiries:

- **Easiness.** How easy it is to perform the annotation.
- **Within-subject reliability**. The possibility that the annotations are nearly the same a month later.
- **Between-subject reliability**. The possibility that the annotations are nearly the same as those of others.

All answers are on a five-point scale ranging from 1 to 5 (strongly disagree to strongly agree). Table 5.8 shows the average answers of the 603 subjects who answered the three questions. It can be found that the ranking measure is indeed much easier to use than its rival; this result validates the claim that it is easier for humans to rank rather than rate the music emotion. The subjects also express a high confidence level of both within- and between-subject reliability when the ranking measure is used, indicating its ability to reduce the inconsistency of emotion annotation. The fact that all the results of the rating measure are below the borderline further confirms the necessity and importance of the ranking approach. We have interchanged the order of rating and ranking measures and found that the results are nearly the same.

We also evaluate whether the difference between the rating and ranking measures is significant by the two-tailed t-test [133]. The two-tailed t-test evaluates whether the new result is significantly larger or smaller than the old result, whereas the one-tailed t-test test is directional; one can only test whether the new result is significantly larger or significantly smaller than the old result. The results show that the differences between ranking and rating are significant (p-value < 0.01) under the two-tailed t-test for all three inquiries.

Table 5.8 Comparison of Annotation Methods

Method	Subjective Evaluation			Objective Evaluation
	Easiness	Within Reliability	Between Reliability	Within Reliability (Test-Retest)
Rating	2.82	2.92	2.81	0.635
Ranking	4.07	3.78	3.36	0.708

Note: The scores are on a five-point scale where 3 means neutral.

Next, we conduct a test-retest reliability study to examine whether the annotations of a subject are similar after a span of time [65]. This way, we can objectively evaluate the within-subject reliability by computing the correlation between the two courses of annotations. More specifically, we conduct a second course of subjective test one month after the first course and reinvite 98 subjects to annotate online the pieces they have annotated. We compute the Spearman rank correlation coefficient [304] for every subject. The value is in $[-1, 1]$; a higher value indicates a higher correlation. As Table 5.8 shows, the average correlation of the ranking measure (0.708) is indeed higher than that of the rating measure (0.635). However, unlike the subjective evaluation, the difference between the ranking and rating measures is insignificant in the objective evaluation. A possible explanation is that in the subjective evaluation the subjects overestimate the within-subject reliability because they find the annotation easy to perform.

We do not make an objective evaluation of the between-subject reliability of db2 because its annotations are fairly sparse (707 music pieces are annotated by fewer than four different subjects). As for db1, the average Pearson correlation coefficient in the between-subject reliability is 0.416 for valence and 0.751 for arousal. The latter is significant ($p<0.05$) under the two-tailed t-test. The small correlation of valence annotations also suggests that valence perception is more subjective.

We also use the ratings to order music pieces and compare the resulting order to that of the ranking measure. The Spearman correlation coefficient reaches 0.667 if we compare all the music pieces and 0.765 if we compare only the pieces that fall into the upper and lower quartiles. This result indicates that the annotations of the ranking and rating measures are similar.

5.6.2 Accuracy of Emotion Recognition

We then evaluate the accuracy of emotion recognition of the computational model in terms of the Gamma statistic [304], the widely used statistical measure for estimating the ordinal correlation of two random variables that contain ties. It is defined by the number of concordant (correctly ranked) pairs C and the number of discordant (incorrectly ranked) pairs D, ignoring tied pairs, as follows:

$$G = \frac{C - D}{C + D}. \tag{5.15}$$

For two objects d_i and d_j, there is a concordant pair in $\mathbf{s}$ and $f(\mathbf{x})$ if $(f(\mathbf{x}_i) - f(\mathbf{x}_j))(s_i - s_j) > 0$ and a discordant pair if $(f(\mathbf{x}_i) - f(\mathbf{x}_j))(s_i - s_j) < 0$. There is a tied pair in $\mathbf{s}$ if $s_i = s_j$. When there are tied pairs, the Gamma statistic is often used instead of the Spearman rank correlation coefficient or the Kendall's τ, which is equal to $\frac{C-D}{N(N-1)/2}$ [304]. The value of the Gamma statistic equals 1 for perfect agreement, -1 for total disagreement, and 0 if the rankings are independent. Note that unlike MSE, the Gamma statistic places more importance on the relative emotion rankings than on exact emotion values.

5.6.2.1 Comparison of Different Feature Representations

We first compare the prediction accuracy using different feature representations. We conduct the experiment on the smaller data set db1 because it has both valence and arousal annotations (cf. Table 5.4). As this data set has been partitioned into four subsets for subjective test, we also use one of the subsets as the test set and the remaining ones for training (in a sense similar to fourfold cross-validation) and repeat the process four times until each subset is held out once. The ϵ-support vector regression (SVR) described in Section 4.3.3.2 is employed to train the model. We implement SVR based on the free LIBSVM library [54], with a RBF kernel and the scale parameter γ (cf. 4.12) empirically set to 0.01 after a grid search.

The average accuracy is shown in the first three rows of Table 5.9. It can be observed that the accuracy of arousal prediction is much higher than that of valence, and the difference is significant (p-value<0.01). This is not surprising since there are a number of features closely related to arousal perception, but only a few relevant to valence perception [173, 217]. By investigating the combination of the feature sets (rows 4–7 of Table 5.9), it can be found that using all the feature sets yields good accuracy for both valence and arousal prediction (0.424 and 0.676, respectively).

We then employ feature selection [112] to find an optimal feature subset that gives the maximal accuracy. While many feature selection methods have been proposed for classification (e.g., information gain and signal-to-noise ratio), few have been designed for regression and learning-to-rank [104]. One exception is the RReliefF algorithm [333], which measures the importance of a feature according to its ability to separate two training instances whose predicted values (i.e., ranking scores) differ a lot. As RReliefF has been shown effective in other MER work (e.g., [364]), we also

Table 5.9   The Gamma Statistic of Valence and Arousal Prediction of SVR Using Different Feature Representations

Feature Set	# of Features	Valence Prediction	Arousal Prediction
Harmony	10	0.319	0.691
Timbre	142	0.390	0.667
Rhythm	5	0.171	0.471
{Harmony, timbre}	152	0.424	0.667
{Harmony, rhythm}	15	0.295	0.686
{Timbre, rhythm}	147	0.395	0.671
{Harmony, timbre, rhythm}	157	0.424	0.676
{Harmony, timbre, rhythm}	15	0.319	0.752
+ feature selection (RReliefF)	70	0.471	0.738
	100	0.419	0.691

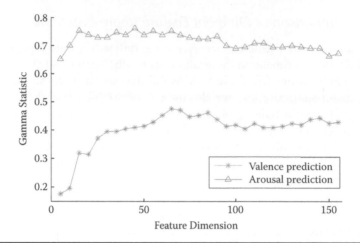

Figure 5.4 **The Gamma statistic of valence and arousal prediction with different numbers of features selected by the feature selection algorithm RReliefF.**

employ it here. As Table 5.9 shows, the best accuracies (0.471 for valence and 0.752 for arousal) are achieved when the top 70 and top 15 features selected by RReliefF are used. Using more features introduces noises to the system and degrades the accuracy, as shown in Figure 5.4. Moreover, we find that the top selected features for valence are mostly related to inharmonicity (dissonance), SFM, and SCF (tonalness), while those for arousal are related to chromagram center (pitch) and MFCC (timbre). This result is consistent with the findings of music psychologists [101].

According to Eq. 5.15, the percentage of correctly ranked pairs $C/(C + D)$ can also be calculated as $(G + 1)/2$. By this conversion, we know that the accuracies of valence and arousal prediction correspond to 73.6% and 87.6%, respectively, which are comparable to that of the state-of-the-art music emotion classification systems [140, 217] (cf. Table 1.3).

5.6.2.2 Comparison of Different Learning Algorithms

We then compare the performance of SVR and ListNet with different kernels/neural network functions using the following four settings. In the first db1→db1 setting, we use one of the four subsets of db1 for testing and the remaining ones for training. In the second db2→db2 setting, we randomly sample one-fourth of db2 for testing and the remaining ones for training. The above procedure is repeated 100 times to get the average result. In the third db2→db1 setting, we use the whole db2 as the training set and the whole db1 for testing. Likewise, in the fourth db1→db2 setting, we use db1 for training and db2 for testing. We consider the result of the last two settings as more important because they evaluate how well an MER system can be trained and evaluated using separate data sets. Note that RankSVM is not evaluated here because of its high computational cost [123, 359]. Moreover, it has been reported that its performance is inferior to that of ListNet for MER [356].

**Table 5.10   The Gamma Statistic of Valence Prediction
of Different Learning Algorithms**

Method	Function	db1 →db1	db2 →db2	db2 →db1	db1 →db2
Random	—	0.002	0.000	0.000	0.001
SVR	linear	0.319	0.367	0.139	0.208
SVR	RBF	0.471	0.376	0.245	0.245
ListNet	linear	0.243	0.353	0.165	0.267
RBF-ListNet	RBF	0.292	0.317	0.326	0.213

As arousal prediction has been shown easier, we focus on valence prediction and use the top 70 features selected by RReliefF from {harmony, timbre, rhythm} as the feature representation. In all settings, feature normalization is done by standardizing the training data to zero mean and unit variance (i.e., z-score normalization) and applying the normalization parameters to the test set. The convergent threshold δ is set to 1e−4, the learning rate η is set to 0.01 and 10000/N for ListNet and RBF-ListNet, and the number of radial basis functions K is set to 10 (a parameter sensitivity test is described later). In addition, we set the maximum number of iterations of ListNet and RBF-ListNet to 40 to prevent overfitting. We also implement a baseline method that randomly orders the music pieces.

Table 5.10 shows the experimental results. For db1→db1, the SVR of RBF kernel performs the best. The algorithms that employ RBF function generally perform better than those that use linear function; this validates previous findings that the characteristics of music are often better modeled with a nonlinear function. All four algorithms outperform the random permutation baseline by a great margin.

For db2→db2, however, the performance difference between the four algorithms becomes small, suggesting that valence prediction for this setting is relatively easier. The large number of training data in this setting (930 pieces) may account for this result.

For db2→db1, interestingly, the performance of all algorithms degrades significantly, except for RBF-ListNet. This degradation of performance may result from the differences of the two data sets in sample length, annotation method, and even the language of music pieces. In spite of these differences, it is found that RBF-ListNet performs consistently well and reaches the highest Gamma statistic of 0.326.

To qualitatively examine the result, we show the titles of the music pieces ranked topmost and bottommost in the db2→db1 setting in Table 5.11. It can be found that when RBF-ListNet is used, the music pieces with higher ranks are usually of positive emotions (happy, cheerful, or bright), while those with lower ranks are of negative emotions (sad, gloomy, or dark). The same trend can be observed from the result of other settings. However, when SVR is used, the music pieces with lower ranks are not always of negative emotions (e.g., "A Whole New World"). Notably,

Table 5.11   Estimated Order (Positive to Negative Valence) of Songs of DB1 by the MER System Trained with DB2 (DB2→DB1)

	Ranked by RBF-ListNet	Ranked by SVR
1	"I Feel Good" (0.433)	"I Want to Hold Your Hand" (0.507)
2	"Like a Virgin" (0.357)	"I Feel Good" (0.433)
3	"We Wish You the Merriest" (0.515)	"We Wish You the Merriest" (0.515)
4	"C'est La Vie" (0.498)	"Tell Laura I Love Her" (0.131)
5	"Oh Pretty Woman" (0.478)	"Dancing Queen" (0.449)
56	"Gloomy Sunday" (−0.243)	"She" (0.039)
57	"Mad World" (−0.396)	"Labita" (−0.035)
58	"Stay" (−0.264)	"A Whole New World" (0.530)
59	"Hallelujah" (−0.331)	"I Will Always Love You" (0.203)
60	"Your Song" (0.125)	"When a Man Loves a Woman" (−0.272)

Note: The number in the parenthesis indicates the average ground truth rating of the song.

if we look at the music pieces whose valence ratings are negative (suppose to be ranked lower), the Gamma statistics of RBF-ListNet and SVR are 0.157 and −0.06, respectively. The low value of SVR indicates its inability to rank songs of negative valence, which may result from the fact that there are multiple ties in the lowermost ranks of db2. Because the subjects are not asked to compare the music pieces that are ranked lower in the first level of emotion tournament (e.g., the a, d, e, g in Figure 5.1), 285 music pieces are in fact ranked the lowermost and 170 music pieces are ranked the second lowermost. The use of MSE as the cost function makes SVR sensitive to these ties. RBF-ListNet, on the contrary, performs effectively despite of the multiple ties in the ground truth.

Finally, for db1→db2, the performance difference of the four algorithms becomes small again. Furthermore, comparing with the results obtained under the db2→db1 setting, we can see that the advantage of RBF-ListNet over SVR decreases. This is partly because the training data is small and partly because the training data is annotated in a rating-based way.

5.6.2.3 Sensitivity Test

We further examine the performance by randomly sampling different numbers of music pieces from db2 as the training data. As shown in Figure 5.5, the prediction accuracy of RBF-ListNet is low when the number of training data is small, approaches 0.3 with 300 training pieces, and reaches a plateau after that. When a sufficient number of training data is gathered, increasing the number of training data does not significantly improve the accuracy of either RBF-ListNet or SVR. Therefore, we can use a mild scale database to build a dimensional MER system.

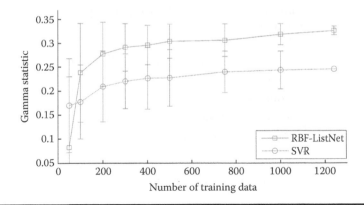

Figure 5.5   The Gamma statistic of valence prediction with different numbers of training data under the db2→db1 setting. Each error bar represents one standard error of 100 trials.

Finally, we conduct a sensitivity test on the parameters of RBF-ListNet under the db2→db1 setting. The result is shown in Table 5.12. It can be found that setting δ too small overfits the data, while setting δ too big underfits the data; both degrade the accuracy. Therefore, we set δ to $1e-4$ as a compromise. It is also noted that the prediction accuracy is rather sensitive to the value of η. Setting η too small results in slow convergence, while setting η too large results in an oscillation of parameters and thus degrades the performance. Moreover, we find that the optimal value of η depends on the number of training data N. Setting η to $1e4/N$ seems to perform well in all four settings (for db2→db1, $\eta \simeq 10.8$). The value of K also affects the prediction accuracy. Since the time complexity increases linearly with K, we set K to 10 in balance of computational time and accuracy. The computational cost of RBF-ListNet is slightly higher than SVR; for db2→db1 RBF-ListNet and SVR take 4.2 second and 1.6 second, respectively.

Table 5.12   The Gamma Statistic of RBF-ListNet with Different Parameter Settings for db2→db1

	$K = 5$		$K = 10$		$K = 20$	$K = 40$
$\eta \setminus \delta$	*1e–4*	*1e–3*	*1e–4*	*1e–5*	*1e–3*	*1e–3*
1e3/N	0.214	0.176	0.196	0.198	0.189	0.187
5e3/N	0.348	0.286	0.361	0.360	0.346	0.329
1e4/N	0.321	0.343	0.326*	0.293	0.318	0.324
1e5/N	0.271	0.277	0.277	0.287	0.265	0.153

Note: The entry marked with * corresponds to the parameter setting used in the other experiments of this study.

Table 5.13 Subjective Satisfaction of the Prediction Result

Method	Satisfaction
Random baseline	2.79
Ground truth	6.04
ListNet – prediction result	6.45
SVR – prediction result	6.43

Note: The scores are on an 11-point scale where 5 means neutral.

5.6.3 Subjective Evaluation of the Prediction Result

Finally, we evaluate the subjective satisfaction of the prediction result of MER by conducting another subjective evaluation that places 15 randomly chosen music pieces from db2 on a displayed axis according to valence values. Subjects are asked to listen to the pieces and then express the satisfaction of the distribution of the pieces on an 11-point scale ranging from 0 to 10 (strongly unsatisfactory to strongly satisfactory). We train the MER system under the db2→db2 setting and compare the following four methods of obtaining the valence values: (a) a baseline method that determines the valence value randomly, (b) the ground truth ranking-based annotations, (c) the prediction result of ListNet using ranking-based annotations, and (d) the prediction result of SVR using rating-based annotations. For methods b and c the rankings are converted to ratings in a linear fashion, as described in Section 5.4.

Table 5.13 shows the average result of the 134 subjects. All methods score higher than 5 (borderline) except for the random baseline. Both SVR and ListNet outperform the ground truth one, likely because of the excessive number of ties of the ground truth that reduces the satisfaction. More importantly, it is noted that the satisfaction of ListNet and that of SVR are comparable; both of them are around 6.45. This result implies that a good emotion-based visualization can be obtained by focusing on the relative emotion values only.

5.7 Discussion

The dimensional approach to MER aims at representing each song as a point in the 2D emotion space. However, it is unclear whether humans perceptually evaluate the accuracy of such representation with respect to the *exact* position of each song or the position *relative* to one another. In fact, as emotion perception is subjective, it is also unclear whether the exact valence and arousal values of a song can even be determined. The ranking approach to MER described in this chapter explores the possibility of representing songs in the emotion space according to the relative emotion rankings, which simplifies both the annotation and model training processes of MER (both the human subjects and computer need to pay attention to the relative rankings only). However, the strategy of converting emotion rankings to emotion values in a linear way may be overly simplified. For future work one may consider using emotion ratings to regulate the conversion—for example, to determine which songs have neutral emotion values.

As for the emotion tournament scheme, one can include a *reverse* tournament to enhance the resolution in the lowermost ranks of the ground truth. For example, one can ask half of the subjects to rank songs in ascending order of emotion values and half in descending order. One can also allow the result of a match to be a tie. For example, if songs a and b in Figure 5.1 are tied, one can randomly select one of them as a surrogate to compare with the winner between songs c and d. This would further relieve the burden on the subjects since in some cases the emotions of two songs are just not comparable. Moreover, the computational model described in this chapter does not explicitly deal with *contradiction*. It is possible that a is ranked higher than b by one subject and ranked lower by another. This is not an issue in the implemented system described in this chapter because the songs annotated by two subjects seldom overlap, but may deserve attention in other MER systems.

5.8 Summary

In this chapter, we have described a ranking approach to dimensional MER. Instead of directly computing the emotion values of each music piece, the ranking approach first ranks a collection of music pieces by emotion and then determines the emotion values of each music piece by its relative emotion with respect to other music pieces. This approach facilitates the collection of ground truth, protects us from the issues (e.g., reduction of the range of emotions) associated with rating-based methods, and in turn improves the performance of the MER system.

We have also described an empirical evaluation of the ranking approach. Experimental results show that the music emotion tournament greatly simplifies the annotation process and enhances the reliability of ground truth. Subjects reported a high degree of easiness and reliability of using the ranking measure. In addition, results show that the learning-to-rank algorithm RBF-ListNet performs consistently well for different data sets. By utilizing a ranking-based cost function, RBF-ListNet is insensitive to the ties of the ground truth and therefore superior to regression algorithms such as SVR for ranking songs based on the emotion annotations collected in a ranking-based manner. When evaluated on a data set consisting of 1240 music pieces, the use of RBF-ListNet for model learning and the top 70 features selected by RReliefF for feature representation achieves a Gamma statistic of 0.326 for valence prediction. Finally, the high subjective satisfaction of the prediction result validates that one can obtain a good emotion-based visualization of music pieces by focusing on the relative emotion values only.

6

Fuzzy Classification of Music Emotion

Emotion perception is intrinsically subjective, and people usually perceive different emotions in the same song. This subjectivity issue makes the performance evaluation of an MER system fundamentally difficult because a common agreement on the classification result is hard to obtain. An MER system that neglects the subjectivity issue and assigns emotion labels or values to music pieces in a deterministic fashion cannot perform well in practice, since it is likely that a user is not satisfied with the prediction result. The following four chapters describe a number of methods that have been developed to address the subjectivity issue, including techniques for soft assignment and personalization. We begin with a fuzzy approach that is developed for categorical MER in this chapter. This approach estimates the likelihood of perceiving an emotion when listening to a music piece, thereby making the prediction result less deterministic.

6.1 Motivation

Due to the subjective nature of human perception, classification of the emotion of music is a challenging problem. Cultural background, age, gender, personality, training, and so forth can influence the emotion perception [16, 147]. Because of these factors, classification methods (e.g., [217, 336, 352]) that simply assign one emotion class to each song in a deterministic manner do not perform well in practice.

The subjective nature of emotion perception suggests that fuzzy logic is an appropriate mathematical tool for emotion detection [83, 155]. For example, *fuzzy classifiers* can be employed to measure the strength of an emotion class in association with the music piece under classification. Based on the measurement, the user knows how likely a music piece belongs to an emotion class. In this way, the classification result is less deterministic and more acceptable to users.

The idea of applying fuzzy classifiers to the categorical approach to MER is first proposed in [365], which represents one of the first attempts to take the subjective nature of human perception into consideration for MER. This chapter provides the details of this fuzzy approach. Another approach that utilizes the probabilistic estimate of support vector machine (SVM) [254] to make soft assignment of classification result is later proposed in [344]. This prediction result of the probabilistic approach is the probability distribution of a music piece over the Hevner's eight emotion classes, which is called the *emotion histogram*. As described in Chapter 9, the idea of making soft predictions has also been applied to the dimensional approach to MER.

6.2 Fuzzy Classification

Compared with traditional classifiers that only assign one class to a test sample, a fuzzy classifier assigns a *fuzzy vector* that indicates the relative strength of each class. For example, assuming our emotion taxonomy consists of four emotion classes, a fuzzy vector of $[0.1\ 0.0\ 0.8\ 0.1]^{\top}$ indicates a fairly strong emotion strength for the third class, while $[0.1\ 0.4\ 0.4\ 0.1]^{\top}$ shows an ambiguity between the second and the third classes. The ambiguity that fuzzy vectors carry is very important because emotion perception is intrinsically subjective.

Many algorithms have been developed for fuzzy classification. Below we describe two of the most popular algorithms, fuzzy k-nearest neighbor and fuzzy nearest-mean.

6.2.1 Fuzzy k-NN Classifier

The (crisp) k-nearest neighbor (k-NN) classifier is commonly used in pattern recognition [78]. A test sample is assigned to the class that represents the majority of class labels of the k-nearest neighbors of the test sample, where the distance between samples is measured in the feature space. However, only a class label is assigned to the test sample. There is no indication of its strength of membership in that class.

Fuzzy k-NN classifier [165], a combination of fuzzy logic and k-NN classifier, is designed to solve the above problem. It contains two steps: *fuzzy labeling* that computes the fuzzy vectors of training samples (done in model training) and *fuzzy classification* that computes the fuzzy vectors of test samples (done in testing).

In **fuzzy labeling**, we compute μ_i, the fuzzy vector of a training sample. Several methods have been developed to compute the fuzzy vector [115, 165]. These methods can be generally described by the following formula:

$$\mu_{ic} = \begin{cases} \beta + \frac{n_c}{k}(1 - \beta), & \text{if } c = v \\ \frac{n_c}{k}(1 - \beta), & \text{otherwise} \end{cases} \tag{6.1}$$

where v is the ground truth class of $\mathbf{x}_i$, n_c is the number of samples that belong to class c in the k-nearest training samples of $\mathbf{x}_i$, and β is a bias parameter indicating how v takes part in the labeling process ($\beta \in [0, 1]$). When $\beta = 1$, this is the crisp labeling that assigns each training sample full membership in the ground truth class v. When $\beta = 0$, the memberships are assigned according to the k-nearest neighbors.

In **fuzzy classification**, we assign a fuzzy membership μ_{uc} of each class c to a test sample $\mathbf{x}_u$ as a linear combination of the fuzzy vectors of the k-nearest training samples of a test sample,

$$\mu_{uc} = \frac{\sum_{i=1}^{k} w_i \mu_{ic}}{\sum_{i=1}^{k} w_i}, \tag{6.2}$$

where μ_{uc} is the fuzzy membership of a training sample $\mathbf{x}_i$ in class c, $\mathbf{x}_i$ is one of the k-nearest samples, and w_i is the weight inversely proportional to the distance d_{ui} between $\mathbf{x}_u$ and $\mathbf{x}_i$,

$$w_i = d_{ui}^{-2} = \|\mathbf{x}_u - \mathbf{x}_i\|^{-2}. \tag{6.3}$$

With Eq. 6.2, we compute the $C \times 1$ fuzzy vector μ_u indicating music emotion strength of the test sample as

$$\mu_u = [\mu_{u1}, \ldots, \mu_{uc}, \ldots, \mu_{uC}]^{\top}, \sum_{c=1}^{C} \mu_{uc} = 1. \tag{6.4}$$

The class label of $\mathbf{x}_u$ can then be assigned by picking the class that has the maximal μ_{uc} (i.e., majority voting).

Example MATLAB® codes of fuzzy k-NN are shown in Tables 6.1 and 6.2.

6.2.2 Fuzzy Nearest-Mean Classifier

For the fuzzy nearest-mean classifier, we need to calculate the centroid of each class in the model training process by

$$\mu_c = \frac{1}{N_c} \sum_{i=1}^{N_c} \mathbf{x}_{ic}, \tag{6.5}$$

where μ_c is the centroid of all the training samples of class c, $\mathbf{x}_{ic}$ is the i-th music piece of class c, and N_c is the total number of music pieces that belong to class c.

In testing, we compute the sum of the distance between the test sample $\mathbf{x}_u$ and the centroid of each class. The class whose centroid is closest to $\mathbf{x}_u$ is assigned. That is,

$$C(\mathbf{x}_u) = \{y \mid \min(d_{uc}, c \in \{1, \ldots, C\})\}, \tag{6.6}$$

Table 6.1   An Example MATLAB Code for Fuzzy *k*-NN

```
%% TRAINING PHASE---------------------------------------------
% feature extraction
X = extract_feat('DIR_TR');      % features (N by M)
[X p_mu p_std] = zscore(X);
[N M] = size(X);                 % (N by M)

% emotion annotation
C = 4;                           % number of classes
Y = annotate_emotion;            % ground truth (N by 1)
             % 1: happy, 2: angry, 3: sad, 4: relaxing

% fuzzy labeling
K = 10;
beta = 0.5;
U = zeros(N,C);
for i=1:N                        % see Table 6.2
    [idx dist] = find_nearest_neighbors(X,X(i,:),K+1);
    idx(1) = [];                 % remove the nearest one
                                 % since it must be i
    nc = zeros(1,C);
    for c=1:C
        nc(c) = sum(Y(idx)==c);
    end
    for c=1:C                    % cf. Eq. 6.1
        U(i,c) = (1-beta)*nc(c)/K;
        if c==Y(i)
            U(i,c) = U(i,c) + beta;
        end
    end
end

%% TEST PHASE-------------------------------------------------
Xtest = extract_feat('DIR_TE');  % features (Ntest by M)
for j=1:M, Xtest(:,j) = (Xtest(:,j)-p_mu(j))/p_std(j); end
Ntest = size(Xtest,1);
Ypred = zeros(Ntest,1);          % to be predicted
Upred = zeros(Ntest,C);

% fuzzy classification
for i=1:Ntest
    [idx dist] = find_nearest_neighbors(X,Xtest(i,:),K);
```

(*continued*)

Table 6.1   An Example MATLAB Code for Fuzzy *k*-NN (Continued)

```
    wei = zeros(1,K);
    for k=1:K                      % cf. Eq. 6.2
        wei(k) = 1/(dist(k)^2);
        Upred(i,:) = Upred(i,:) + U(idx(k),:)*wei(k);
    end
    Upred(i,:) = Upred(i,:)/sum(wei);
                                   % majority voting
    Ypred(i) = find(Upred(i,:)==max(Upred(i,:)));
end
```

where $C(\mathbf{x}_u)$ denotes the predicted class of $\mathbf{x}_u$, and $d_{uc} = ||\mu_c - \mathbf{x}_u||$ is the distance between $\mathbf{x}_u$ and the mean of class c. The fuzzy vector of the test sample is obtained by computing the inverse of the distance,

$$\mu_{uc} = \frac{d_{uc}^{-\varrho}}{\sum_{i=1}^{C} d_{ui}^{-\varrho}}, \tag{6.7}$$

where ϱ, the degree of fuzziness [315], is empirically chosen.

An example MATLAB code for fuzzy nearest-mean is shown in Table 6.3.

Table 6.2   A Subroutine of the MATLAB Code in Table 6.1

```
function [idx dist] = find_nearest_neighbors(X, Xin, K)
% input: X: features of training data (N by M)
%        Xin: features of an input instance (1 by M)
%        K: number of nearest neighbors
% output: idx: indexes of training data that are
%              nearest to the input data (1 by K)
%        dist: the distance between the nearest training
%              data and the input instance (1 by K)
N = size(X,1);
dist = zeros(1,N);

for i=1:N                         % L2 distance
    dist(i) = sqrt((X(i,:)-Xin)*(X(i,:)-Xin)');
end

% sort by distance
[dist idx] = sort(dist,'ascend');

% pick the K nearest ones
idx = idx(1:K);
dist = dist(1:K);
```

Table 6.3   An Example MATLAB Code for Fuzzy Nearest-Mean

```
%% TRAINING PHASE-----------------------------------------
% feature extraction
X = extract_feat('DIR_TR');      % features (N by M)
[X p_mu p_std] = zscore(X);
[N M] = size(X);                 % (N by M)

% emotion annotation
Y = annotate_emotion;            % ground truth (N by 1)
            % 1: happy, 2: angry, 3: sad, 4: relaxing

% compute centroid
V = zeros(C,M);
for c=1:C
    idx = find(Y==c);
    V(c,:) = mean(X(idx,:));
end


%% TEST PHASE----------------------------------------------
Xtest = extract_feat('DIR_TE');  % features (Ntest by M)
for j=1:M, Xtest(:,j) = (Xtest(:,j)-p_mu(j))/p_std(j); end
Ntest = size(Xtest,1);
Ypred = zeros(Ntest,1);          % to be predicted
Upred = zeros(Ntest,C);

varrho = 2;                      % the degree of fuzziness

% compute fuzzy vector
for i=1:Ntest
    dist = zeros(1,C);
    for c=1:C
        dist(c) = (Xtest(i,:)-V(c,:))*(Xtest(i,:)-V(c,:))';
        dist(c) = sqrt(dist(c));
        Upred(i,:) = 1/(dist^varrho);
    end
    Upred(i,:) = Upred(i,:)/sum(Upred(i,:));
                                 % majority voting
    Ypred(i) = find(Upred(i,:)==max(Upred(i,:)));
end
```

6.3 System Overview

The fuzzy approach consists of two parts: model training and testing. In model training, a computational model is generated using the training samples, whereas in testing the computational model is applied to predict the emotion of a test sample. More specifically, the fuzzy vector of a test sample is first computed using Eq. 6.2 for FKNN or Eq. 6.7 for FNM. The maximum element in the vector is then chosen as the final decision of classification. In the case of equal music emotion strength in two or more classes, the class of the nearest sample is chosen.

6.4 Implementation

To evaluate the fuzzy approach, a categorical MER system is implemented. The emotion taxonomy consists of four emotion classes — happy, angry, sad, and relaxing—each corresponding to a quadrant of the emotion plane. The details of each system component are described below.

6.4.1 Data Collection

The data set consists of 243 popular songs selected from Western, Chinese, and Japanese albums. Each song is converted to 22,050 Hz, 16-bit, mono channel PCM WAV format for fair comparison. For each song, a 25-second segment that is representative of the whole song is chosen. A subjective test is conducted to have subjects label the emotion class of the music segments. If a 50% agreement cannot be reached, the segment is considered too emotionally subjective and thus gets removed. After this removal, 195 segments are retained, each labeled with a class voted by the subjects (determined by majority vote). See Table 6.4 for the class distribution of the music segments.

6.4.2 Feature Extraction and Feature Selection

We use the toolbox PsySound (version 2) [44] to extract the 15 music features recommended in [211,282,341]. The features are listed in Table 4.4. These features are also used in the system described in Section 4.5.

To improve the classification accuracy, feature selection is applied to remove irrelevant or redundant features. Specifically, the stepwise backward selection method [293] is employed. It begins with all the 15 features and then greedily removes the worst feature sequentially until no more accuracy improvement is obtained. The method we adopt to evaluate the classification accuracy is the 10-fold cross-validation technique [78]. That is, 90% of the segments are randomly selected as training samples to generate the model, and the remaining 10% are used for testing. The above process is repeated 50 times before the average accuracy is computed.

Table 6.4   Class Distribution of the Music Pieces

	Class 1	Class 2	Class 3	Class 4
# music pieces	49	48	49	49
Total		1	95	

6.5 Performance Evaluation

6.5.1 Accuracy of Emotion Classification

We first evaluate the performance of FKNN using different values of β in Eq. 6.1. The number of neighbors k is empirically set to 11 for better performance. From Table 6.5 it can be found that the highest accuracy, 68.22%, is achieved when β is set to 0.75.

The results of FNM are shown in Table 6.6. We see that FNM brings about better accuracy (71.34%) than FKNN, especially for class 1 (71% vs. 56%). To examine the result more carefully, a scatter plot of the first two principal components of the data set is created, as shown in Figure 6.1. It can be found that the samples of class 1 overlap a lot with the samples of class 2. FKNN relies more on local neighbors of the test samples than does FNM. Therefore, maybe it is the overlapping that causes FKNN to misclassify the samples of class 1.

Tables 6.7 and 6.8 show the result of FKNN and FNM after feature selection. We see great improvement in the overall accuracy. Moreover, we note that FNM still performs better than FKNN (78.33% vs. 70.88%).

6.5.2 Music Emotion Variation Detection

Music emotion varies within a song (see Sections 2.1.3 and 2.2.3). To track the emotion variation, we segment a music piece every 10 seconds, with 1/3 overlapping between segments to increase correlation, and sequentially classify the segments using FNM. Figure 6.2 shows how the segmentation is performed. We can then exploit the geometric relationship of the four emotion classes and transform a fuzzy vector to valence and arousal values, as described in Section 4.2.2, by the following formula:

$$\begin{cases} \text{valence of } \mathbf{x}_u = \mu_{u1} + \mu_{u4} - \mu_{u2} - \mu_{u3}, \\ \text{arousal of } \mathbf{x}_u = \mu_{u1} + \mu_{u2} - \mu_{u3} - \mu_{u4}. \end{cases} \tag{6.8}$$

Table 6.5 The Classification Accuracy of FKNN under Different Values of β

β	$1 \to 1$	$2 \to 2$	$3 \to 3$	$4 \to 4$	*Average*
0.0	46%	92%	39%	66%	60.60%
0.25	51%	93%	51%	68%	65.86%
0.50	54%	93%	59%	66%	67.95%
0.75	**56%**	**92%**	**61%**	**64%**	**68.22%**
1.0	57%	89%	61%	63%	67.39%

Table 6.6 The Classification Accuracy of FNM

β	$1 \rightarrow 1$	$2 \rightarrow 2$	$3 \rightarrow 3$	$4 \rightarrow 4$	*Average*
FNM	71%	88%	61%	66%	71.34%

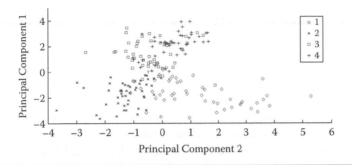

Figure 6.1 Scatter plot of the first two principal components of the data set.

Table 6.7 The Classification Accuracy of FKNN ($\beta = 0.75$) after Stepwise Backward Feature Selection

	Class 1	*Class 2*	*Class 3*	*Class 4*
Class 1	53.36%	41.63%	3.57%	1.42%
Class 2	2.08%	94.16%	3.43%	0.31%
Class 3	3.16%	9.89%	59.28%	25.91%
Class 4	0.1%	3.77%	21.12%	75%
Overall	70.88%			

Table 6.8 The Classification Accuracy FNM after Stepwise Backward Feature Selection

	Class 1	*Class 2*	*Class 3*	*Class 4*
Class 1	74.32%	18.24%	7.42%	0%
Class 2	4.83%	94.45%	0.7%	0%
Class 3	2.04%	6.12%	72.81%	19.02%
Class 4	0%	0%	28.24%	71.75%
Overall	78.33%			

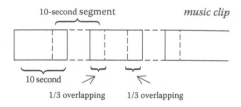

Figure 6.2 **Segmentation of music clip for MEVD.**

We use Eq. 6.8 to translate the resulting fuzzy vectors into valence and arousal values and separately plot the valence and arousal values of the music segments as time unfolds. For example, Figure 6.3 shows the result of Rene Liu's "Love You Very Much." By considering the time points with rapid change of arousal or valence as the *boundaries* between different emotions and dividing the song into several *sub-emotion units* (denoted as I, II, III, IV, V, VI, and VII), an interesting relationship between music structure and valence and arousal values can be observed. We find that the higher-arousal subunits II, IV, and VI correspond to the chorus sections of the song, whereas other subunits correspond to the intro, verse1, verse2,

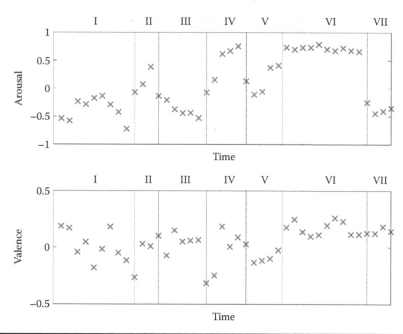

Figure 6.3 **Arousal (top) and valence (bottom) variation of Rene Liu's "Love You Very Much" using FNM. An interesting relationship between music structure and emotion values can be observed. The high-arousal subunits II, IV, and VI correspond to the chorus sections of the song, whereas other subunits correspond to the intro, verse1, verse2, middle-eight, and outro sections of the song, respectively.**

middle-eight, and outro sections of the song, respectively. This result shows an interesting link between MER and music structure analysis, which can be investigated further in future work.

6.6 Summary

In this chapter, we have described a fuzzy approach to categorical MER that measures the relative strength of emotion perception in association with the music piece under classification. This approach performs better than conventional deterministic approaches because it considers the subjective nature of emotion perception and makes the classification result soft. We have also shown how to apply this approach to compute the valence and arousal values and to track the emotion variation in a song.

Although this approach is developed for categorical MER, the idea of computing the likelihood of different emotions being perceived in a music piece can be utilized to dimensional MER as well. See Chapter 9 for more details.

7

Personalized MER
and Groupwise MER

While Chapter 6 describes the fuzzy approach that intends to address the subjectivity issue of categorical MER, the following three chapters describe approaches that are developed to address the subjectivity issue of dimensional MER. We begin with two intuitive methods proposed in [366] for personalization in this chapter: a personalized MER scheme that trains a personalized model for emotion prediction using a user's feedback and a groupwise MER scheme that trains a number of groupwise regressors for users possessing different personal factors. Although these two methods have limited performance, they provide useful insights into the subjectivity issue of MER and inspire the development of more effective methods.

7.1 Motivation

As described in Chapter 4, regression algorithms can be employed in a dimensional MER system to train the computational model for predicting the valence and arousal (VA) values. Typically, a *general* regressor is trained based upon the average emotion ratings of music pieces from the subjective test. After training, the general regressor is applied to predict the emotion values of input music pieces. This approach, however, neglects the fact that human perception of emotion is by nature subjective and different people can perceive differently in a music piece. Even though the accuracy of emotion recognition reaches 100%, it only means that the computational model accurately predicts only the *average* emotion perception for a music piece, not the emotion perception of an individual user for the music piece.

Figure 7.1 shows the annotations of the 60 music pieces used in Chapters 5, 7–9. In this figure, each circle corresponds to the annotation of a subject for a music piece over the 2D valence-arousal emotion plane. Evidently, simply assigning one emotion value to a music piece in a deterministic manner does not perform well in practice because the emotion perception varies greatly from person to person.

To deal with this subjectivity issue, a reasonable approach is to build an MER system that makes different emotion predictions for different users. This chapter describes two methods to achieve this:

- Personalized MER (**PMER**): One of the most intuitive methods to resolve the subjectivity issue is to personalize the MER system. This can be done by asking a user to explicitly annotate his/her emotion perception of a number of music pieces and then using these annotations as ground truth to train a *personalized* regressor. For the specific user, the personalized regressor should perform better than the general regressor.subjectivity does play an important role.

- Groupwise MER (**GWMER**): Another intuitive method groups users according to personal factors such as demographic properties, music experience, and

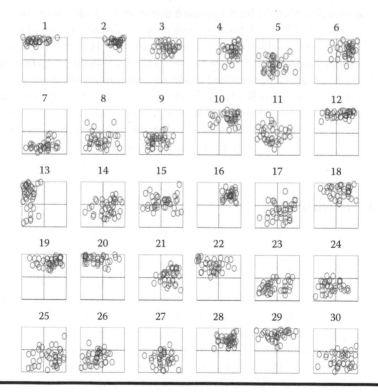

Figure 7.1   The annotations of the 60 songs used in Chapters 5, 7–9.

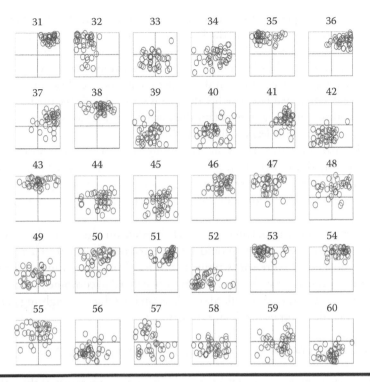

Figure 7.1   (Continued.)

personality and then trains a *groupwise* regressor for each user group. One can interpret the prediction accuracy of a groupwise regressor as the importance of the corresponding personal factor. For example, if the prediction accuracy is significantly improved when different regressors are used for people of different genders, it implies that the emotion perception of music is significantly different between male and female and such differentiation is useful.

This chapter provides the details of these two methods and presents an empirical performance comparison of the two methods with the general (baseline) method.

7.2 Personalized MER

Though it is great to develop a general MER system that performs equally well for each user, it may be unnecessary. As pointed out in [252], most of the time it is only necessary that one's personal computer is able to recognize his or her emotion. As emotion perception is by nature subjective, it should be beneficial to personalize the MER system. Personalized MER (PMER) explores whether the prediction accuracy for each individual is significantly improved by personalization.

A critical issue of personalization is the introduction of user burden. Personalization is usually done by exploiting the listening history [110] or using user feedback mechanisms such as relevance feedback [128], mostly because these methods involve presumably smaller user burden. For MER, one may assume that the emotion values for music pieces a user listened to in the same time period are close, or one may use relevance feedback to evaluate whether the user is satisfied with the prediction result. However, both methods cannot obtain the exact VA values a user perceives in the music pieces and are thus less applicable to MER.

PMER personalizes the MER system by asking a user to pre-annotate the emotion values for a limited number of music pieces in advance. A personalized regressor is then trained based on these annotations. Since the personalized regressor is trained for the specific user, its performance for the user should be better than that of the general regressor.

However, to prevent putting too much burden on the user, the number of songs pre-annotated by a user should be kept reasonably small. Therefore, it is likely that the general regressor is trained with much more training data than the personalized regressor. In such a case, it may be beneficial to combine the result of the general regressor and the personalized one. We can introduce a weighting parameter $w \in [0, 1]$ that determines the degree of personalization,

$$r_{\text{PMER}}(\mathbf{x}_i) = (1 - w) \cdot r_{\text{general}}(\mathbf{x}_i) + w \cdot r_{\text{personalized}}(\mathbf{x}_i), \qquad (7.1)$$

where $r_{\text{general}}(\mathbf{x}_i)$ and $r_{\text{personalized}}(\mathbf{x}_i)$ represent the prediction result of the i-th input instance by the general regressor and personalized regressor, respectively. Clearly, as w approaches 1 PMER becomes more personalized, whereas as $w = 0$ it becomes namely the general model.

A system diagram of PMER is shown in Figure 7.2. PMER uses an additional annotation process to collect the emotion annotation from the test user and uses an additional regressor training process to train the personalized regressor. The prediction of a test music piece is computed as the weighted sum of the results of the general regressor and the personalized one.

7.3 Groupwise MER

It has been pointed out that the incorporation of personal information improves the performance of music retrieval systems (e.g., [52, 367]). The psychologist Huron has also pointed out that emotion perception is influenced by personal factors such as cultural background, generation, sex, and personality [147]. Groupwise MER (GWMER) aims at incorporating such personal factors to the MER system.

The ground truth needed to train a regressor is typically formed by averaging subjects' annotations. For GWMER, the ground truth is set in a different way. The users are grouped into a number of user groups according to personal factors such as

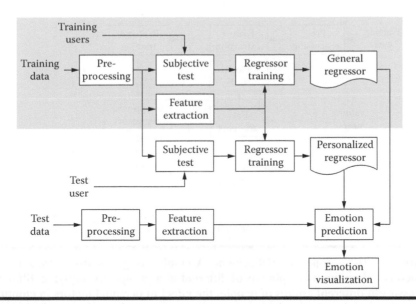

Figure 7.2 **The personalized MER scheme. A personalized regressor is trained for a specific user, who is asked to annotate a number of music pieces. The prediction results of the personalized regressor and the general regressor are linearly combined to get the final prediction.**

demographic properties, music experience, and personality. A number of groupwise regressors are then trained for each user group based on the average ratings of the subjects that belong to the user group.

Based on the following two observations, one may consider the prediction accuracy of each groupwise regressor as the importance of the associated personal factor to MER. First, if individual difference is large for a personal factor, dividing users according to this personal factor should reduce the individual difference. Second, if individual difference has remarkable impact on the performance of MER, the reduction of individual difference should improve the prediction accuracy of MER.

Note GWMER represents a compromise between a general MER system and a personalized one. By grouping users based on personal factors, GWMER reduces individual differences without resorting to too much user burden (that is, only some personal information is asked from a user). Moreover, GWMER is fairly generic since there is no restriction on the personal factors that can be considered. Different implementations of GWMER may consider different sets of personal factors.

A system diagram of GWMER is shown in Figure 7.3. Each groupwise regressor is trained based on the average opinion of the subjects belonging to the user group. In practice, a groupwise regressor is chosen from the set of groupwise regressors to respond to a specific user according to the personal information of the user.

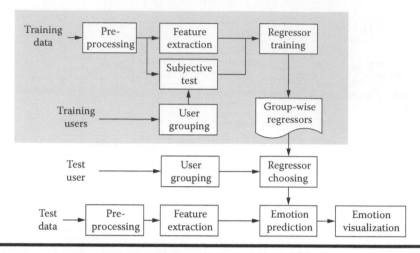

Figure 7.3 The groupwise MER scheme. A number of groupwise regressors are trained based on the user opinions of different user groups. By applying different regressors to different groups of people, the effect of personal factors in emotion perception is reduced, thereby improving the accuracy of emotion prediction.

7.4 Implementation

This section describes an implementation of PMER and GWMER. The implemented system is utilized in the performance evaluation described in the next section.

7.4.1 Data Collection

The data set consists of 60 famous popular songs from English albums. For fair comparison, each song is converted to a uniform format (22,050 Hz, 16 bits, and mono channel PCM WAV) and normalized to the same volume level. In addition, to reduce the emotion variation and lessen the burden on the subjects, each song is truncated to a 30-second segment by manually picking the chorus part. Note that the scale of this data set is kept small to have each song annotated by as many subjects as possible. A total of 99 subjects (46 male, 53 female) are recruited from the campus of National Taiwan University, making each song annotated by 40 subjects. This is in contrast to other work that employs few (typically less than five) subjects for emotion annotation [203, 217, 297, 316].

A user interface called "AnnoEmo" is utilized in the subjective test. With this user interface, which is implemented in the Java programming language, a subject annotates the VA values for each song by using a mouse to click a point in the emotion plane displayed by computer. After clicking on a point, a rectangle is formed on the specified point. The subject can then click on the rectangle to listen to the associated music piece again, or drag and drop the rectangle to other places since after listening

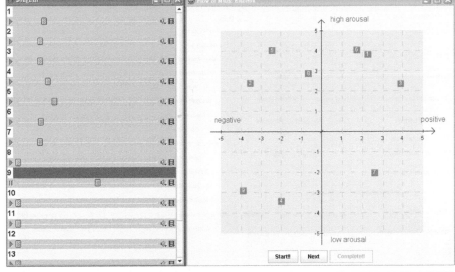

Figure 7.4 **Screen capture of a user interface AnnoEmo for annotating the VA values.**

to other songs the subject may want to modify the annotation of previous songs. Once formed, the rectangle would exist throughout the subjective test. Therefore, as the subject annotates more songs, more rectangles are presented on the emotion plane, making it easy for the subject to compare the annotations of different music pieces. In this implementation, the subjects are allowed to listen to the music pieces multiple times (by clicking on the rectangle or on a song list). No limitation is given to the total duration of the annotation process. Typically, the annotation of 15 songs could be finished in 15 minutes. Figure 7.4 shows a screen capture of AnnoEmo for annotating the VA values.

The data set is partitioned into four subsets, each with 15 music pieces whose emotions are roughly uniformly distributed in the emotion plane. For each subject, one of the subsets is randomly picked for annotation. The subjects are asked to annotate the VA values with the graphic interface AnnoEmo in a silent computer lab. Many subjects find the annotation pleasant and volunteer to annotate more. In that case, we remove the rectangles and select another subset of music to annotate. A total of six subjects annotate the entire data set. These six subjects are treated as the test users in the performance evaluation of PMER (see Section 7.5.3). In sum, we get 2400 annotations; each of the 60 songs is annotated by 40 subjects.

See Table 5.5 for the titles and Figure 7.1 for the ground truth ratings of the 60 songs. The data set (including annotations and features) and the software AnnoEmo are publicly available on the Web. [Online] http://mpac.ee.ntu. edu.tw/~yihsuan/hcm07/.

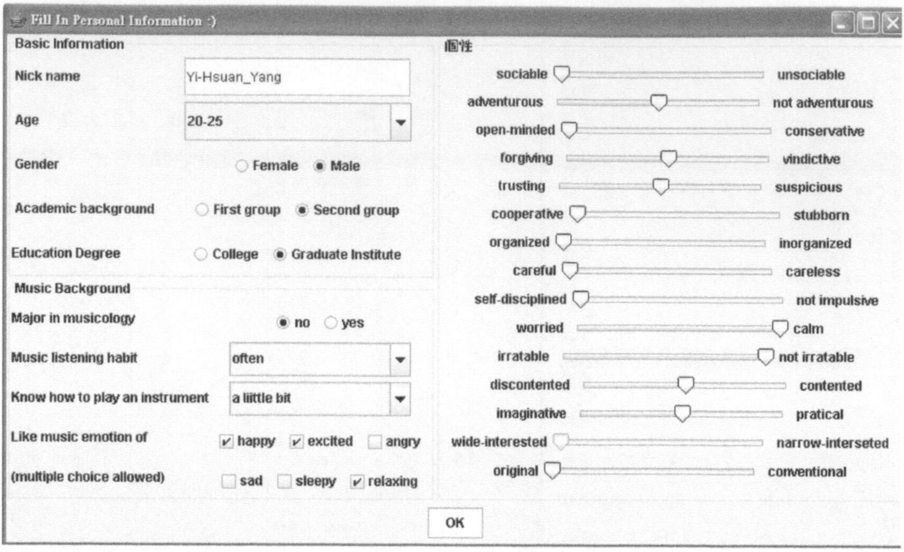

Figure 7.5   Screen capture of AnnoEmo for collecting the personal information of a subject.

7.4.2 Personal Information Collection

For GWMER, we need to collect the personal information of each subject. A screen capture of AnnoEmo for collecting personal information is shown in Figure 7.5. In this implementation, the following personal factors are considered:

Demographic property. The subjects are grouped by gender and the academic background. The latter is defined as follows: The first academic group includes colleges of liberal arts, social science, management, and law, whereas the second academic group includes colleges of engineering, science, life science, medicine, and computer science. Note that we do not consider personal factors such as cultural background, generation, and the level of education in this study because the subjects are mainly Chinese students between the ages of 20 and 25. This also explains why the academic background is considered.

Music experience. The perception of music is influenced by music experiences including music expertise, musicianship, taste, and familiarity with the music piece [198]. In this implementation, we represent music experience in terms of the habit of music listening (rare to frequent), the ability to play an instrument (can or cannot), and the desire to listen to music of the following six prototypical emotions: happy, exciting, angry, sad, sleepy, or relaxing. In other words, the first two factors evaluate how a subject loves to listen to or play music, whereas the last six factors evaluate which types (emotions) of music the subject prefers.

Personality. We use the Big Five personality traits [106] to describe personality. The Big Five are five broad factors or dimensions of personality discovered through empirical psychological research. They are as follows:

- **Extraversion** vs. introversion: energy, positive emotions, and the tendency to seek stimulation in the company of others.
- **Agreeableness** vs. antagonism: a tendency to be compassionate and cooperative rather than suspicious and antagonistic toward others.
- **Conscientiousness** vs. lack-of-direction: a tendency to show self-discipline, to act dutifully, and to aim for achievement.
- **Neuroticism** vs. emotional-stability: a tendency to experience unpleasant emotions easily, such as anger, anxiety, or depression.
- **Openness-to-experience** vs. closeness-to-experience: the appreciation for art, emotion, adventure, unusual ideas, curiosity, and variety of experience.

Typically the Big Five personality traits are measured using self-report questionnaires. A subject is asked to answer a number of questions, and the solution to each question contributes to a rating to one of the five personality traits. However, to prevent subjects from being exhausted by a lengthy questionnaire, we measured the personality by the self-report personality inventory [65] instead. Specifically, we ask subjects to rate a list of adjectives related to personality in the following way: If the adjective describes his/her personality well, rate +1; if the opposite adjective does, rate −1; otherwise, rate 0. For example, the adjectives *sociable*, *adventurous*, and *open-minded* are used to measure extraversion. If a subject rates all three adjectives as +1, he or she gets a rating of +3 for extraversion. Table 7.1 lists the adjectives that are used for self-report personality inventory [65].

A total of 15 personal factors are considered. They are listed in Table 7.1 along with possible values, which take a binary form. For the five personality factors, we converted the numerical ratings to zero or one according to whether the value is nonnegative. That is, a person is considered an extravert if he or she rated more extraversion-related adjectives as +1 rather than −1.

In this implementation, we consider using only one personal factor each time to partition users into two groups, since the objective is to evaluate the importance of each personal factor. For extension, one may cluster users into more than two groups by considering several personal factors together or cluster users using their emotion annotations directly [367].

7.4.3 Feature Extraction

For feature extraction, two toolkits, PsySound [44] and Marsyas [324], are employed. A total of 45 features are extracted to represent each music piece in the feature space. Each feature is normalized linearly to [0, 1] before the regressor training. To fairly compare the performance of each regressor, no feature selection algorithm is applied.

PsySound extracts features based on a number of psychoacoustical models [44]. Therefore, it can generate features that are more relevant to emotion perception. We use PsySound to generate the 15 features listed in Table 4.3 including spectral centroid, loudness, sharpness, timbral width, volume, spectral dissonance, pure tonal, complex tonal, multiplicity, tonality and chord.

Marsyas is a generic software framework for rapid development and evaluation of computer audition applications [324]. We use it to generate 19 spectrum features (spectral centroid, spectral rolloff, spectral flux, time domain zero-crossing, and MFCC), six rhythm features (by beat and tempo detection), and 5 pitch features (by multi-pitch detection). See Chapter 3 for more descriptions of these features.

7.5 Performance Evaluation

The generalization performances of the regression models are evaluated by the leave-one-out (LOO) cross-validation technique [78], which is known to provide an almost unbiased estimate of the generalization error even with a small data set. As the name suggests, LOO uses one data instance of the data set as the testing data and the remaining instances as training data to train the regressor. This procedure is repeated until each instance is held out once as the testing data. The R^2 statistics for valence and arousal are computed separately.

Due to its superior performance, ϵ-support vector regression (SVR) is adopted for model training. For general MER, a general (baseline) regressor is trained based on the average rating of all the subjects in the subjective test. For GWMER, a number of groupwise regressors are trained for each user group based on the average rating of subjects belonging to that user group. For PMER, a personalized regressor is trained for each user using his or her annotations. The implementation of SVR is based on the library LIBSVM [54].

7.5.1 Performance of the General Method

For the baseline general SVR regressor, the R^2 statistic reaches 17% for valence and 79.9% for arousal, respectively. The lower accuracy for valence is consistent with the result of other MER work (e.g., see Section 4.6.1). Moreover, Figure 7.6 shows that subjects can easily distinguish high-arousal songs from low-arousal songs (there are two evident clusters along the arousal axis), but not for the valence dimension. The almost neutral valence values come from the averaging of subjects' opinions: Half of them find the song positive, whereas others find it negative.

To gain more insights into the prediction accuracy, the following three performance levels are defined in terms of the mean absolute error η,

$$\eta = \frac{1}{N} \sum_{i=1}^{N} \text{abs}(y_i - r(\mathbf{x}_i)), \qquad (7.2)$$

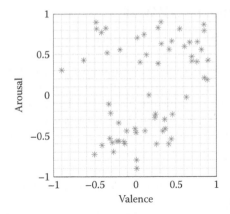

Figure 7.6 **Distribution of the ground truth data. While many neutral values are assigned to valence, there are two evident clusters along the arousal axis, implying that arousal is easier to predict than valence.**

where $r(\cdot)$ is the regressor, $\mathbf{x}_i$ is the feature representation for the music piece d_i, y_i is the ground truth, and $r(\mathbf{x}_i)$ is the prediction result. As shown in Figure 7.7, a performance level l represents that the average absolute error of the VA values is lower than $0.1 \times l$ (that is, within each associated red circle). The smaller l the better. Figure 7.7 shows the corresponding value of the R^2 statistics for each performance level. It can be observed that the prediction accuracy of the general regressor reaches performance level two for arousal and performance level three for valence.

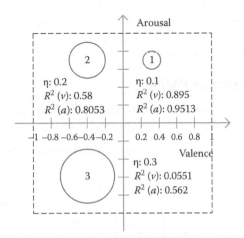

Figure 7.7 **The performance levels and the R^2 statistics for valence (v) and arousal (a) corresponding to three levels of mean absolute error η.**

7.5.2 *Performance of GWMER*

We evaluate the importance of each personal factor one by one. Specifically, for each personal factor, we partition the subjects into two groups 0 or 1 (according to the *Value* column shown in Table 7.2) and train regressors for each of the two user groups. The prediction accuracy for each user group is evaluated separately.

Experimental results are shown in Table 7.3. The first column specifies which kind of subject is categorized to group 1 of the personal factor; the second column shows the number of subjects (out of 99) that are categorized to group 1. Note that the groupwise regressors of the two groups (0 or 1) are trained with the same number of training pieces. The two regressors only differ in the pool of subjects that contribute to the ground truth emotion ratings. The following observations are made from Table 7.3:

■ Only few groupwise regressors outperform the baseline regressor, and the improvement is not significant. It seems that removing the effect of each personal factor alone does not improve the accuracy. Difference cannot be removed by each single personal factor; this result implies that the subjectivity issue cannot be resolved by considering one personal factor alone. For future work one may investigate the combination of personal factors or exploit other personal factors that better describe subjectivity.

■ While the R^2 statistics for arousal are roughly the same (range from 0.716 to 0.808), the R^2 statistics for valence vary a lot (range from -0.022 to 0.206). This finding implies again that personal difference in perceiving valence is much larger than in perceiving arousal.

■ Interestingly, for some personal factors, the differences in valence accuracy between group 1 and group 0 are fairly large. It is much easier to predict the valence perception for people who *often listen to the music*, who *belong to the first academic group*, who *love neither sad nor sleepy songs*, and who *are less neurotic* compared to the counterparts.

7.5.3 *Performance of PMER*

To evaluate whether the removal of individual difference improves the prediction accuracy, we train a personalized regressor for each user. In this evaluation, we assume

Table 7.1 The Adjectives for Self-Report Personality Inventory

Personality Trait	Adjective
Extraversion	Sociable, adventurous, open-minded
Agreeableness	Forgiving, trusting, cooperative
Conscientiousness	Organized, careful, self-disciplined
Neuroticism	Worried, irritable, discontented
Openness to experience	Imaginative, wide-interested, original

Table 7.2   The Personal Factors Considered in GWMER

#	Type	Name	Value (0/1)
1	Demographic property	Gender	Male / female
2		Academic group	First / second
3	Music experience	Music listening	Rare / often
4		Instrument play	Cannot / can
5		Love happy songs	No / yes
6		Love exciting songs	No / yes
7		Love angry songs	No / yes
8		Love sad songs	No / yes
9		Love sleepy songs	No / yes
10		Love relaxing songs	No / yes
11	Personality (The Big Five)	Extraversion	Low/ high
12		Agreeableness	Low/ high
13		Conscientiousness	Low/ high
14		Neuroticism	Low/ high
15		Openness to experience	Low/ high

that the user burden is not an issue and exploit the maximal available number of pre-annotated songs. Therefore, we use the six subjects who have annotated all 60 songs as the test users, and the remaining ones as training users. Specifically, for each of the six subjects, we train a personalized regressor using the annotations of the test subject, and a general regressor using the annotations of the other subjects. Then we use the weighted combination of the prediction VA values of the general regressor and personalized regressor to compute the emotion values of the test songs.

First, we evaluate the accuracy of PMER when 59 songs are used for training and one song for testing, an experiment setting that is similar to LOO. This evaluation is repeated until each song is used for testing once. In this evaluation, the ground truth of the test song is set according to the rating of the test subject *alone*. That is to say, even though the general regression models well the average emotion ratings of music pieces, it may fail to predict the emotion perception of the test user, since the subjectivity issue is not taken into account.

We evaluate the R^2 statistics when w varies from 0, 0.5, to 1. The following observations are made from Table 7.4:

■ The average performance of the general regressor for predicting the emotion perception of the six subjects drops from 0.170 to 0.088 for valence and from 0.802 to 0.667 for arousal, comparing to the performance of predicting the average emotion perception of all subjects (cf. Table 7.3). This result shows that personalization is indeed important for an MER system to be effective in practice.

Table 7.3   The R^2 Statistics of Each Personal Factor for the GWMER Approach

Description of Group 1	# Subjects in Group 1	Valence Prediction		Arousal Prediction	
		Group 1	Group 0	Group 1	Group 0
Baseline		0.170	0.170	0.802	0.802
Female	50	0.160	0.111	0.761	0.808
Second academic group	42	0.046	0.193	0.779	0.797
Often listen to music	67	0.206	0.065	0.779	0.776
Can play an instrument	44	0.087	0.146	0.777	0.747
Love happy songs	68	0.141	0.174	0.799	0.774
Love exciting songs	38	0.198	0.122	0.738	0.800
Love angry songs	6	0.157	0.131	0.798	0.787
Love sad songs	29	0.067	0.179	0.799	0.795
Love sleepy songs	11	−0.015	0.172	0.728	0.804
Love relaxing songs	63	0.157	0.073	0.800	0.767
High extraversion	46	0.061	0.132	0.760	0.800
High agreeableness	54	0.135	0.119	0.752	0.778
High conscientiousness	49	0.129	0.096	0.773	0.805
High neuroticism	23	−0.022	0.174	0.716	0.795
High openness to experience	47	0.074	0.174	0.773	0.786

Table 7.4   The R^2 Statistics for the Six Subjects for the PMER Approach

Subject	Valence Prediction			Arousal Prediction		
	$w = 1$	$w = 0.5$	$w = 0$	$w = 1$	$w = 0.5$	$w = 0$
1	0.027	0.048	−0.202	0.742	0.750	0.681
2	0.261	0.284	0.211	0.739	0.727	0.689
3	0.224	0.235	0.183	0.815	0.815	0.787
4	0.074	0.156	0.097	0.628	0.641	0.571
5	0.228	0.237	0.124	0.669	0.684	0.658
6	0.216	0.205	0.115	0.660	0.674	0.619
avg	0.172	0.194	0.088	0.709	0.715	0.667

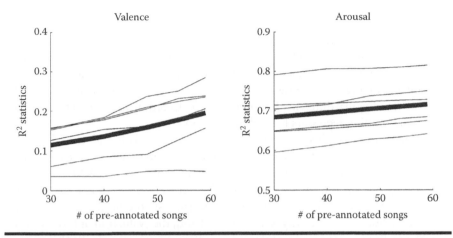

Figure 7.8   Degradation of the R^2 statistics as the number of pre-annotated songs by the user decreases. The light line represents the R^2 statistics for each user, and the heavy line represents the average of the six users.

■ Compared to the baseline method ($w = 0$), personalization generally produces better prediction accuracy for both valence and arousal. Moreover, PMER consistently outperforms the baseline method for the six subjects. The improvement for valence is salient.

■ The best performance is obtained when w is set to 0.5, which leads to partial personalization (the results of general regressor and personalized regressor are averaged). The R^2 of valence prediction is improved from 0.088 to 0.194, and that of arousal prediction is improved from 0.667 to 0.715.

Next, we evaluate the accuracy of PMER with different numbers of pre-annotated songs. As shown in Figure 7.8, the number of songs pre-annotated by the test subject correlates positively with the prediction accuracy, especially for valence. Such correlation is observed for all six subjects. This result shows the effectiveness of personalized MER.

It should be noted that, for PMER to be more feasible in practice, the number of pre-annotated songs should be kept lower to reduce user burden. A user study may be needed to study how many songs a user is willing to pre-annotate, when the user is told that his/her annotations help improve the prediction accuracy for him/her. The prediction accuracy of the MER system should also be improved, perhaps by investigating new features that are relevant to our emotion perception. A reasonable goal may be to have the prediction accuracy of valence reach performance level 2 and that of arousal reach level 1, with as few user inputs as possible.

7.6 Summary

In this chapter, we have described two simple methods that address the subjectivity issue of dimensional MER. The first method, personalized MER (PMER), personalizes the MER system by asking users to pre-annotate a number of songs and training a personalized regressor, whereas the second method, groupwise MER (GWMER), reduces the individual difference by grouping users according to a number of personal factors and training regressors for each user group.

We have also described an empirical evaluation of PMER and GWMER. Despite the incorporation of personal factors such as gender, academic background, music experience, and personality to the computational model, GWMER does not significantly outperform the general method in terms of prediction accuracy. This finding implies the subtlety of subjectivity and suggests the need to explore other methods to describe subjectivity. On the other hand, the evaluation of PMER shows that personalization is indeed useful to address the subjectivity issue. PMER outperforms the general method by a great margin, especially for valence prediction. Best performance is achieved by partial personalization.

8

Two-Layer Personalization

In the previous chapter, we have shown that personalization is an effective way to deal with the subjectivity issue of MER. In this chapter, we move on to discuss more advanced methods that are useful for addressing the subjectivity issue, including the bag-of-users model and the residual modeling. Based on these two methods, a two-layer personalization scheme is developed. A first-layer regressor is trained to predict the general perception of a music piece, and a second-layer regressor is trained to predict the difference between the general perception and a user's individual perception. This two-layer personalization scheme is more effective than the single-layer one (that is, personalized MER) because the music content and the individuality of the user are treated separately.

8.1 Problem Formulation

One can differentiate the following two dimensional MER problems:

- **General prediction**: Given a music piece d_i, predict the emotion value y_i generally perceived by every user. This is what the general regressor described in Chapter 7 aims to predict.
- **Personalized prediction**: Given a music piece d_i and a user u_j, predict the emotion value y_{ij} perceived by the user. This is what the personalized regressor described in Chapter 7 aims to predict.

Following Chapters 4 and 7, this chapter also formulates MER as a regression problem. Given N inputs $(\mathbf{x}_i, y_i)$, $1 \leq i \leq N$, where $\mathbf{x}_i$ is a feature vector of the i-th music piece d_i, and $y_i \in [-1, 1]$ is the emotion value obtained by averaging the annotations of subjects, a general regressor $r(\cdot)$ is trained by minimizing the squared error between y_i and $\hat{y}_i$, where $\hat{y}_i = r(\mathbf{x}_i)$ is the prediction result for d_i. We also use this method as the baseline in this chapter. On the other hand, according to the personalized MER (PMER) scheme described in Chapter 7, a personalized regressor $r_j(\cdot)$ is trained by minimizing the squared error between y_{ij} and $r_j(\mathbf{x}_i)$.

The baseline method and the PMER scheme described above, however, do not make the best use of available data for model training. Below we describe two more advanced methods that were developed in [361] to improve the performance of general prediction and personalized prediction, respectively. The first method, bag-of-users model (BoU), improves general prediction by better utilizing the annotations collected from subjective tests. The second method, a two-layer personalization scheme, improves personalized prediction by modeling music content and the individuality of user in two stages. As shown in Section 8.4, BoU and the two-layer personalization scheme significantly outperform the baseline method and the single-layer scheme (i.e., PMER), respectively.

8.2 Bag-of-Users Model

The ground truth data needed for training a general regressor is typically obtained by averaging the opinions of subjects. This procedure, however, makes little use of the individual annotations assigned by each subject, which provide abundant cues of the affective content of a music piece. Figure 7.1 illustrates that simply averaging annotations loses the information that for some music pieces the perceived emotion values are fairly sparse.

The bag-of-users (BoU) model trains a regressor $r_j(\cdot)$ for each subject u_j using his/her annotations and obtains a bag of models $\{r_1(\cdot), r_2(\cdot), \ldots, r_U(\cdot)\}$, where U denotes the number of subjects. The BoU model then aggregates the models using a *super* regression model to make a general prediction. Let $\hat{\mathbf{y}}_i = [\hat{y}_{i1}, \hat{y}_{i2}, \ldots, \hat{y}_{iU}]^\top$ denote a vector of the prediction results for d_i, where $\hat{y}_{ij} = r_j(\mathbf{x}_i)$. The super model $r^*(\cdot)$ is trained by minimizing the error between y_i and $r^*(\hat{\mathbf{y}}_i)$. The estimate $r^*(\hat{\mathbf{y}}_i)$ can be regarded as the aggregation of the opinions of the U subjects.

The strength of BoU is that it is able to assign different weights to different subjects through the super model $r^*(\cdot)$. A lower weight would be assigned to a subject u_j (more accurately, the corresponding regressor $r_j(\cdot)$) whose annotations are considered less reliable or less consistent, thereby removing the effect of outliers to the ground truth data.

Tables 8.1 and 8.2 show example MATLAB® codes for the baseline method and the BoU model, respectively. It can be found that the two methods differ in the way user annotations are utilized and the way regressor models are trained. Note that both methods are designed for general prediction, not personalized prediction.

Table 8.1   An Example MATLAB Code for the Baseline Method

```
%% TRAINING PHASE----------------------------------------------
% assume that we have U users annotate all the N songs
% in the database
% the annotations are stored in a matrix Y
Y = annotate_emotion;
[N U] = size(Y);

% take average
Yavg = mean(Y,2);                    % (N by 1)

% feature extraction and normalization
X = extract_feat('DIR_TR');      % features (N by M)

% model training
% use support vector regression implemented in LIBSVM
model_general = svmtrain( Yavg, X, '-s 3');

%% TEST PHASE----------------------------------------------
% feature extraction
Xtest = extract_feat('DIR_TE');  % features (Ntest by M)
[Ntest M] = size(Xtest);

% prediction
Ypred = svmpredict( zeros(Ntest,1), Xtest, model_general);
```

8.3 Residual Modeling and Two-Layer Personalization Scheme

Given the general perception y_i of a music piece d_i, we can compute the *perception residual* of a user u_z as the difference between the general perception and the personalized one, $\psi_{iz} = y_{iz} - y_i$. In other words, the personalized perception y_{iz} can be considered as the combination of general perception y_i and perception residual ψ_{iz}. The former is more related to the content of the music piece, while the latter is more related to the individuality of the user. This way, personalized prediction can be decomposed into the prediction of general perception and the prediction of perception residual.

The prediction of perception residual is called *residual modeling*. It is trained in an on-the-fly fashion as a test user interacts with the MER system. More specifically, the system asks a test user u_z to annotate his/her perceived emotions of a number of music pieces Φ and uses the annotations to train a personalized model $r_z^{\Delta}(\cdot)$ that minimizes the error between ψ_{iz} and $r_z^{\Delta}(\mathbf{x}_i)$, $d_i \in \Phi$. Note that Φ needs to be a subset of the training data because the general perception of Φ needs to be known prior to computing the perception residual. Once the personalized regressor

Table 8.2   An Example MATLAB Code for the Bag-of-Users Model

```
%% TRAINING PHASE---------------------------------------------
% assume that we have U users annotate all the N songs
% in the database
Y = annotate_emotion;
[N U] = size(Y);
Yavg = mean(Y,2);                    % take average (N by 1)


% feature extraction and normalization
X = extract_feat('DIR_TR');      % features (N by M)


% model training
% train a bag of U models
models_BoU = cell(U,1);
Ypred_tr = zeros(N,U);
for j = 1:U
    models_BoU{j} = svmtrain( Y(:,j), X, '-s 3');
    % apply the model to the training data itself
    Ypred_tr(:,j) = svmpredict( zeros(N,1), X,
                    models_BoU{j});
end

% train the super model to aggregate the U models
model_super = svmtrain( Yavg, Ypred_tr, '-s 3');

%% TEST PHASE--------------------------------------------------
% feature extraction
Xtest = extract_feat('DIR_TE');   % features (Ntest by M)
[Ntest M] = size(Xtest);

% prediction
Ypred_te = zeros(Ntest,U);
tmp = zeros(Ntest,1);
for j = 1:U
    Ypred_te(:,j) = svmpredict( tmp, Xtest, models_BoU{j});
end
Ypred = svmpredict( tmp, Ypred_te, model_super);
```

is trained, the personalized emotions of the other music pieces can be computed simply by summing the results of the general regressor and the personalized one, $\hat{y}_{iz} = r(\mathbf{x}_i) + r_z^{\Delta}(\mathbf{x}_i)$. We can also combine BoU with RM, $\hat{y}_{iz} = r^*(\hat{\mathbf{y}}_i) + r_z^{\Delta}(\mathbf{x}_i)$. The former is denoted as baseline+RM, whereas the latter is denoted as BoU+RM.

Another strength of the two-layer personalization scheme is that it makes better use of the ground truth data in the model training process. Unlike PMER, which trains a personalized regressor using only the annotations provided by the test user,

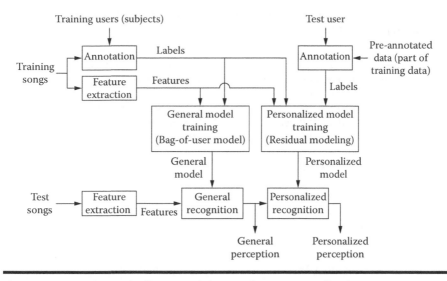

Figure 8.1   A schematic diagram of the two-layer personalized system.

the two-layer personalization scheme utilizes all the ground truth data in both the first and the second layers. In the first layer all the ground truth is used for training the general regressor, whereas in the second layer the ground truth is utilized to compute the perception residual. Therefore, the two-layer scheme has a similar or even stronger ability to harness available data for training as the partial personalization method (which performs better than total personalization) described in the previous chapter.

Figure 8.1 shows a schematic diagram of an MER system that adopts the two-layer personalization scheme. An example MATLAB code of the baseline+RM scheme is also shown in Table 8.3.

8.4 Performance Evaluation

The data set utilized in the performance evaluation is the same as the one described in Section 7.4.1. It consists of 60 popular songs selected from English albums. A total of 99 subjects are recruited from the campus, making each song annotated by 40 subjects. Each song is represented by 80-dimension Mel-frequency cepstral coefficients (MFCCs). Features are linearly normalized to the range of 0 to 1. The ϵ-support vector regression (SVR) described in Section 4.3.3.2 is adopted to train the regression models [301]. The implementation of SVR is also based on the library LIBSVM [54].

A standard measure of the goodness of fit for a regression model is the squared sample correlation coefficient R^2, or the coefficient of determination, between the

Table 8.3   An Example MATLAB Code for the Two-Layer Personalization Scheme Baseline+RM

```
%% TRAINING PHASE------------------------------------------
% train a general regressor by the baseline method
% (this can be replaced by using the BoU model)
Y = annotate_emotion;
Yavg = mean(Y,2);                 % take average (N by 1)
X = extract_feat('DIR_TR');       % features (N by M)
model_general = svmtrain( Yavg, X, '-s 3');

% a test user z is asked to annotate a subset 's_idx'
  of songs
% in the database
% the annotations are stored in a matrix Yz
Yz = annotate_emotion_test;

% compute perception residual
psi = Yz - Yavg(s_idx);

% residual modeling
          % The features of the songs annotated by the
          % test subject is X(s_idx,:)
model_RM = svmtrain( psi, X(s_idx,:), '-s 3');

%% TEST PHASE----------------------------------------------
% feature extraction
Xtest = extract_feat('DIR_TE');   % features (Ntest by M)
[Ntest M] = size(Xtest);

% emotion prediction
Ypred_ge = svmpredict( zeros(Ntest,1), Xtest, model_general);
Ypred_RM = svmpredict( zeros(Ntest,1), Xtest, model_RM);
Ypred = Ypred_ge + Ypred_RM;
```

ground truth $\mathbf{y}$ and the estimates $\hat{\mathbf{y}}$ [291],

$$R^2(\mathbf{y}, \hat{\mathbf{y}}) = \left(\frac{E((\mathbf{y} - \mu_{\mathbf{y}})(\hat{\mathbf{y}} - \mu_{\hat{\mathbf{y}}}))}{\sigma_{\mathbf{y}} \sigma_{\hat{\mathbf{y}}}} \right)^2. \tag{8.1}$$

The value of R^2 ranges from 0 to 1; an R^2 of 1.0 means perfect fit. Note the definition of R^2 used in this and the next chapters is different from the ones used in Chapters 4 and 7, whose value ranges from $-\infty$ to 1 (cf. Section 4.6). The one adopted here is also the default one implemented in LIBSVM.

For general prediction, we compare the performance of the BoU model against the baseline model. We randomly select 10 songs as test data and the remaining ones as training data. The overall procedure is repeated 100 times to get the averaged result. While the R^2 of arousal for both is around 0.70, the BoU model improves the R^2 of valence from 0.1590 to 0.1771, a +11.4% relative improvement. The performance difference is significant (p-value<1%) under the two-tailed t-test [232].

To evaluate personalized prediction, we use the six subjects who have annotated all the 60 songs as test users and the remaining ones as training users. The annotations made by the six subjects are shown in Figure 8.2. We randomly select 10 songs as the test data and the remaining ones as training data. The annotations of a test user u_z for $|\Phi|$ randomly selected songs (which are a subset of the training data) are used to train a personalized model $r_z(\cdot)$ or $r_z^\Delta(\cdot)$, and the annotations of the same user for the 10 test songs are used to evaluate $r_z(\cdot)$.

Table 8.4 shows the accuracy of personalized valence prediction of PMER (described in Chapter 7), baseline+RM, and BoU+RM, with different numbers of pre-annotated songs $|\Phi|$. A star denotes a significant improvement over the baseline model at the $\alpha = 0.01$ significance level [232]. The following observations can be made from the result:

■ Both two-layer personalization methods (baseline+RM and BoU+RM) greatly outperform direction personalization (PMER), especially when $|\Phi|$ is small. With only 10 pre-annotated songs, baseline+RM improves the R^2 from 0.1590 to 0.1709, comparing to the baseline model. Although the performance of PMER and baseline+RM becomes closer as $|\Phi|$ increases, PMER is considered less favorable because it requires too many user annotations for the personalization to be effective. This result shows that the two-layer scheme is indeed superior.

■ The performance of all three personalization methods increases as the number of $|\Phi|$ increases. This result is consistent with the result described in Section 7.5.3. We can predict the emotion perception of a test subject more accurately if we have more user feedback from him/her.

■ Among the three personalization methods, BoU+RM performs the best. It significantly improves the prediction accuracy to 0.1885 (+18.6% relative improvement) when $|\Phi|$ reaches 20, and to 0.2041 (+28.4%) when $|\Phi|$ reaches 50.

■ Interestingly, as also shown in Figure 8.3, BoU+RM constantly outperforms baseline+RM by about 0.01 (in terms of absolute difference in R^2), regardless of the number of $|\Phi|$. This result shows that the accuracy of general prediction also plays an important role in the two-layer personalization scheme.

This evaluation validates the effectiveness of the two-layer scheme for personalized valence prediction. The two-layer scheme, however, does not improve personalized arousal prediction (the R^2 is around 0.65), possibly because the perception of arousal is less subjective than that of valence.

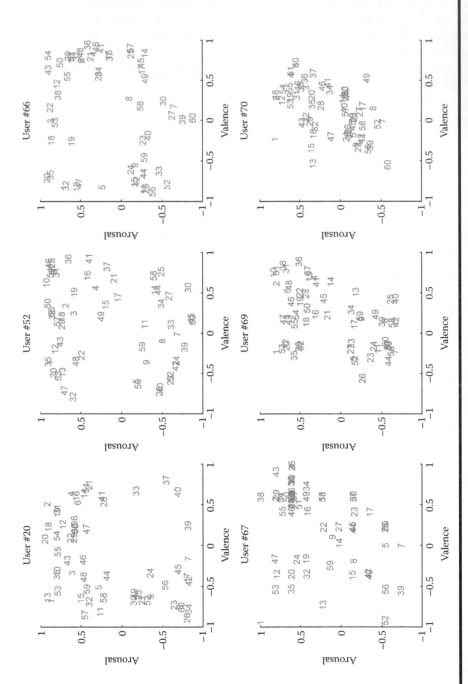

Figure 8.2 The emotion annotations of the six test subjects who annotate all 60 songs. The number in the figures corresponds to the song ID (cf. Table 5.5).

Table 8.4 Accuracy (R^2) of Personalized Valence Prediction

Method	$|\Phi| = 5$	$|\Phi| = 10$	$|\Phi| = 20$	$|\Phi| = 30$	$|\Phi| = 40$	$|\Phi| = 50$
Baseline	0.1590	0.1590	0.1590	0.1590	0.1590	0.1590
Bag-of-users (BoU)	0.1771*	0.1771*	0.1771*	0.1771*	0.1771*	0.1771*
PMER	0.1517	0.1544	0.1674	0.1788*	0.1853*	0.1953*
Baseline + RM	0.1613	0.1709*	0.1778*	0.1823*	0.1878*	0.1930*
BoU + RM	0.1732*	0.1800*	0.1885*	0.1934*	0.1988*	0.2041*

*Significant improvement over the baseline at $\alpha = 0.01$ level.

8.5 Summary

In this chapter, we have described two methods that accommodate the individual differences of emotion perception. The bag-of-users (BoU) model provides a better way to aggregate the individual perceptions of the subjects, whereas the two-layer personalization scheme personalizes the MER system by focusing on music content and user perception in different stages. The perspectives introduced in this chapter are also applicable to other applications that involve subjective human perception.

The two-layer scheme is a simple and effective personalization process because the music content and the individuality of the user are modeled separately. It does not require too many inputs from the user and is therefore superior to the personalized MER scheme described in Chapter 7. Moreover, because the two-layer

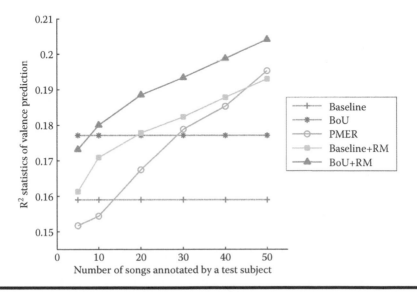

Figure 8.3 Accuracy (R^2) of personalized valence prediction.

personalization scheme harnesses the ground truth data in the model training process, it has a similar strength as the partial personalization described in the previous chapter.

To make the two-layer scheme more sophisticated, one may take into account the demographic property, music preference, or listening context of the user in the process. Another interesting research direction is to integrate the two-layer personalization scheme with the groupwise MER scheme described in the previous chapter to combine the advantages of the two methods: The former is an effective personalization method, whereas the latter requires the training only of a limited number of regressors instead of potentially infinite regressors (i.e., one for each user).

9

Probability Music Emotion Distribution Prediction

This chapter describes a new approach to dimensional MER that assigns *soft* (probabilistic) emotion values instead of *hard* (deterministic) emotion values to music pieces. This approach considers the affective content of a music signal as an emotion distribution in the emotion plane and trains a computational model to predict the music emotion distribution. In this way, one can model how subjective the perceived emotion of a music piece is and how likely a specific emotion (defined by valence and arousal values) would be perceived by a person while listening to the music piece. To our best knowledge, this is the first approach to dimensional MER that computes soft emotion values. This chapter also presents an extensive performance evaluation of this approach and describes how this approach can be applied to enhance our understanding of music emotion.

9.1 Motivation

As we have discussed in the previous chapters, simply representing a song as a single point in the emotion plane according to the mean valence and arousal (VA) values is not enough due to the subjectivity of emotion perception. As Figure 9.1 shows, the perceived emotions of a song in fact constitute an *emotion distribution* in the emotion plane. For some songs the distribution is dense and monomodal, whereas for others it is sparse and multimodal.

Motivated by the above observation, this chapter describes a new perspective that considers the perceived emotion of a music piece as a probabilistic distribution

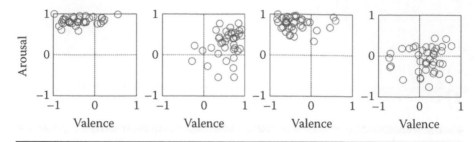

Figure 9.1 Emotion annotations in the 2D valence-arousal emotion plane [272] for four songs: (a) "Smells Like Teen Spirit" by Nirvana, (b) "A Whole New World" by Peabo Bryson and Regina Belle, (c) "The Rose" by Janis Joplin, and (d) "Tell Laura I Love Her" by Ritchie Valens. Each circle corresponds to a subject's annotation of the song. It can be observed that emotion perception is indeed subjective and that different subjects' annotations of a song constitute an "emotion distribution" in the emotion plane. (Data from Y.-H. Yang, et al. *Proc, ACM Int. Workshop on Human-Centered Multimedia.* 2007).

instead of a single point in the emotion plane. Modeling music emotion distribution is central to the understanding of music emotion and the design of an emotion-based music retrieval system, as the disparate emotion distribution is a natural consequence of the interplay between musical and personal factors of emotion perception [100]. In addition, this probabilistic model provides a solid basis for personalized emotion-based retrieval. An emotion distribution can be considered as a collection of users' perceived emotions of a music piece, whereas the perceived emotion of a specific user can be considered as a sample of the distribution. Based on the probabilistic model, one can formulate MER and personalized emotion-based music retrieval under a unified probabilistic framework.

Essential to this idea is the development of the computational model for predicting the emotion distribution of a music piece *directly* from music features. That is, given a music signal (and its feature representation), the computational model predicts its *emotion mass* at every point in the emotion plane, with the values summed to one. Here the term *emotion mass* refers to the probability that a listener's perceived emotion of a music piece locates at a specific point. The formulation of MER as the prediction of emotion mass calls for novel ways of generating the ground truth data, training the machine learning model, and representing the result. Below we provide the details of the methods that have been developed to tackle these issues.

9.2 Problem Formulation

We begin with the mathematical formulation of music emotion distribution prediction. Given the feature representation $\mathbf{x}_s$ of an input song d_s, the goal is to predict the probability of the perceived emotion of the song being $e^{ij} = [v^i, a^j]^\top$, where

$[v^i, a^j]^\top \in [-1, 1]^2$ are the VA values. Formally speaking, we aim at predicting the emotion distribution $P(\mathbf{e}|d_s)$ of song d_s, subject to

$$\int_{i=-1}^{i=1} \int_{j=-1}^{j=1} P\left(e^{ij}|d_s\right) didj = 1, \quad P\left(e^{ij}|d_s\right) \geq 0. \tag{9.1}$$

However, this requires an infinite number of predictions. To make the problem tractable, each dimension is quantized into G equally spaced discrete samples (emotion points), leading to a $G \times G$ grid representation of the emotion plane. That is, the spacing between two neighboring points is $\Delta = \frac{2}{G}$ and the VA values of a point $\bar{e}^{ij}$ equals $[(i - \frac{1}{2})\Delta - 1, (j - \frac{1}{2})\Delta - 1]^\top$. This way, the task becomes the prediction of $P(\bar{e}^{ij}|d_s)$, $(i, j) \in \{1, \ldots, G\}^2$, subject to

$$\sum_{i=1}^{i=G} \sum_{j=1}^{j=G} P\left(\bar{e}^{ij}|d_s\right) = 1, \quad P\left(\bar{e}^{ij}|d_s\right) \geq 0. \tag{9.2}$$

Note that we use $\bar{e}$ to denote the quantized emotion here. While $P(e^{ij}|d_s)$ is called emotion density, $P(\bar{e}^{ij}|d_s)$ is referred to as emotion *mass*. Because $P(\bar{e}^{ij}|d_s)$ is a real value in the range $[0, 1]$, regression algorithms [291] can be employed to train G^2 regressors for each of the emotion points, under the assumption that the emotion mass values of different emotion points are independent. We denote $f^{ij}(\cdot)$ as the regressor for predicting the emotion mass of $\bar{e}^{ij}$. Accordingly, the prediction result is expressed as $\hat{P}(\bar{e}^{ij}|d_s) = f^{ij}(\mathbf{x}_s)$.

The new problem formulation of MER leads to the following three issues. First, how do we obtain the ground truth data needed to train the regressors? We need to have ground truth emotion mass for each of the discrete samples. Second, how do we choose a regression algorithm to train the regressors and how do we choose the feature representation of music? Third, given the prediction result $\hat{P}(\bar{e}^{ij}|d_s)$, how do we recover the continuous emotion distribution $\hat{P}(e^{ij}|d_s)$? It is important to have the continuous emotion distribution as the output because a user can click on any point in the emotion plane. These issues cannot be resolved by the methods introduced in the previous chapters.

There are two approaches that can be applied to address the aforementioned issues. The *KDE-based* approach applies kernel density estimation (KDE) [39, 320] to approximate the ground truth emotion mass for each of the discrete samples from the annotations collected through the subjective test. Based on the ground truth and extracted features, a total of G^2 regressors are trained to learn the mapping between feature space and music emotion distribution; each predicts the emotion mass for a discrete sample of the emotion plane. Given an input test music piece, we extract features, apply regressors, and use Gaussian process regression [263] to generate the output of emotion distribution that is approximately continuous.* A system diagram of the KDE-based approach is shown in Figure 9.3. Each system component is described in detail in the next section. An illustration of the flow chart of this approach is depicted in Figure 9.3.

An alternative is to model the emotion distribution by some known probability function and apply machine learning to predict the parameterization of the distribution from music features. For example, we can model each emotion distribution as a bivariate Gaussian and train five regressors to predict the mean, variance, and covariance of valence and arousal (note we need to predict the emotion distribution directly from features because we do not have users' annotations for a test song). This *single-Gaussian* approach is computationally more efficient and allows easier performance analysis. However, its prediction accuracy may be limited by the single Gaussian assumption. Modeling the emotion distribution as a mixture of Gaussian distributions would be more accurate, but that requires a decision regarding the number of mixture components and the weight associated with each of them, which is difficult to make automatically. Moreover, there may be multiple parameterizations of the Gaussian mixture model that fit the emotion distribution of a song, making the prediction problem ill-posed. Section 9.5 presents an empirical performance comparison of the KDE-based approach and the single-Gaussian approach.

9.3 The KDE-Based Approach to Music Emotion Distribution Prediction

In music emotion distribution prediction, the emotion of each music piece is represented as a probability distribution in the emotion plane and computational models are applied to predict the emotion mass for each discrete sample. This section provides the details of the KDE-based approach to music emotion distribution prediction.

9.3.1 Ground Truth Collection

In the annotation process, a subject is asked to annotate the VA values of a music piece by clicking on a point in the emotion plane displayed by computer [366] (see Section 9.4.1 for more details). Therefore, for each music piece we have several subjects' annotations of the VA values, as represented by the circles in Figure 9.2(a). Based on these annotations, we want to estimate the emotion mass $P(\bar{e}^{\,ij}|d)$ of each grid point $\bar{e}^{\,ij}$, $(i, j) \in \{1, \ldots, G\}^2$. Clearly, the value of G has an important effect on the system performance. If G is too small, the emotion distribution will suffer from insufficient resolution, whereas if G is too large, the computational cost will be exceedingly high. As a compromise, one may set G to 8 and estimate the density of

---

* Note that a more correct term might be *continual*, because even a very fine resolution is still not, strictly speaking, continuous.

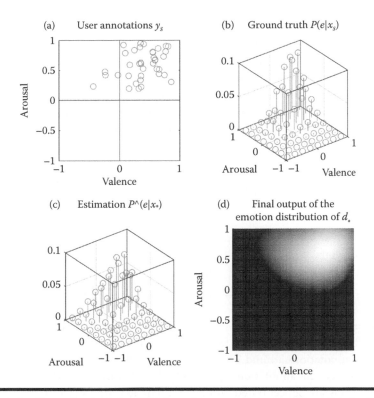

Figure 9.2 **Flow chart of the KDE-based approach to emotion distribution prediction: (a)→(b)→(c)→(d).**

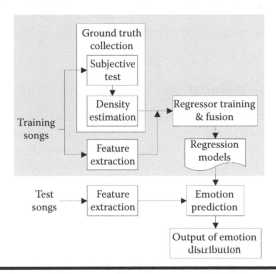

Figure 9.3 **A schematic diagram of the KDE-based approach to emotion distribution prediction.**

the 8×8 grid points ($\Delta = \frac{2}{G} = 0.125$). See Section 9.5 for an empirical performance comparison of different numbers of G.

To estimate $P(\bar{e}^{ij}|d)$ from the emotion annotations, KDE is employed. KDE is a popular non-parametric way of estimating the probability density function of a random variable [39]. Given the user annotations $[z_{s1}, z_{s2}, \ldots, z_{s U_s}]$ of a music piece d_s, where $z_{s1} \in [-1, 1]^*$ is the VA values assigned by a subject and U_s is the number of subjects that annotate the music piece,* the kernel density approximation of the probability density function is

$$P\left(\bar{e}^{ij}|d_s\right) = \frac{1}{U_s} \sum_{u=1}^{U_s} K\left(\bar{e}^{ij} - z_{su}\right), \tag{9.3}$$

where $K(\cdot)$ is a kernel function, typically chosen as the bivariate Gaussian with zero mean and diagonal covariance,

$$K(\mathbf{z}) = \frac{1}{2\pi |\Sigma|^{1/2}} \exp\left(-\frac{1}{2}\mathbf{z}^\top \Sigma^{-1} \mathbf{z}\right), \tag{9.4}$$

where $\Sigma = \text{diag}([h_v, h_a])$, and h_v, h_a are scaling parameters that can be optimally chosen [38]. It can be found that the density is estimated by summing the *affinity* of subjects' annotations around $\bar{e}^{ij}$, weighted inversely proportionally to the scaled distance between the annotation z_{su} and $\bar{e}^{ij}$. The density $P(\bar{e}^{ij}|d_s)$ is large when the annotations are concentrated around $\bar{e}^{ij}$. The resulting 2D histogram is then normalized to a probability distribution. Figure 9.2(b) shows a sample result. Note that kernel density estimation can be considered as an extension of the classical Parzen window method [78], which simply counts the number of annotations that fall within an L2 ellipse centered at $\bar{e}^{ij}$, with horizontal axis of length h_v and vertical axis of length h_a.

9.3.2 Regressor Training

Under the independence assumption, we train G^2 regressors for each of the emotion points. Given N inputs $(\mathbf{x}_s, y_s)$, $s \in \{1, \ldots, N\}$, where $\mathbf{x}_s$ is the feature vector and y_s is the real value to be predicted (here the emotion mass $P(\bar{e}^{ij}|d_s)$), a regressor $f^{ij}(\cdot)$ is created by minimizing the mismatch ϵ (i.e., mean squared error) between ground truth and prediction [291],

$$\epsilon = \frac{1}{N} \sum_{s=1}^{N} \left(P\left(\bar{e}^{ij}|d_s\right)\right) - f^{ij}(\mathbf{x}_s))^2. \tag{9.5}$$

---

* Here it is assumed that the annotations of a song are independent and identically distributed random variables.

As the regression theory has been well studied, many good regression algorithms are readily available. Below we describe the two state-of-the-art methods that are employed in the performance evaluation: the v-support vector regression (v-SVR) [69, 281] and the Gaussian process regression (GPR) [263]. Note that the v-SVR introduced here is slightly different from the ϵ-SVR described in Section 4.3.3.2.

9.3.2.1 v-Support Vector Regression

Since the 1990s, support vector machines (SVMs) have been widely used in different classification and regression tasks [69, 281]. SVM nonlinearly maps input feature vectors $\mathbf{x}$ to a higher dimensional feature space $\phi(\mathbf{x})$ by the kernel trick and learns a nonlinear function by a linear learning machine in the kernel-induced feature space, where data are more separable [69]. For regression, we look for a function $f(\mathbf{x}_s) = \mathbf{m}^\top \phi(\mathbf{x}_s) + b$ that has at most ε deviation from the ground truth y_s for all the training data and meanwhile is as flat as possible (i.e., $\mathbf{m}^\top \mathbf{m}$ is small) [281]. Moreover, under the soft margin principle [40], we introduce slack variables ξ_s and ξ_s^* to allow the error to be greater than ε. Consequently, we have the following optimization problem:

$$\underset{\mathbf{m}, b, \xi, \xi^*, \varepsilon}{\arg\min} \ \frac{1}{2}\mathbf{m}^\top \mathbf{m} + C\left(v\varepsilon + \frac{1}{N}\sum_{s=1}^{N}\left(\xi_s + \xi_s^*\right)\right),$$

$$\text{subject to } \left(\mathbf{m}^\top \phi(\mathbf{x}_s) + b\right) - y_s \leq \varepsilon + \xi_s, \tag{9.6}$$

$$y_s - \left(\mathbf{m}^\top \phi(\mathbf{x}_s) + b\right) \leq \varepsilon + \xi_s^*,$$

$$\xi_s, \xi_s^* \geq 0, s = 1, \ldots, N, \varepsilon \geq 0,$$

where the parameter C controls the trade-off between the flatness of $f(\cdot)$ and the amount up to which deviations larger than ε are tolerated, and the parameter $v \in [0, 1]$ controls the number of support vectors (the points lying on the boundaries) [281]. A common kernel function is the radial basis function (RBF): $K(\mathbf{x}_p, \mathbf{x}_q) \equiv \phi(\mathbf{x}_p)^\top \phi(\mathbf{x}_q) = \exp(-\gamma \|\mathbf{x}_p - \mathbf{x}_q\|^2)$, where γ is a scale parameter [69]. Typically the parameters of SVR are determined empirically by doing a grid search. The above quadratic optimization problem can be efficiently solved by known techniques [40].

The main difference between the v-SVR described here and the ϵ-SVR described in Chapters 4 is the introduction of the parameter v, which better controls the number of support vectors and training errors. Our empirical evaluation shows that v-SVR slightly outperforms ϵ-SVR for music emotion distribution prediction.

9.3.2.2 Gaussian Process Regression

GPR can be interpreted as a Bayesian version of SVR [263]. A Gaussian process generates data located throughout some domain such that any finite subset of the range follows a multivariate Gaussian distribution with zero mean and certain covariance, or $y_* \sim \mathcal{N}(0, K(\mathbf{X}_*, \mathbf{X}_*))$.* A popular covariance function is the squared exponential (SE),

$$\text{cov}(f(\mathbf{x}_p), f(\mathbf{x}_q)) = K_{\text{SE}}(\mathbf{x}_p, \mathbf{x}_q) = \sigma_y^2 \exp\left(-\frac{\|\mathbf{x}_p - \mathbf{x}_q\|^2}{2l^2}\right), \qquad (9.7)$$

where σ_y^2 is called the signal variance, and l is the characteristic length-scale. For noisy inputs we have $K(\mathbf{x}_p, \mathbf{x}_q) = K_{\text{SE}}(\mathbf{x}_p, \mathbf{x}_q) + \sigma_n^2 \delta(\mathbf{x}_p, \mathbf{x}_q)$, where σ_n^2 is the noise variance and $\delta(\cdot, \cdot)$ is the Kronecker delta function. When $\mathbf{x}_p$ and $\mathbf{x}_q$ are far away from each other, $K(\mathbf{x}_p, \mathbf{x}_q) \simeq 0$. Given the training data $\mathbf{y}, \mathbf{X}$ and the test inputs $\mathbf{X}_*$, we have

$$\begin{bmatrix} \mathbf{y} \\ \mathbf{y}_* \end{bmatrix} \sim \mathcal{N}\left(\mathbf{0}, \begin{pmatrix} K(\mathbf{X}, \mathbf{X}) & K(\mathbf{X}_*, \mathbf{X})^\top \\ K(\mathbf{X}_*, \mathbf{X}) & K(\mathbf{X}_*, \mathbf{X}_*) \end{pmatrix}\right). \qquad (9.8)$$

It can be shown that

$$\mathbf{y}_* | \, \mathbf{X}, \mathbf{X}_*, \mathbf{y} \sim \mathcal{N}\left(\mathcal{K}_* \mathcal{K}^{-1} \mathbf{y}, \mathcal{K}_{**} - \mathcal{K}_* \mathcal{K}^{-1} \mathcal{K}_*^\top\right), \qquad (9.9)$$

where we have used the shorthand $\mathcal{K} = K(\mathbf{X}, \mathbf{X})$, $\mathcal{K}_* = K(\mathbf{X}_*, \mathbf{X})$, and $\mathcal{K}_{**} = K(\mathbf{X}_*, \mathbf{X}_*)$. Our best estimate of y_* is the mean of this distribution,

$$\hat{\mathbf{y}}_* = f(\mathbf{X}_*) = \mathcal{K}_* \mathcal{K}^{-1} \mathbf{y}. \qquad (9.10)$$

Moreover, with the Bayesian formalism, GPR provides a principled way to select the parameters $\theta = \{l, \sigma_y, \sigma_n\}$ by maximizing the marginal likelihood,

$$\log p(\mathbf{y}|\mathbf{X}, \theta) = -\frac{1}{2}\mathbf{y}^\top \mathcal{K}^{-1}\mathbf{y} - \frac{1}{2}\log|\mathcal{K}| - \frac{n}{2}\log 2\pi. \qquad (9.11)$$

Gaussian process models are attractive mainly because of their flexible non-parametric nature. The major drawback of heavy computational scaling (e.g., the need to compute the inverse of the $N \times N$ matrix $\mathcal{K}$) has recently been alleviated by the introduction of generic sparse approximations [263].

In practice some prediction result may be negative because SVR does not constrain the estimate to be nonnegative. To make the prediction result of a song a probability distribution, the negative estimates are truncated to zero and then all the estimates are normalized to sum-to-one.

---

* We write $y \sim \mathcal{N}(\mu, \sigma^2)$ when a random variable y is distributed normally with mean μ and variance σ^2.

9.3.3 Regressor Fusion

A key issue in developing an MER system is the design of highly discriminant features. However, what intrinsic element of music, if any, creates a specific emotional response from the listener is still far from well understood. Moreover, the importance of different features depends on the emotion we are trying to predict. For example, while the tempo of a music piece is related to arousal perception, the musical mode is related to valence perception [159]. Due to these considerations, one may extract a number of music features and employ model fusion algorithms to aggregate the different perceptual dimensions of music listening, such as harmony, timbre, and rhythm.

Consider that we have T feature representations of music $\mathbf{X}^t = \{\mathbf{x}_1^t, \ldots, \mathbf{x}_N^t\}$, $t = \{1, \ldots, T\}$, where $\mathbf{x}_s^t$ is the t-th feature representation of a music piece d_s. Our goal is to train T regressors $f_t(\cdot)$, $t = \{1, \ldots, T\}$, to predict the emotion mass of a specific emotion point based on each of the feature representations, and to find the best strategy to combine these T regressors so that the overall accuracy is improved. In other words, we look for the optimal combination operator $f_o(\cdot)$ among the set of functional operators that minimizes a cost function expressed in the form $L(\mathbf{y}, f_o([f_1(\mathbf{x}^1), \ldots, f_T(\mathbf{x}^T)]^\top))$, where $L(\cdot, \cdot)$ is some cost function. This problem is called *regressor fusion*.

In the machine learning community, several *aggregation* operators have been proposed, such as the mean, the product, or the maximum of the values returned by all machine learning models [170]. As past work has shown that the mean operator usually performs well [170], we describe two methods for aggregating the regressors by a linear weighted mean operator as follows:

$$\hat{P}\left(\bar{e}^{ij} | d_s\right) = \sum_{t=1}^{T} w_t^{ij} f_t^{ij}\left(\mathbf{x}_s^t\right), \tag{9.12}$$

where w_t^{ij} is the weight assigned to the t-th regressor, $w_t^{ij} > 0$, $\sum_{t=1}^{T} w_t^{ij} = 1$, and $f_t^{ij}(\cdot)$ is the t-th regressor for predicting the emotion mass of $\bar{e}^{ij}$. The task is to find the optimal weight w_t^{ij} associated with each regressor.

9.3.3.1 Weighted by Performance

For classifier fusion, it has been shown that the optimal weight of each classifier is proportional to the empirical average classification accuracy of each classifier, if the cost function is the probability of misclassification [309]. The optimality is theoretically justifiable under the assumption that the classification accuracy follows a Gaussian distribution. As an extension of this work, weighted-by-performance weights each regressor according to the prediction accuracy of the regressor. More specifically, the method *weighted-by-λ* assumes that the mean squared error (MSE) ϵ of a regressor (cf. Eq. 4.4) follows an exponential distribution and weights each regressor by the mean λ of the exponential distribution,

$$\lambda_t^{ij} = \frac{1}{\epsilon_t^{ij}} = \frac{N}{\sum_{s=1}^{N} \left(P\left(\bar{e}^{ij} | d_s \right) \right) - f_t^{ij} \left(\mathbf{x}_s^t \right) \right)^2}. \tag{9.13}$$

The weights are normalized so that $w_t^{ij} = \lambda_t^{ij} / \sum_{t=1}^{T} \lambda_t^{ij}$. The idea of weighting multiple machines/servers according to the mean of exponential distributions can also be found in the field of load sharing in distributed computer systems [25].

The method *weighted-by-R^2* weights regressors according to the R^2 statistics, another standard metric for evaluating regressors [291]. As we have described in Section 8.4, an R^2 of 1.0 means the model perfectly fits the data, while $R^2 = 0$ indicates no linear relationship between the ground truth and the estimate.

Accordingly, we set

$$w_t^{ij} = \frac{R^2 \left(\mathbf{y}^{ij}, f_t^{ij}(\mathbf{X}^t) \right)}{\sum_{t=1}^{T} R^2 \left(\mathbf{y}^{ij}, f_t^{ij}(\mathbf{X}^t) \right)},$$

$$\mathbf{y}^{ij} = \left[P\left(\bar{e}^{ij} | d_1 \right), \ldots, P\left(\bar{e}^{ij} | d_N \right) \right]^\top, \tag{9.14}$$

$$f_t^{ij}(\mathbf{X}^t) = \left[f_t^{ij}(\mathbf{x}_1^t), \ldots, f_t^{ij}(\mathbf{x}_N^t) \right]^\top,$$

where $\mathbf{y}^{ij}$ and $f_t^{ij}(\mathbf{X}^t)$ are the ground truth and the estimates, respectively.

Note that for the above two methods λ and R^2 are estimated from the training data and used to compute the weights, which are then applied to the test data.

9.3.3.2 Optimization

We can also use the R^2 statistics as the cost function and directly optimize $L(\mathbf{y}^{ij}, \sum_{t=1}^{T} w_t^{ij} f_t^{ij}(\mathbf{X}^t))$. Specifically, one can formulate the following constrained optimization problem to determine the weights (the superscripts ^{ij} are suppressed for brevity),

$$\underset{\mathbf{w}}{\arg\max} \frac{\text{cov}\left(\mathbf{y}, \Sigma_{t=1}^{T} w_t \hat{\mathbf{y}}_t \right)^2}{\text{var}(\mathbf{y}) \text{var}\left(\Sigma_{t=1}^{T} w_t \hat{\mathbf{y}}_t \right)}, \tag{9.15}$$

subject to $\mathbf{w} > 0$, $\mathbf{w}^\top \mathbf{w} = 1$,

where $\mathbf{w} = [w_1, \ldots, w_T]^\top$. By writing $u_t = \text{cov}(\mathbf{y}, \hat{\mathbf{y}}_t)^2$ and $v_t = \text{var}(\mathbf{y}) \text{var}(\hat{\mathbf{y}}_t)$, we get an equivalent problem,

$$\underset{\mathbf{w}}{\arg\min} \frac{-\mathbf{u}^\top \mathbf{w}}{\mathbf{w}^\top \text{diag}(\mathbf{v}) \mathbf{w}}, \tag{9.16}$$

subject to $\mathbf{w} > 0$, $\mathbf{w}^\top \mathbf{w} = 1$, where $\mathbf{u} = [u_1, \ldots, u_T]^\top$, and $\mathbf{v} = [v_1, \ldots, v_T]^\top$. The above problem can be easily solved by any off-the-shelf solver, such as the fmincon function of the MATLAB optimization toolbox [9]. As a nonconvex problem, the solution of Eq. 9.16 is sensitive to the initial values of $\mathbf{w}$ [40]. One may run a number of trials with different (random) initializations and take the one with the lowest cost $L(\mathbf{y}, \hat{\mathbf{y}})$. This method is called *optimize-R^2*. Likewise, we also develop *optimize-ϵ* by using MSE as the cost function. As weighted-by-performance, the weights are learned from the training data.

Table 9.1 shows an example MATLAB® code for weighted-by-R^2.

Table 9.1   An Example MATLAB Code for the Regressor Fusion Method Weighted-by-R^2

```
% regressor fusion is done for each discrete sample
% separately here we use only one discrete sample for example
Y;                              % ground emotion mass (N by 1)

% extract features of different perceptual dimensions
Xs = extract_feat('DIR_TR');   % cell array (T by 1)
T = length(Xs);                % T: # of perceptual dimensions

% model training
models = cell(T,1);
Ypred_tr = zeros(N,T);
for t = 1:T
    models{t} = svmtrain( Y, Xs{t}, '-s 3');
    Ypred_tr(:,t) = svmpredict( zeros(N,1),Xs{t},models{t});
end

% learn the weights using weighted-by-R^2
W = zeros(T,1);
for t = 1:T
    W(t) = calc_r2(Y,Ypred_tr(:,t));   % compute the R^2
end
W = W/sum(W);

%% TEST PHASE---------------------------------------------------
Xtests = extract_feat('DIR_TE');
Ntest = size(Xtest,1);
Ypred_te = zeros(Ntest,T);
tmp = zeros(Ntest,1);

% prediction
for t = 1:T
    Ypred_te(:,t) = svmpredict( tmp, Xtests{t}, models{t});
end

% fusion
Ypred = Ypred_te * W;          % (Ntest by 1)
```

9.3.4 Output of Emotion Distribution

The emotion distribution of an 8×8 grid is too coarse to meet user satisfaction, since in practice a user can click on any point in the emotion plane. To resolve this issue, we need to approximate the continuous representation by estimating the emotion mass of a 100×100 finer grid ($\Delta = 0.02$, which is presumably small enough) from the 8×8 grid.

In geo-statistics, the technique of interpolating the value of a random field (e.g., elevation, ore-grade, or the emotion mass here) at an unobserved location (mostly on 2D and 3D input spaces) from observations of its value at nearby locations is often known as "kriging" [71]. Gaussian process regression (GPR) is a standard solution to this problem [263]. Specifically, to apply GPR, the locations of the songs in the emotion plane are treated as input features $\mathbf{X}$ and the emotion masses $\hat{P}(\tilde{e}^{ij}|d)$ are treated as ground truth $\mathbf{y}$. Eq. 9.10 is then applied to estimate the emotion mass of each test point $e_* = [v_*, a_*]^\top$. Using a 100×100 grid is in fact a compromise between resolution and computational cost. In our implementation, which is based on the GPML (Gaussian process for machine learning) toolkit [263], generating the output of emotion distribution of a song took less than 1 second on a regular dual-core Pentium PC.

An algorithmic description of emotion distribution prediction is shown in Table 9.2.

Table 9.2   Algorithmic Description of the KDE-Based Approach to Music Emotion Distribution Prediction

TRAINING PHASE
INPUT: The T feature representations $\mathbf{X}^1, \ldots, \mathbf{X}^T$ of the N training samples $d_1, \ldots, d_N$ ($\mathbf{X}^t = \{\mathbf{x}_1^t, \ldots, \mathbf{x}_N^t\}$)
% *Ground truth collection (Section 9.3.1)*
collect annotations of the VA values from subjects
for $s = 1$ to N
for $i, j = 1$ to G
estimate $P(\tilde{e}^{ij}|d_s)$ by kernel density estimation
end
end
% *Regressor training & fusion (Sections 9.3.2 and 9.3.3)*
for $i, j = 1$ to G
for $t = 1$ to T
train $f_t^{ij}(\cdot)$ by minimizing the error between $P(\tilde{e}^{ij}|d_s)$ and $f_t^{ij}(\mathbf{x}_s^t)$
using a regression algorithm (e.g., v-SVR)
end

(continued)

Table 9.2   Algorithmic Description of the KDE-Based Approach to Music Emotion Distribution Prediction (Continued)

learn the optimal fusion weights $\mathbf{w}^{ij} = [w_1^{ij}, \ldots, w_T^{ij}]^\top$ so that $\hat{P}(\tilde{e}^{ij}|d_s) = \sum_{t=1}^{T} w_t^{ij} f_t^{ij}(\mathbf{x}_s^t)$ end OUTPUT: The $G^2 T$ regressors $f_t^{ij}(\cdot)$ and G^2 fusion weights $\mathbf{w}^{ij}$
TEST PHASE
INPUT: The T feature representations $\mathbf{x}_*^1, \ldots, \mathbf{x}_*^T$ of a test sample d_* % *Prediction* for $i, j = 1$ to G predict $\hat{P}(\tilde{e}^{ij}|d_*) = \sum_{t=1}^{T} w_t^{ij} f_t^{ij}(\mathbf{x}_*^t)$ end % *Output generation (Section 9.3.4)* interpolate the emotion mass of a finer grid by GPR OUTPUT: emotion distribution prediction of d_*

9.4 Implementation

This section describes the implementation details of the KDE-based approach and the single-Gaussian approach to music emotion distribution prediction. We present the qualitative and quantitative evaluations of the two approaches in the next section.

9.4.1 Data Collection

The data set utilized in this implementation is the same as the one used in the previous two chapters (cf. Section 7.4.1). It consists of 60 famous popular songs selected from English albums, each of them truncated to a 30-second segment by manually picking the chorus part. Accordingly, we predict the emotion distribution of the segment and consider the prediction result as that of the entire song. Moreover, we partition the data set to four subsets, each with 15 music pieces whose emotions are roughly uniformly distributed in the emotion plane, and randomly select one of the subsets for a subject to annotate. A total of 99 subjects (46 male, 53 female) are recruited from the campus, making each music piece annotated by 40 subjects in the end. See Section 7.4.1 for more details of the data set.

Since annotations that are largely different from the others are usually less reliable, we employ the algorithm described in [111] to remove these outliers and to reduce the number of effective annotations from 2400 to 2364.

9.4.2 Feature Extraction

As Table 9.3 shows, several features are extracted to represent the following five perceptual dimensions of music listening: harmony, spectrum, temporal, rhythm,

Table 9.3   Extracted Feature Sets

Feature Set	Feature Dimension	Features
Harmony	10	Salient pitch, chromagram center, key clarity, mode, and harmonic change [182]. Take mean and standard deviation for temporal integration [228].
Spectrum	90	32 spectral flatness measures, 32 spectral crest factors [324], and 26 Mel-scale frequency cepstral coefficients [246].
Temporal	6	Zero-crossing rate, temporal centroid, and log attack time [31]. Take mean and standard deviation.
Rhythm	61	Rhythm histogram and average tempo [206].
Lyrics	60	Probability distribution over 60 latent topics [129]. See Table 9.4.

and lyrics. We then train regressors using features of each perceptual dimension. Since the details of many features have been described in Chapters 3 and 10, we only briefly introduce them below:

Harmony. We use the MIR toolbox [182] to generate two pitch features (salient pitch, chromagram center) and three tonal features (key clarity, mode, harmonic change). All these features are extracted for each short time frame (23 ms, 50% overlapping) and then aggregated by taking the mean and standard deviation [228].

Spectrum. We use Marsyas [324] to extract 32 spectral flatness measures (SFM) and 32 crest factors (SCF), which are both related to the tonalness of audio signal [21]. They are extracted by computing the values in 24 subbands for each frame and then taking the mean and standard deviation for each second. The sequence of feature vectors is then collapsed into a single vector representing the entire signal by taking again the mean and standard deviation. We consider only the values in the first eight subbands, for they contain more information. MFCCs are also extracted using the MA toolbox [246]. We take the first 13 MFCC coefficients of each frame and then use the mean and standard deviation for temporal integration [228].

Temporal. We use the sound description toolbox [31] to extract zero-crossing rate, temporal centroid, and log attack time to capture the temporal quality of music. Spectrum and temporal features summarize the timbre content of music.

Rhythm. We use the rhythm pattern extractor [206] to generate a 60-bin rhythm histogram by aggregating the energy in 60 modulation frequencies. The mean of the rhythm histogram is also computed as an estimate of the average tempo.

For a given piece of music, the rhythm histogram is calculated by taking the median of the histograms of every 6-second segment processed.

Lyrics. Complementary to music signal, lyrics are semantically rich and expressive and have profound impact on human perception of music [19]. It is often easy for humans to tell whether a song expresses happiness or sadness from the lyrics. The incorporation of textual features extracted from the lyrics is therefore helpful in modeling our valence perception, as shown in past MER work [139, 183, 288, 363]. In our implementation, the lyrics of 46,218 unlabeled English songs are obtained from the Internet and preprocessed with traditional information retrieval operations such as stop word removal and stemming [290]. We then count the occurrence of terms in the lyrics and trained probabilistic latent topic analysis (PLSA) [129] to obtain the probability distribution of each song over 60 latent topics. The number of latent topics is empirically determined. PLSA reduces the dimension of the feature space and increases the overlapping of semantic terms. See Chapter 10 for more details of PLSA and lyrics processing.

Table 9.4 shows the first 40 latent topics and the associated eight most probable terms in the class-conditional distribution. It can be found that different latent

Table 9.4 The Top Eight Words of the First 40 Latent Topics Learned from 46,218 Lyrics Using PLSA note, these words have been stemmed (c.f. Section 10.2)

ID	Top Eight Terms of Each Topic							
1	fall	tear	rain	pain	fear	reach	shadow	empti
2	hear	old	everybodi	sound	music	parti	ear	guitar
3	call	home	talk	town	line	mother	wake	worri
4	wanna	leav	noth	insid	without	hide	els	reason
5	made	told	knew	lie	hous	daddi	met	fell
6	nig*a	sh*t	f*ck	with	b*tch	a*s	thi	wit
7	year	pass	kid	dog	damn	school	famili	dont
8	heart	song	true	sing	mai	gave	broken	part
9	dai	life	alwai	free	turn	set	til	ani
10	never	need	everyth	someon	miss	anyth	thought	pretend
11	monei	ask	best	pai	bui	caught	act	work
12	hit	hot	cut	kick	drop	top	straight	cuz
13	like	plai	game	train	kinda	with	boss	movi
14	burn	cold	soul	dark	deep	fire	river	gold
15	girl	cry	care	wish	kind	lover	yea	with

(continued)

Table 9.4   The Top Eight Words of the First 40 Latent Topics Learned from 46,218 Lyrics Using PLSA note, these words have been stemmed (c.f. Section 10.2) (Continued)

ID	Top Eight Terms of Each Topic							
16	dream	hold	kiss	close	lone	arm	breath	tight
17	friend	end	fool	fight	doe	sad	stori	begin
18	make	choru	bring	repeat	hate	vers	bridg	bet
19	hei	realli	tonight	wear	treat	dress	doctor	billi
20	head	befor	door	happi	bodi	room	bed	anymor
21	face	place	child	voic	children	wast	speak	futur
22	awai	gone	far	lost	todai	forget	goodby	memori
23	night	everi	wrong	till	until	strong	mess	sight
24	thi	world	chang	togeth	forev	moment	differ	tomorrow
25	time	long	rememb	ago	befor	spend	year	spent
26	sai	good	someth	stai	worth	modern	cheat	special
27	feel	wai	why	mayb	hurt	afraid	explain	shouldn
28	where	late	slow	wall	meet	middl	scare	pack
29	god	heaven	angel	follow	earth	troubl	power	wing
30	anoth	round	ground	feet	everyon	fire	million	whoa
31	road	drink	mama	half	nice	thousand	shoe	countri
32	onli	still	even	mani	young	ladi	lot	isn
33	show	put	start	listen	step	fun	stone	number
34	yeah	huh	oooh	boom	solo	mood	cream	che
35	love	sweet	abov	affair	truli	with	tender	share
36	thei	lord	men	carri	poor	women	lucki	welcom
37	wait	big	ooh	grow	veri	beauti	minut	histori
38	down	watch	break	lai	shake	shout	brother	hell
39	try	help	lose	somebodi	hang	lead	trust	faith
40	ain	stop	nobodi	goin	fast	comin	lookin	nothin

Note: Obscene words have been obscured.

Source: T. Hofmann. *Proc. ACM Int. Conf. Information Retrieval.* 1999.

topics indeed carry different semantic meanings. For example, the first topic seems to be related to the feeling of sorrow, the seventh one seems to be related to kids, the sixteenth is about love, the twenty-second is about leaving, and the sixth topic contains lots of obscene words. Different songs would have different probability distributions over the 60 latent topics according to the terms in their lyrics.

9.5 Performance Evaluation

We run a series of experiments to evaluate the accuracy of emotion distribution prediction. Different regression algorithms, feature representations, and fusion methods are empirically compared in terms of the R^2 statistics (we use R^2 instead of MSE because the latter does not take data variation into account [291]) and the Jensen–Shannon (JS) divergence [271], defined as

$$D_{JS}(\mathbf{y}, \hat{\mathbf{y}}) = \frac{1}{2} \sum_i \left(y_i \log \frac{y_i}{z_i} + \hat{y}_i \log \frac{\hat{y}_i}{z_i} \right), \tag{9.17}$$

where $\mathbf{y}$ and $\hat{\mathbf{y}}$ are two probability distributions (here the ground truth emotion distribution and the estimated one), and $z_i = (y_i + \hat{y}_i)/2$. The calculation of R^2 and D_{JS} involves a conversion of the 2D emotion distribution to a 1D vector by stacking the columns,

$$\mathbf{y} = \text{vec}(P(\bar{e}^{ij}|d)), \hat{\mathbf{y}} = \text{vec}(f^{ij}(\mathbf{X})), (i, j) \in \{1, \ldots, G\}^2, \tag{9.18}$$

where vec($\cdot$) denotes the vectorization of a matrix. Being an extension of the well-known Kullback–Leibler divergence [176], the Jensen–Shannon divergence is symmetric, nonnegative, and small when the two distributions are similar. Likewise, instead of computing $\frac{1}{G^2} \sum_{i,j}^{G} R^2(P(\bar{e}^{ij}|\mathbf{x}_s), f^{ij}(\mathbf{x}_s)))$, we compute $R^2(\mathbf{y}_s, \hat{\mathbf{y}}_s)$.

The performance is evaluated by the leave-one-out (LOO) cross-validation technique, which is known to provide an almost unbiased estimate of the generalization error even with a small data set [78]. LOO uses one music piece as the test data and the remainder as training data in each run of the evaluation. This procedure is repeated for N runs until each music piece is tested once. In each run, feature normalization is done by standardizing the training data to zero mean and unit variance (i.e., z-score normalization) and applying the normalization parameters to the test data. We report the mean R^2 and D_{JS} of the N runs.

9.5.1 Comparison of Different Regression Algorithms

We first evaluate the performance of different regression algorithms, including v-support vector regression (v-SVR), Gaussian process regression (GPR), multiple linear regression (MLR), and a random assignment baseline. Our implementation of GPR is based on the GPML toolkit [263], with the parameters optimized by maximizing the marginal likelihood (see Eq. 9.11). We have tried different kernel functions of GPR and found that the rational quadratic (RQ) covariance function, a mixture of SE covariance functions with different characteristic length-scales, empirically performed the best:

$$K_{\text{RQ}}(\mathbf{x}_p, \mathbf{x}_q) = \left(1 + \frac{(\mathbf{x}_p - \mathbf{x}_q)^2}{2\alpha l^2} \right)^{-\alpha}, \tag{9.19}$$

Table 9.5 Comparison of Different Regression
Algorithms, Using Harmony for Feature Representation

Algorithm	Run Time	R^2	D_{JS}
v-SVR	4.6 sec	**0.5018**	**0.1045**
GPR	41 min	0.4626	0.1103
MLR	1.3 sec	0.4909	0.1079
Random	0.01 sec	0.0172	0.2421

where α, $l > 0$ are parameters of the characteristic length-scales [263]. No sparse approximation is adopted in our implementation to speed up GPR. MLR is implemented in MATLAB. We also implement a baseline method that randomly assigns emotion mass values.

We fix the feature representation to harmony and train the regressors using each regression algorithm. Table 9.5 shows that v-SVR outperforms other algorithms; the R^2 and D_{JS} reach 0.5018 and 0.1159, respectively. Moreover, v-SVR is efficient and takes less than 10 seconds to finish the evaluation process. Consequently, we employ v-SVR in the following experiments.

Although there is no direct reference with which we can compare the result presented here, it should be fair to say that this result is fairly promising, considering the result of research work on predicting the mean VA values of music signals. For example, the R^2 reported in Chapter 4 is 0.28 for valence and 0.58 for arousal, whereas the R^2 reported in Chapter 7 is 0.17 for valence and 0.80 for arousal.

9.5.2 Comparison of Different Distribution Modeling Methods

Next, we compare different distribution modeling methods, including the KDE-based approach with different sample sizes ($G = 6$, 8, 10, and 16) and the simple single-Gaussian approach. The former requires G^2 regressors while the latter requires five. We fix the feature representation to harmony and employ SVR to train the regressors.

Table 9.6 shows that the KDE-based approach outperforms the random baseline regardless of the value of G. R^2 is improved from 0 to 0.5, whereas D_{JS} is reduced from 0.24 to below 0.12. The KDE-based approach attains the best R^2 (0.5018) and D_{JS} (0.1045) when G equals 8. This is reasonable as smaller G cannot offer sufficient resolution for distribution modeling and larger G results in unnecessary complexity. We can also observe that the time needed to accomplish the N evaluations increases with G and that the KDE-based approach is fairly efficient. Even when more features are added—for example, up to 90 features are used in Section 9.5.3—KDE ($G = 8$) still takes less than 15 seconds. On the other hand, although single-Gaussian is more

Table 9.6 Comparison of Different Emotion Distribution Modeling Methods, Using Harmony for Feature Representation

Algorithm	Run Time	R^2	D_{JS}
Random	0.01 sec	0.0172	0.2421
KDE ($G = 6$)	2.7 sec	0.4743	0.1140
KDE ($G = 8$)	4.6 sec	**0.5018**	**0.1045**
KDE ($G = 10$)	8.1 sec	0.4679	0.1206
KDE ($G = 16$)	24 sec	0.4773	0.1150
Single-Gaussian	0.5 sec	0.3962	0.1260

efficient, its prediction accuracy is lower than that of the KDE-based approach.* The difference in R^2 is significant (p-value$<5\%$) under the two-tailed t-test [232]. This is perhaps because the KDE-based approach is specifically optimized to predict the emotion mass, whereas single-Gaussian is not.

Figure 9.4 shows a qualitative evaluation of the prediction result. The songs are sorted from left to right in ascending order of the mean ground truth valence value and from bottom to top in ascending order of mean arousal value. It can be found that the predictions of both approaches resemble the ground truth ones, but the ground truth distribution is denser. Comparing Figures 9.4(b) and (c), we see that single-Gaussian generates denser distributions in the upper plane but sparser distributions in the lower plane. Moreover, we can see that the emotion distributions of many songs in the last three rows of Figure 9.4(b) are inaccurately determined as emotions around the origin. This also explains why single-Gaussian performs worse than the KDE-based approach.

From Figure 9.4(c) we also observe that the prediction accuracy is higher for arousal prediction and lower for valence prediction. This finding is in line with past work on MER (e.g., [80, 173, 364]). It is also observed that the prediction is more accurate for songs with emotion distributed mainly in the first quadrant, comparing to those in the second quadrant. For future work one may explore more features that discriminate positive and negative valence.

In summary, our evaluation shows that the KDE ($G = 8$) outperforms other distribution modeling methods in terms of both R^2 and D_{JS}, with only a modest increase in computational cost.

---

* To evaluate the R^2 and D_{JS} of single-Gaussian, we compute the emotion mass at each discrete sample according to the learned bivariate Gaussian distribution. We find that the sample size also affects the accuracy of single-Gaussian and setting G to 8 results in the best result.

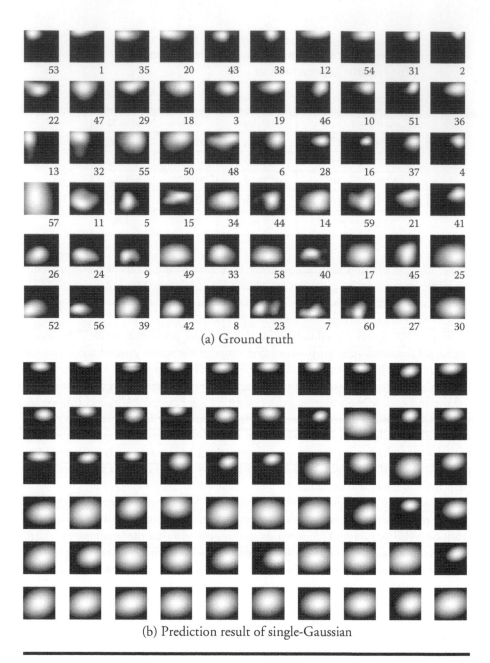

(a) Ground truth

(b) Prediction result of single-Gaussian

Figure 9.4 The (a) ground truth and (b) (c) the predicted emotion distributions of the single-Gaussian approach and the KDE-based approach. We used harmony for feature representation and SVR for regressor training. The songs are arranged according to the mean ground truth VA values. The number in the bottom right of (a) corresponds to the song ID (cf. Table 5.5).

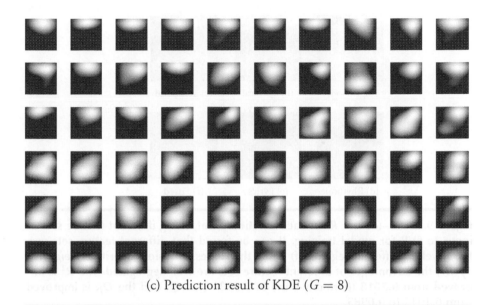

(c) Prediction result of KDE ($G = 8$)

Figure 9.4 **(Continued).**

9.5.3 Comparison of Different Feature Representations

We then evaluate the prediction accuracy using different feature sets as input to SVR. Results shown in Table 9.7 indicate that, despite the relatively small number of features, the feature set *harmony* performs the best. The feature set *spectrum* brings about the second highest R^2 (0.4696) that is not significantly inferior to the result of *harmony*. We also find that audio feature sets generally perform better than *lyrics*, presumably because the former exerts a stronger effect on emotion perception. This is reasonable since we can perceive emotion from songs that are purely instrumental [175].

To examine the performance of different feature sets more carefully, in Figure 9.5 we show the resulting R^2 of different feature sets at separate grid points. It can be

Table 9.7   Comparison of Different Feature Representations

Feature Set	Feature Dimension	R^2	D_{JS}
Harmony	16	0.5018	0.1045
Spectrum	90	0.4696	0.1093
Temporal	6	0.4402	0.1158
Rhythm	61	0.4169	0.1295
Lyrics	60	0.3707	0.1657

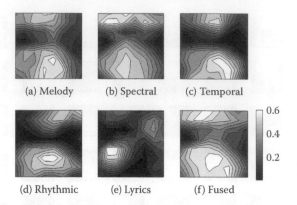

(a) Melody   (b) Spectral   (c) Temporal

(d) Rhythmic   (e) Lyrics   (f) Fused

Figure 9.5 (a)–(e) **The R^2 at each emotion point, using different feature sets as input to SVR for model training. It can be found that different feature sets perform well in different regions. (f) Using the regressor fusion algorithm *weighted-by-R^2*, the advantages of different feature sets are well aggregated. The R^2 is improved from 0.5018 (harmony-only) to 0.5434 (fused), and the D_{JS} is improved from 0.1045 to 0.0985.**

found that the performance of the feature sets is location-dependent. For example, *harmony* performs generally well in both the upper and lower emotion plane, *spectrum* performs relatively well in the first and second quadrants, and *temporal* performs well in the fourth quadrant. Furthermore, it is observed that the *lyrics* feature set performs particularly well in the third quadrant, presumably because there are many words that characterize the emotion of sad. To sum up, Figure 9.5 shows that the feature sets are related to different emotion perceptions of music and that a proper fusion method should aggregate the advantage of them and further improve the accuracy.

9.5.4 Evaluation of Regressor Fusion

Finally, we compare the performance of different methods of regressor fusion, including the four methods described in Section 9.3.3 and the following three baseline methods: the harmony-only baseline, the early fusion baseline that concatenates all the features into a single 252D feature vector before model training, and the late fusion baseline that simply averages the result of different regressors (namely, $w_t = 1/T$ in Eq. 9.12). Results shown in Table 9.8 lead to the following observations:

■ The performance of early fusion is even inferior to the harmony-only baseline, showing that directly concatenating features of different perceptual dimensions is not effective. We have employed the RReliefF algorithm [333] to conduct feature selection but found that the accuracy is not improved.

■ Simply averaging the result of the feature sets (i.e., late fusion) improves R^2 but slightly degrades D_{JS}.

Table 9.8 Comparison of Different Regression Fusion Methods

Regression Fusion	R^2	D_{JS}
Harmony only	0.5018	0.1045
Early fusion	0.4273	0.1208
Late fusion	0.5231	0.1056
Weighted-by-λ	0.5302	0.1034
Weighted-by-R^2	**0.5434**	**0.0985**
Optimize-R^2	0.5321	0.0987
Optimize-ϵ	0.5308	0.1003

■ By assigning weights to each feature set in a location-dependent fashion, all four methods described in Section 9.3.3 better aggregate the advantage of the feature sets and outperform the baseline methods in both R^2 and D_{JS}. The R^2 and D_{JS} of weighted-by-R^2 are 0.5434 (8.3% relative gain over harmony-only) and 0.0985 (5.7% improvement), respectively.

■ By comparing Figures 9.5(a) and (f), we see that weighted-by-R^2 improves the R^2 for almost all locations. Salient improvement is found in the first and the second quadrants, where feature sets such as spectrum and rhythm outperform harmony. Though the improvement is not significant under the t-test, this result shows that the fusion methods described in Section 9.3.3 are indeed effective in aggregating different dimensions of music listening.

9.6 Discussion

In this chapter, we have focused on the *indexing* part of MER—that is, predicting $P(\mathbf{e}|d)$ such that we can organize and represent songs in the emotion plane. The other step not addressed here is the *retrieval* part; that is, when a user u clicks on a point e^{ij}, the return is a list of songs ranked in the descending order of $P(d|e^{ij}, u)$. According to Bayes' rule,

$$P(d|\mathbf{e}, u) = \frac{P(\mathbf{e}|d, u)\,P(d|u)}{P(\mathbf{e}|u)}, \qquad (9.20)$$

where $P(\mathbf{e}|d, u) \sim P(\mathbf{e}|d)$ is a term of personal perception of music emotion, $P(d|u)$ can be regarded as the preference of the user with respect to music type, and $P(\mathbf{e}|u)$ is the emotion preference. This establishes a probabilistic framework of personalized emotion-based music retrieval. Both $P(d|u)$ and $P(\mathbf{e}|u)$ can be learned from the user's listening history. One may consider an emotion distribution $P(\mathbf{e}|d)$

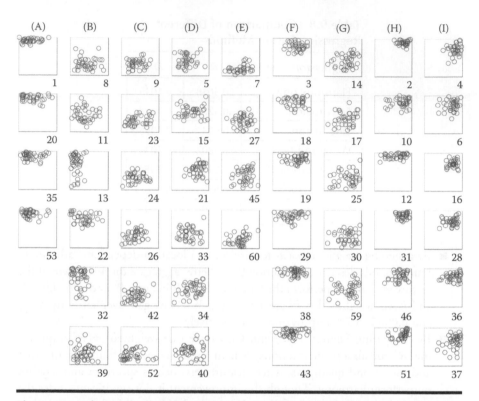

Figure 9.6 The result of applying spectral clustering to group songs into nine clusters according to the similarity of emotion distribution. Each circle corresponds to a subject's annotation of a song and each column corresponds to a cluster. The clusters are sorted from left to right in ascending order of the average valence value. At most six songs are shown for each cluster. The number in the bottom right corresponds to the song ID. (Data from A. Y. Na. et al. *Proc. Neural Information Processing Systems.* 2002.)

as a collection of users' perceived emotions of a song and the perceived emotion of the user $P(e|d, u)$ as a sample of the distribution. However, developing a computational model for $P(e|d, u)$ may be challenging and needs further research.

In addition to personalized emotion-based music retrieval, modeling music emotion as a probability distribution has application in enhancing our understanding of music emotion. For example, we can compute the pairwise similarity between the emotion distributions of songs using 1_{JS} and then cluster the songs using a clustering algorithm such as spectral clustering [236].* Figure 9.6 shows the result when we grouped songs into nine clusters (each column corresponds to a cluster).† Clearly the

---

* See Section 12.3.1 for more details on spectral clustering.

† The number of clusters is set to the one with the highest within-cluster sums of point-to-centroid distances among 2 to 20.

clusters correspond to different patterns of emotion distribution. Songs in clusters A and B are generally of high arousal and negative valence, but songs in cluster A (such as "Smells Like Teen Spirit" by Nirvana) can also be perceived as of positive valence, while songs in cluster B (such as "Sweet Dreams" by Marilyn Manson) can be perceived as of low arousal. Clusters H and I consist of songs whose emotion is of high arousal and positive valence, but songs in cluster H ("Are We the Waiting" by Green Day) are more likely to be perceived as of negative valence than songs in cluster I ("Oh Happy Day"). Cluster C ("Barriers" by Aereogramme) corresponds to songs of low arousal and negative valance, while cluster G ("I Will Always Love You" by Whitney Houston) corresponds to songs of low arousal and positive valance. It can be found that the emotion distributions of songs of low arousal are generally sparser than those of high arousal. Finally, songs belonging to the middle three clusters are of neutral valence but largely differ in arousal. Songs of cluster F ("Sweet Child O' Mine" by Guns N' Roses) have the highest arousal, while songs of cluster E ("As Time Goes By") have the lowest arousal. Songs of cluster D (such as "The Drugs Don't Work" by The Verve) have fairly sparse emotion distributions, showing that their emotion perceptions are very subjective. We would not have such a rich description of music emotion if songs were represented as points rather than distributions.

Another example application is to investigate the relationship between the Euclidean distance in the emotion plane and the *perceptual distance*. Although being widely adopted in the literature, it is unclear whether the emotion plane is Euclidean perceptually. For example, is the distance between two valence values 0.6 and 0.8 the same as that between two other valence values −0.1 and 0.1 in a listener's mind? As the emotion distributions of songs of neutral valence are often sparser, the latter may have a smaller perceptual distance. We used a mass, spring, and damper force-based algorithm [85] to study this. Specifically, considering that songs with similar emotion distributions should be perceptually similar, we initialized the position of each song by its mean VA values and then applied an electrostatic-like force between every pair of songs that is proportional to the inverse of their JS divergence. This way, songs with similar emotion distributions are drawn closer while still trying to stick to the initial positions. We implemented the algorithm using the NEATO utility of the Graphviz package, which runs an iterative solver to minimize a global energy function of the spring system [85]. The result is shown in Figure 9.7, with the grid lines deformed accordingly using a moving least squares method of rigid transformation [277]. By comparing the original and modified positions of the songs, it can be found that the range of valence values in the lower plane is compressed from 1 to around 0.7, showing that the perceptual distance is shorter than the Euclidean distance in the lower plane. It can also be observed that the songs in the first quadrant are drawn close to the origin, whereas songs in the second quadrant underwent fewer changes (possibly because their distributions are relatively distinct from others). This result shows that the perceptual distance between songs is different from the Euclidean distance of the mean VA values.

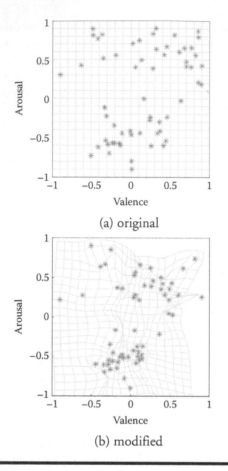

(a) original

(b) modified

Figure 9.7 (a) **The positions of the 60 songs according to the mean VA values. Each star represents a song. (b) The modified positions. Songs with similar emotion distributions are drawn closer. Clearly the distance between songs is different in (a) and (b), showing that the perceptual distance between songs is different from the Euclidean distance of mean VA values.**

Another interesting direction is to treat the average emotion distribution as an *emotion prior* $P(\bar{e}^{ij})$ of the computational model. From Figure 9.5 it can be found that the prediction accuracy is particularly low for the region along the negative valence axis, whereas from Figure 9.4 it can be observed that the probability values in this area are zero in the ground truth distributions of most songs, but nonzero in many of the predicted ones. This mismatch degrades both R^2 and D_{JS}. In fact, as Figure 9.8(a) shows, the average emotion mass of the ground truth distributions of the 60 songs is not uniformly distributed. The average probability of perceiving emotions with zero VA values (i.e., around the origin or along the axes) is

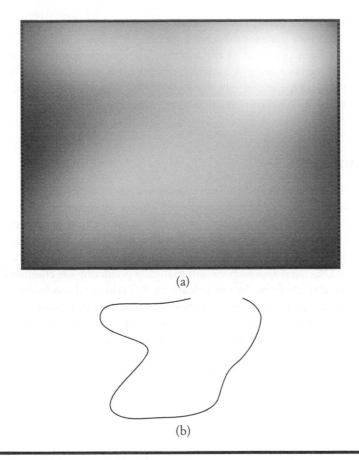

(a)

(b)

Figure 9.8   (a) The average emotion distribution, created by summing up the emotion distributions of all 60 songs. It can be considered as a prerequisite for emotion distribution, namely, $P(\tilde{e}^{ij})$. The contour shown in (b) encircles the emotion points whose $P(\tilde{e}^{ij})$ values are above the average.

fairly low. Interestingly, the observation that emotion is not uniformly distributed in the emotion plane has also been made in the field of video emotion recognition [117], where perceived emotions are found to lie inside a contour similar to the one shown in Figure 9.8(b), which encircles the emotion points whose $P(\tilde{e}^{ij})$ values are above the average. One may incorporate this emotion prior to the model training process, or one may sample the emotion plane according to the prior instead of uniformly. Both may improve the prediction accuracy of the computational model.

Another interesting research direction is to break the assumption that the regressors for different emotion points are independent. The emotion probabilities of neighboring emotion points could be highly correlated, and such correlation can be incorporated into the model training process to improve accuracy. Several algorithms have been proposed in the machine learning community to model the dependency of regressor outputs, such as multitask GPR, twin GPR, and dependent GPR [35, 36, 41]. One may apply these algorithms and see whether the resulting increase of computational complexity is worthwhile.

9.7 Summary

In this chapter, we have described a novel computational framework for dimensional MER that considers the perceived emotion of a music piece as a probabilistic distribution in the emotion plane rather than a single point. Instead of deterministically assigning an emotion value to a music piece, the probability of the perceived emotion of the song at every discrete sample of the emotion plane is computed. We have also described a KDE-based approach for automatically predicting the emotion distribution of a song directly from the music features. Experimental results show that the prediction accuracy of this approach is promising, achieving average R^2 of 0.5434 for music emotion distribution prediction. We have also shown that modeling the perceived emotion of a music piece as a distribution opens a new window to music understanding and provides opportunities to resolve the subjectivity issue of MER by a rigorous probabilistic framework.

10

Lyrics Analysis and Its Application to MER

The viability of an MER system largely lies in the accuracy of emotion recognition. However, due to the semantic gap between the object feature level and the human cognitive level of emotion perception, it is difficult for the machine to accurately compute the emotion values, especially the valence values. Consequently, many efforts have been made to incorporate mid-level features of music to MER. For example, B. Schuller et al. incorporated genre, ballroom dance style, chord progression, and lyrics in their MER system and found that many of them contribute positively to the prediction accuracy [286–288]. Similar observations have also been made by many other researchers [60, 139, 183, 207]. The following three chapters describe how such mid-level features, including lyrics, chord progression, and genre metadata, can be utilized to improve MER. For simplicity, we focus on categorical MER in the following three chapters. We begin with the use of text features extracted from lyrics in this chapter.

10.1 Motivation

A popular approach to categorical MER uses audio features such as MFCCs to represent a music signal and employs machine learning techniques to classify the emotion embedded in a music signal. The progress of such a *monomodal* approach, however, has been stagnant due to the so-called semantic gap — the chasm between raw data (signals) and high-level semantics (meanings). While mid-level audio features such as chord, mode, articulation, and instrumentation carry more semantic information [30, 60, 63, 217], robust techniques for extracting such features need to be developed.

Complementary to music signal, lyrics are semantically rich and expressive and have profound impact on human perception of music [20]. It is often easy for us to tell from the lyrics whether a song expresses love, sadness, happiness, or something else. Incorporating lyrics to the analysis of music emotion is feasible because most popular songs sold in the market come with lyrics and because most lyrics are written in accordance with music signal [94]. One can also analyze lyrics to generate text feature descriptors of music.

The application of text analysis to song lyrics has been explored for singer identification [216], structure analysis, similarity search [222], and genre classification [226]. The use of features extracted from the lyrics to improve MER have received increasing attention in the MIR community, and many different lyrics features have been proposed. Earlier approaches (e.g., [62,64,352]) use either manually or automatically generated affect lexicons to analyze lyrics. These lexicon-based approaches are considered less favorable since they are not applicable to songs of any language. Later approaches [138,183,219,288,326,353,363] are mainly based on statistical natural language processing (NLP) [225], which is more general and well grounded.

This chapter presents a *multimodal* approach to categorical MER. Features extracted from both the music signal and the associated lyrics are utilized to model our emotion perception. Specifically, NLP techniques such as bag-of-words [290] and probabilistic latent semantic analysis (PLSA) [129] are adopted to extract text features from the lyrics. These feature extraction algorithms are general and can be applied to lyrics of any language. This chapter also describes a number of multimodal fusion methods that properly integrate the extracted text and audio features. Evaluation results show that the incorporation of lyrics indeed improves the accuracy of MER. In particular, the multimodal fusion method *late fusion by subtask merging* significantly outperforms the conventional audio-based approach; a +21% relative improvement gain in classification accuracy is observed.

10.2 Lyrics Feature Extraction

Lyrics are normally available on the Web and downloadable with a simple script-based URL (uniform resource locator) lookup [45,103]. Many websites have a fixed pattern such as "http://[...]/?artist=[...]&song=[...]" that can be utilized to search for lyrics. One can query the website by putting artist name and song title in the URL pattern. Alternatively, the famous website LyriWiki [8] provides an application programming interface (API) that allows programmatic access to the content of its lyrics database [183].

The acquired lyrics are then preprocessed with traditional information retrieval operations such as stopword removal, stemming, and word segmentation [290]. *Stopword removal* is the process of filtering out common words, such as *a, the, and, can, it,* and *we,* to name a few. These words are removed because they are so common that they are less likely to be useful for information retrieval or text classification. Many English stopword lists are available on the Web.

Stemming is the process of reducing the various forms of a word to its stem, or root word. For example, *listening, listened, listens,* and *listener* are reduced to *listen,* and *studying, studied,* and *studies* are reduced to *studi.* Removing these redundant words helps reduce the size of the vocabulary and match synonyms. For English, one of the most famous stemming algorithms is the Porter stemming algorithm [259]. Its code is available on the Web in most programming languages.

Finally, *word segmentation,* or tokenization, is typically used for languages that do not have spaces between words, such as Chinese and Japanese [235, 251, 351]. Before running any word- or token-based linguistic processing, it is necessary to break the stream of text into tokens (meaningful word elements). For Chinese, the toolkit LingPipe provides a good utility to perform Chinese word segmentation [7].

After preprocessing, natural language processing techniques can be applied to generate text features [225, 233]. Below we describe three popular text features that are utilized in the performance evaluation described in Section 10.4.

10.2.1 Uni-Gram

A standard text feature representation counts the occurrence of uni-gram terms (words) in each document and constructs the bag-of-words model that represents a document as a vector of terms [290]. This process generates a *co-occurrence table.* The terms (i.e., the entries of the table) are usually weighted by a tf-idf (term-frequency inverse-document-frequency) function defined as follows [18, 179],

$$tf - idf(t_i, d_j) = \#(t_i, d_j) \log \frac{|D|}{\#D(t_i)}, \tag{10.1}$$

where $\#(t_i, d_j)$ denotes the frequency with which a term t_i occurs in document d_j, $\#D(t_i)$ denotes the number of documents in which t_i occurs, and $|D|$ is the size of the corpus (i.e., the number of documents). The intuition is that the importance of a term increases proportionally to its occurrence in a document, but is offset by its occurrence in the entire corpus to filter out common terms (that are not included in the stopword list). In this way, a good combination of popularity (tf) and specificity (idf) is obtained [290]. Despite its simplicity, the uni-gram-based bag-of-words model has shown superior performance in many information retrieval problems. In our implementation, we computed the tf-idf for each term and selected the M most frequent terms as our features (M is empirically set to 4000 by a validation set in our implementation).

Lyrics, however, are different from regular documents such as news articles in the following aspects:

■ First, lyrics are usually brief and are often built from a small vocabulary. Because of this *short text problem,* often there are words in a test set that do not appear in the training set [261]. In such cases, the performance of the uni-gram model may drop.

■ Second, lyrics are often composed in a poem-like fashion. The rich *metaphors* can make word sense disambiguation [290] difficult and degrade the performance of the uni-gram model.

■ Third, lyrics are in nature recurrent because of the stanzas (groups of lines arranged together in metrical length). This *recurrent structure* is not modeled by bag-of-words since word orders have been disregarded.

■ Fourth, unlike normal articles, which contain a variety of topics (e.g., politics, sports, entertainment, and weather), lyrics are *almost always about love and sentiment*. This makes common stopword lists not applicable.

■ Finally, *negation terms* such as *no* and *not* can play a more important role in lyric analysis. For example, whether there is a *not* precedent to *regret* greatly alters the semantic meaning.

A part of the aforementioned issues are addressed by the following two text feature extraction algorithms.

10.2.2 Probabilistic Latent Semantic Analysis (PLSA)

PLSA is known for its ability to discover *polysems* (words that have multiple senses and multiple usages in different contexts) and synonyms (i.e., different words that share a similar meaning) [129, 131, 368]. It has been shown that PLSA increases the overlapping of semantic terms and improves the accuracy of classifying short documents [261]. It has also been successfully applied to other multimedia retrieval problems such as scene classification [37, 134], image indexing [231], and collaborative filtering [130].

In PLSA [129], the joint probability between documents $\mathcal{D}$ and terms $\mathcal{T}$ is modeled through a *latent variable z*, which can be loosely regarded as a *hidden class* or *topic*. As shown in Figure 10.1, a PLSA model is parameterized by $P(t|z)$ and $P(z|d)$, which are estimated using the iterative expectation maximization (EM) algorithm [74] to fit the training corpus. Under the conditional independence assumption, the

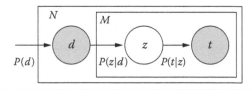

Figure 10.1 **Graphical representation of the PLSA model.** *M* denotes the number of terms in the corpus and *N* the size of the corpus. Shaded nodes highlight the observable random variables *t* for the occurrence of a term and *d* for the respective document. *z* denotes the hidden topic variable.

joint probability of t and d can be defined as

$$P(d, t) = P(d) P(t|d) = P(d) \sum_{z \in Z} P(t|z) P(z|d), \qquad (10.2)$$

where Z denotes the set of latent topics. After training, $P(t|z)$ are used to estimate $P(z|q)$ for new (test) document q through a folding-in process [129]. Each component of $P(z|q)$ represents the likelihood that the document q is related to a prelearned latent topic z. Similarity in this *latent vector space* can be regarded as the semantic similarity between two documents. Therefore, PLSA can be viewed as a dimension reduction method ($|Z| \ll M$) that converts the bag-of-words model into a semantically compact form in a generative process. $|Z|$ is set to 100 in our implementation.

The EM algorithm learns $P(t|z)$ and $P(z|d)$ by alternating the following two coupled steps: expectation (E) and maximization (M). It can be derived [129] that the E-step equation follows

$$P(z|d, t) = \frac{P(z) P(d|z) P(t|z)}{\sum_{z' \in Z} P(z') P(d|z') P(t|z')} \qquad (10.3)$$

and the M-step equation follows

$$P(d|z) \propto \sum_{d \in D} \#(t, d) P(z|d, t),$$

$$P(t|z) \propto \sum_{t \in T} \#(t, d) P(z|d, t), \qquad (10.4)$$

$$P(z) \propto \sum_{d \in D} \sum_{t \in T} \#(t, d) P(z|d, t).$$

Typically the EM algorithm is early-stopped to avoid overfitting [129]. Table 10.1 shows an example MATLAB® code for PLSA. This feature descriptor is also used in Chapter 9. See Table 9.4 for example latent topics derived from the lyrics.

10.2.3 Bi-Gram

N-gram are sequences of N consecutive words [51, 290]. An N-gram of size one is called a *uni-gram* (single word), whereas that of size two is called a *bi-gram* (word pairs). N-gram models are widely used to model the dependency of words. Since negation terms often reverse the meaning of the words next to them, it seems reasonable to incorporate word pairs to the bag-of-words model to take the effect of negation terms into account. In our implementation, we selected the M most frequent uni-gram and bi-gram in the bag-of-words model and obtained a new feature

Table 10.1   An Example MATLAB Code for Probabilistic Latent Semantic Analysis

```
% construct the co-occurrence table
X = build_cooccurrence;
[N M]=size(X);
inv_denomi_X = 1/sum(sum(X));

% parameters
Z = 100;
p.MAX_ITR = 100;
p.MIN_dLi_ratio = 1e-3;

% initialization
Pw_z = rand(M,Z);  Pw_z=Pw_z./repmat(sum(Pw_z),M,1);
Pd_z = rand(N,Z);  Pd_z=Pd_z./repmat(sum(Pd_z),N,1);
Pz = rand(1,Z);    Pz = Pz/sum(Pz);

% EM iterations
Li = zeros(1,p.MAX_ITR);
for iter=1:p.MAX_ITR
    Pw_z_ = Pw_z;
    Pd_z_ = Pd_z;
    Pz_ = Pz;

    sum_Pz_dw = Pd_z_*diag(Pz_)*Pw_z_'+eps;
    inv_sum_Pz_dw = 1./sum_Pz_dw;

    Pd_z = Pd_z_*diag(Pz_).*((X.*inv_sum_Pz_dw)*Pw_z_);
    Pw_z = Pw_z_*diag(Pz_).*((X.*inv_sum_Pz_dw)'*Pd_z_);
    Pz = sum(Pd_z)+eps;

    div = 1./Pz;
    Pd_z = Pd_z.*repmat(div,N,1);
    Pw_z = Pw_z.*repmat(div,M,1);
    Pz = Pz*inv_denomi_X;

    Li(iter) = -sum(sum(X.*log(sum_Pz_dw)));
    disp(sprintf('iter=%d, Li=%f',iter,Li(iter)))

    if(iter>1)
        dLi=abs(Li(iter)-Li(iter-1))/Li(iter-1);
        if(dLi<p.MIN_dLi_ratio), break; end;
    end
end
```

Source: Data from T. Hofmann. *Proc. ACM Int. Conf. Information Retrieval.*
        1999.

representation. To avoid double counting terms in uni-gram and bi-gram, we selected frequent bi-gram first and uni-gram next, fixing the total number of uni-gram and bi-gram to 4000 ($|T| = M = 4000$).

10.3 Multimodal MER System

A system diagram of the training phase of the multimodal approach to MER is shown in Figure 10.2, where audio features extracted from the waveform and text features extracted from the lyrics are both used to represent a music piece. Two emotion classifiers are trained using different modalities of the feature set and then integrated by multimodal fusion methods. The classification models are then utilized to classify the emotion of test music pieces.

Defining emotions according to the four quadrants of the 2D valence-arousal emotion plane, the following multimodal fusion methods can be applied to fuse the audio and text features. The emotion classes include *happy, angry, sad,* and *relaxing.* Note that we can consider the four-class emotion classification problem as two binary classification problems of classifying positive/negative valence and classifying high/low arousal (see Figure 10.3 for illustration). This view is used in multimodal fusion and system evaluation.

To enhance readability, we denote the classification model trained by audio and text features as M_A and M_T, respectively.

- Audio-only (**AO**): Use audio features only and apply M_A to classify emotion. This method can be considered as the baseline method because most research work on MER also adopts it.
- Text-only (**TO**): Use text features only and apply M_T to classify emotion. This method can be used to assess the importance of the text modality.
- Early-fusion-by-feature-concatenation (**EFFC**): Concatenate the audio and text features to a single feature vector and train a single classification model. Early fusion yields a truly multimodal feature space, but it could suffer from the difficulty to combine modalities into a common representation [302].

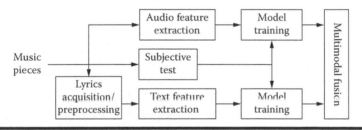

Figure 10.2   System diagram of the training phase of the multimodal MER system.

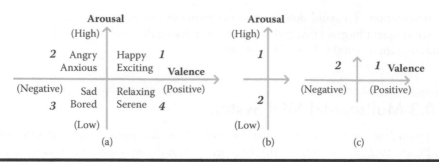

Figure 10.3 (a) 2D valence-arousal emotion plane [272, 310]. Each quadrant of the emotion plane corresponds to an emotion class. One can also divide the four-class emotion classification problem to two binary classification problems: (b) arousal classification and (c) valence classification using the geometric relationship of the four emotion classes. (Data from J. A. Russell. *J. Personality & Social Psychology*. 39(6): 1161–1178, 1980 and R. E. Thayer. *The Biopsychology of Mood and Arousal*. Oxford University Press, New York, 1989.)

■ Late-fusion-by-linear-combination (**LFLC$_\alpha$**): Train M_A and M_T separately and combine their predictions afterward in a linear way. For example, support vector classification (SVC) [69] can be employed to produce probability estimation [54, 143] of the class membership in each class. The probability estimates of two SVC models (M_A and M_T) are then fused linearly as follows:

$$M_{\text{LFLC}_\alpha}(\mathbf{x}) = (1 - \alpha) M_A(\mathbf{x}) + \alpha M_T(\mathbf{x}), \qquad (10.5)$$

where $M_A(\mathbf{x})$ and $M_T(\mathbf{x})$ are vectors indicating the likelihood that each emotion is perceived in the music piece, and $\alpha \in [0, 1]$ is the weight of the two modalities ($\alpha > 0.5$ weights the text modality more). For example, if the probability estimates of the emotion of a music piece by M_A and M_T are $\{0, 0.1, 0.5, 0.4\}^T$ and $\{0, 0.1, 0.7, 0.2\}^T$, then the combination with $\alpha = 0.5$ would be $\{0, 0.1, 0.6, 0.3\}^T$. The final class assignment is made by majority voting, that is, class 3. Late fusion focuses on the individual strength of modalities, yet it introduces additional training efforts and the potential loss of correlation between modalities [302].

■ Late-fusion-by-subtask-merging (**LFSM**): Use M_A and M_T to classify valence and arousal separately and then merge the result. For example, a negative arousal (predicted by M_A) and negative valence (predicted by M_T) would be merged to class 3. One may make the two modalities focus on different emotion classification subtasks because audio and text features may be complementary to one another and useful for different subtasks. In addition, training models for valence and arousal separately have been shown adequate before [364]. Table 10.3 shows an example MATLAB code for LFSM.

Table 10.2 Adopted Feature Extraction Algorithms

Modality	Method	Number of Features	Feature Description
Text	Uni-gram [290]	4000	Bag-of-words
	PLSA [129]	100	Latent vectors
	Bi-gram [290]	4000	Bag-of-words
Audio	Marsyas [324]	52	MFCCs
	PsySound [44]	54	Spectral centroid, moment, roughness

10.4 Performance Evaluation

In our implementation, the music data set is made up of 1240 Chinese pop songs, whose emotions are labeled by one subject. Note that the songs are the same as the ones used in Chapter 5, but the annotations are different. The lyrics of the songs are downloaded from the Internet by script-based URL lookup. We build our own Chinese stopword list for stopword removal and employ the free library LingPipe [7] for Chinese word segmentation. Stemming is not needed for Chinese.

The audio features and text features utilized in this implementation are summarized in Table 10.2. For audio features, we use Marsyas to generate the MFCCs and PsySound to generate some spectrum features. For text features, the three features described in Section 10.2 are used. SVC is adopted to train classifiers for its superb performance shown in previous MER work (e.g., [184, 352]). Our implementation of SVC is based on the library LIBSVM, with default parameter settings [54]. Classification accuracy is evaluated by randomly selecting 760 songs as training data and 160 songs as test data, with the number of songs of each emotion class uniform. Because of this randomization, 1000 iterations are run to compute the average classification accuracy.

10.4.1 Comparison of Multimodal Fusion Methods

To evaluate the multimodal MER system, we treat AO and TO as the two baselines and compare the classification accuracy of different multimodal fusion methods. We first use the features extracted by Marsyas and PsySound for audio feature representation, and the uni-gram-based bag-of-words model for text feature representation.

The results are shown in Table 10.4. It can be observed from the first and second rows that audio features and text features are fairly complementary. While AO yields higher accuracy for arousal classification (78%), TO performs better for valence (73%). This result implies that it is promising to fuse the two modalities since they encode different parts of semantics. Note that the result that audio modality yields

Table 10.3   An Example MATLAB Code for the Multimodal Fusion Method Late-Fusion-by-Subtask-Merging

```
%% TRAINING PHASE----------------------------------------------
% feature extraction
X = extract_feat('DIR_TR');    % features (N by M)
[N M] = size(X);               % N: # of training data
                               % M: # of training data
% emotion annotation
Y = annotate_emotion;          % [1,2,3,4]
Y_ = zeros(N,2);
Y_(:,1) = double(Y==1|Y==4);   % 1,4-> positive; 2,3->negative
Y_(:,2) = double(Y==1|Y==2);   % 1,2-> positive; 3,4->negative

% feature normalization
[X p_mu p_std] = zscore(X);

% model training
models = cell(2,1);
for va = 1:2                    % -s 0 -- C-SVC
    models{va} = svmtrain( Y_(:,va), X, '-s 0');
end

%% TEST PHASE--------------------------------------------------
Xtest = extract_feat('DIR_TE'); % features (Ntest by M)
Ntest = size(Xtest,1);
for j=1:M, Xtest(:,j) = (Xtest(:,j)-p_mu(j))/p_std(j); end

Ypred = zeros(Ntest,1);
Ypred_ = zeros(Ntest,2);

% prediction
for va = 1:2
    Ypred_(:,va) = svmpredict( zeros(Ntest,1), Xtest,
                    models{va});
end

% late-fusion-by-subtask-merging
for i = 1:Ntest
    if Ypred_(i,1)==1 & Ypred_(i,2)==1, Ypred(i)=1;
    elseif Ypred_(i,1)==0 & Ypred_(i,2)==1, Ypred(i)=2;
    elseif Ypred_(i,1)==0 & Ypred_(i,2)==0, Ypred(i)=3;
    else, Ypred(i)=4;
    end
end
```

Table 10.4 Performance Comparison of a Number of Multimodal Fusion Methods for Four-Class Emotion Classification, Arousal Classification, and Valence Classification

Methods	Number of Features	Four-Class Accuracy	Valence Accuracy	Arousal Accuracy
AO	106	46.63%	61.15%	78.03%
TO	4000	40.01%	73.32%	61.95%
EFFC	4106	52.48%	70.54%	77.06%
LFLC$_{0.5}$	106/4000	55.34%	74.83%	77.88%
LFSM	106/4000	57.06%	73.32%	78.03%

good accuracy for arousal classification but worse accuracy for valence is consistent with the result described in previous chapters. Our experiment further shows that lyrics are relevant to valence but relatively less relevant to arousal. This is reasonable since lyrics contain less melodic or rhythmic information.

Table 10.4 also indicates that the four-class emotion classification accuracy can be significantly improved by multimodal fusion. Among the fusion methods (rows 3–5), LFSM achieves the best classification accuracy (57.06%) and brings about 21% relative improvement over the audio-only baseline. It can also be observed that late fusion yields better results than early fusion. This seems to imply that the individual strength of the two modalities should be emphasized separately. Besides, although LFLC$_{0.5}$ is slightly worse than LFSM, its classification accuracy for valence (74.83%) is the highest among the five fusion methods. This indicates that valence can be better modeled by considering both modalities (in a late-fusion manner), whereas arousal can be modeled well by audio features alone. We also vary the value of α from 0 to 1 at a step of 0.1 and find that the accuracy reaches 75.18% by setting α to 0.6, which indicates again that lyrics are useful for valence prediction.

Note that another related work for analyzing the affect of text can be found in the field of blog analysis [15, 199]. In their work [199], G. Leshed et al. also adopted bag-of-words as feature representation and SVC for model learning. Interestingly, the accuracy of valence classification they obtained is also about 74%, which is very close to the result presented here.

10.4.2 Performance of PLSA Model

We then train a PLSA model with 21,661 unlabeled lyrics to convert the bag-of-words feature space to the latent vector space of dimension 100 ($|Z|=100$). We conduct performance comparison of bag-of-words and PLSA feature representations for valence classification with different numbers of training data (the number of test data is fixed to 160) to simulate different levels of shot text problem, which is more

Table 10.5 Performance Comparison of Uni-gram and PLSA
Feature Representations for Valence Classification

Methods	Number of Features	Number of Training Data		
		760	400	200
Uni-gram	4000	73.21%	67.78%	58.70%
PLSA	100	72.85%	70.59%	66.53%

Note: The number of test data is fixed to 160.

severe with smaller number of training data since more words in the test set would not have occurred in training.

Table 10.5 shows that the classification accuracy of bag-of-words degrades significantly as the number of training data decreases. In contrast, because of the incorporation of unlabeled data and the more compact feature representation, PLSA exhibits robust performance. This result shows that PLSA can be applied to effectively mitigate the short text problem. However, as the number of training data is sufficient and the short text problem is less severe, the performance of bag-of-words and PLSA becomes close.

10.4.3 Performance of Bi-Gram Model

To assess the negation-term problem, first we deliberately add common negation words such as *no* and *not* to the stopword list and remove them from the bag-of-words model. Surprisingly, the removal of these negation words did not degrade the classification accuracy much, implying that the effect of negation terms is not well modeled by uni-gram.

To address this issue, another text-only classifier is trained by using both uni-gram and bi-gram. However, the incorporation of bi-gram only slightly improves the classification accuracy of valence from 73.32% to 73.79%. The performance difference is evidently not significant. To better model the effect of negation terms, more advanced methods are needed.

10.5 Summary

In this chapter, we have described a multimodal approach to MER that exploits features extracted from the audio part and the lyrics of a music piece. We have also described how to use natural language processing (NLP) techniques such as bag-of-words, probabilistic latent semantic analysis (PLSA), and *N*-gram to generate text features from lyrics. A number of multimodal fusion methods have also been described. Experimental results show that lyrics indeed carry semantic information complementary to that of the music signal and the integration of the two modalities improves the prediction accuracy of the computational model. Comparing the audio-only method, using the late-fusion-by-subtask-merging method for multimodal fusion improves the four-class classification accuracy from 46.6% to 57.1%. In particular, using text features significantly improves the accuracy of valence classification from 61.2% to 73.3%.

11

Chord Recognition and Its Application to MER

Chord is one of the most important mid-level features of music. With chord sequence, songs that are similar in various aspects can be identified and retrieved more effectively. This chapter describes the extraction of chord features from the chord sequence of music pieces to improve MER. We begin with the introduction of a chord recognition system for recognizing the chord sequence from low-level music features and then describe two features that are computed from the chord sequence. Empirical evaluation shows that these chord features improve the accuracy of valence classification.

11.1 Chord Recognition

A chord is a set of harmonically related musical pitches (notes) that sounded almost simultaneously, and the sequence of chords determines the harmonic progression and the tonal structure of a song. Similar chord sequences can be observed in songs that are close in genre or emotion. The use of chord for cover song detection [194] and music segmentation [30] has also been shown effective. However, to obtain the chord sequence of a song, an automatic chord recognition system needs to be built because the chord sequence is hidden in the audio waveform.

In this section, we describe a chord recognition system that is based on the N-gram model and the hidden Markov model (HMM) [144]. This system is conceptually consistent with musical theory [30], effective, and more time-efficient than conventional chord recognition systems. Its simplicity and time-efficiency is desirable for practical applications.

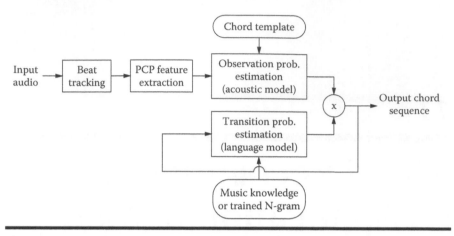

Figure 11.1   A schematic diagram of the chord recognition system.

Figure 11.1 shows a schematic diagram of the chord recognition system. In the training phase, an *N*-gram model is trained based on ground-truth chord transcriptions to learn the common rules of chord progression. For each segment of the input audio in the testing phase, the chord with maximum likelihood is estimated using the pretrained acoustic and language models. More details of the system are described below.

11.1.1 Beat Tracking and PCP Extraction

For an input music piece, a beat tracking system called BeatRoot [76] is applied to detect the beat times. The music piece is then segmented according to the beat times. That is, each music segment is considered to have a consistent chord.

Each music segment is represented by the pitch class profile (PCP), which represents the frequency spectrum by 12 bins according to the 12 distinct semitones (or chroma) of the musical octave (see Section 3.5 for more details of PCP). PCP is commonly adopted in chord recognition systems because it contains information of musical pitches (notes). To extract PCP, the algorithm described in [248] can be adopted.

11.1.2 Hidden Markov Model and N-Gram Model

Chord recognition can be effectively modeled using the basic concepts in digital speech processing. Inspired by the way humans recognize chords, the task of chord recognition can be divided into the following two parts: acoustic modeling and language modeling. In acoustic modeling, the hidden Markov model (HMM) is employed to learn the relationship between PCP features and ground truth chord labels, whereas in language modeling, the *N*-gram model is applied to take into account the transition between chords.

- **Acoustic modeling**: The most likely chord is estimated based on the observed PCP feature vector. A 24-state HMM is used to model 24 major/minor triad chords (e.g., C major, E minor). The goal is to find a chord that best fits the perceived music in a certain time interval.
- **Language modeling**: A sequence of chord labels can be regarded as a word sequence in natural language. Chord progression often follows the rules of harmony and appears in some common patterns (e.g., C→F→G→C), just like grammar and phrases in natural language. Therefore, it is reasonable to train a language model that learns the transition probability between consecutive chords.

Two methods can be adopted for language modeling. The first one exploits music knowledge to set the transition probability between chords, whereas the *N*-gram-based method learns the transition probability empirically from the training data by the *N*-gram model. The strengths of the latter method are as follows:

- In chord progression, a chord highly depends on its previous chords since successive chords generally share some common notes, which provide harmonic continuity to a music passage. The *N*-gram model is consistent with the property of chord progression in that the likelihood of an element in the sequence depends on the previous *N* elements. More formally, given a chord sequence $(c_1, c_2, \ldots, c_{i-1})$, the *N*-gram model predicts the next chord c_i based on the probability $P(c_i | c_{i-N}, c_{i-N+1}, \ldots, c_{i-1})$.
- Many HMM-based systems consider the transition probability only between two consecutive chords. However, the information of two adjacent chords is insufficient for recognizing longer chord sequences. The *N*-gram model is a good mathematic tool to model longer dependency between chords.
- The scale of chord lexicon (only 24 major/minor chords in most work) is small compared with the word lexicon of natural language, and so is the number of permutations. This makes the training of the *N*-gram model manageable.

In our implementation, the training of the *N*-gram model is started with $N = 2$ (i.e., bi-gram) based on the circle of fifths [30]. That is, transitions between chords that sound more consonant with each other are initialized with higher probability. Then, the *N*-gram models with *N* equal to 2, 3, and 4 are trained using 152 manually labeled chord transcriptions provided by Harte and Sandler [119]. For each song, we concatenated the labeled chords into text strings and trained the *N*-gram model using the SRI language modeling (SRILM) toolkit [305]. See Figure 11.2 for the bi-gram model learned in our implementation.

Typically, the training of HMM requires the information of chord boundaries. However, the precise time boundary between consecutive chords in music is often ambiguous and thus difficult to obtain. In addition, because labeling chord boundaries is labor-intensive, only a few data sets are available. The approach described above is free of these problems because the *N*-gram model is trained on chord sequences only. Experimental results in Section 11.4 show that this approach is indeed general enough for a large variety of songs.

11.1.3 Chord Decoding

In the testing phase, the chord sequence is decoded from the input audio. Let $\mathbf{O}_i$ be the observed PCP feature vector and c_i the decoded chord of the *i*-th segment. In the case where bi-gram and tri-gram models are used, the chord c_i^* with maximum likelihood is obtained by

$$c_i^* = \text{argmax}_{c_i}(\alpha \log P_{\text{bi}} + \beta \log P_{\text{tri}} + (1 - \alpha - \beta) log P(c_i|\mathbf{O}_i)), \qquad (11.1)$$

where $P_{\text{bi}} = P(c_i|c_{i-1})$, $P_{\text{tri}} = P(c_i|c_{i-2}, c_{i-1})$, and α and β are nonnegative weights given to P_{bi} and P_{tri}, respectively, $\alpha + \beta \leq 1$. Eq. 11.1 shows how HMM and

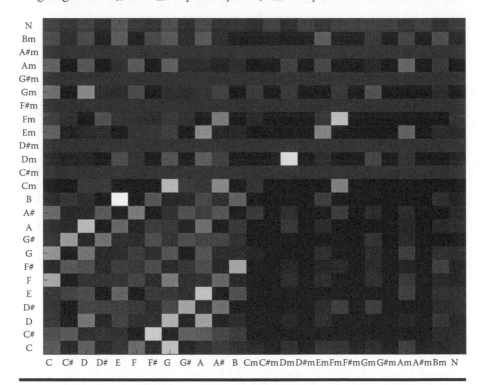

Figure 11.2 The chord transition probability learned by the bi-gram model. *N* denotes "not a chord." For example, from the last row we see that chord C is most likely followed by chord G. Interestingly, C and G are just a fifth apart in music theory.

Figure 11.2 **(Continued.)**

N-gram model are used for acoustic and language modeling, respectively. $P(c_i|\mathbf{O}_i)$, the probability that $\mathbf{O}_i$ is generated by c_i, is estimated by calculating the correlation between $\mathbf{O}_i$ and a set of chord templates as described in [248]. P_{bi} and P_{tri} are given by the *N*-gram model.

The time complexity of this method is one order less than that of the Viterbi algorithm [144, 331]. Consider a song with n segments (determined by estimated beat times). For the Viterbi algorithm, the optimal previous chord for each candidate chord is estimated for each segment, and the paths are stored in a table. Suppose that there are k candidate chords in the HMM; then k^2 such operations are required for each segment, and the total time complexity is $O(k^2 n)$. On the contrary, only k such operations are needed for each segment for the method described here since we simply examine the k candidate chords to determine an optimal one. The total time complexity is $O(kn)$.

11.2 Chord Features

Given the estimated chord sequences of music pieces, the following two methods can be utilized to generate features that describe the property of a chord sequence.

11.2.1 Longest Common Chord Subsequence

To measure the similarity between two chord sequences, we can calculate the longest common chord subsequence (LCCS) via a dynamic programming algorithm [32, 68, 223] that has been widely used in bio-informatics for DNA sequence comparison.

Since the order of chords cannot be rearranged, LCCS as a similarity metric is desirable because it can capture the similarity between sequences while preserving their order. For example, given two chord sequences, $s_1 = $ (C, F, G, C) and $s_2 = $ (C, Am, F, Dm, G), the LCCS of them is $s_{LCCS} = $ (C, F, G). We take the ratio of the length of LCCS to the length of the short sequence (i.e., s_1) to facilitate the comparison of different songs. Given any two songs, the longer the (normalized) LCCS is, the more similar they are.

Below we provide a brief description of how to construct the longest common subsequence (LCS). Given two sequences $X = [x_1, x_2, \ldots, x_N]$ and $Y = [y_1, y_2, \ldots, y_M]$, the following recursive formula can be applied to find the longest common subsequence:

$$c_{i,j} = \begin{cases} 0, & \text{if } i = 0 \text{ or } j = 0 \\ c_{i-1,j-1} + 1, & \text{if } i, j > 0 \text{ and } x_i = y_j, \\ \max(c_{i-1,j}, \ c_{i,j-1}), & \text{if } i, j > 0 \text{ and } x_i \neq y_j \end{cases} \quad (11.2)$$

where $c_{i,j}$ is the length of an LCS of the subsequences $X_i = [x_1, x_2, \ldots, x_i]$ and $Y_j = [y_1, y_2, \ldots, y_j]$, and i and j are two indexes $0 \leq i \leq N, 0 \leq j \leq M$. The recursive procedure ends with $c_{N,M}$ containing the length of the LCS of X and Y. The normalized length of the LCS is therefore $c_{N,M}/min(N, M)$. By using dynamic programming, the running time of computing LCS is $O(NM)$. The dynamic programming approach would maintain a table to simplify the construction of an optimal solution, and the LCS itself can be easily constructed by tracing back the table.

11.2.2 Chord Histogram

Another way to describe a chord sequence is to abandon the temporal information and simply count the number of times a chord presents in the sequence. This feature is called the chord histogram (CH). Figure 11.3 compares the chord histograms of two songs. We can see that the chords C, F, G, and Am appear frequently in both songs. Although these chords may not appear in the same order, they may still express similar emotions. We can also get a sense of tonality from the chord histogram without going through a key detection process in advance. The L2 distance is utilized to measure the similarity between two songs.

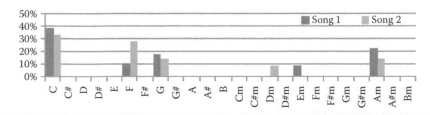

Figure 11.3   A chord histogram showing the chord similarity between two songs.

11.3 System Overview

Figure 11.4 shows a schematic diagram of using chord features to achieve high-level applications. PCP features and other low-level features such as MFCCs are first extracted from the input music signal. PCP features are then utilized to recognize the chord sequence of the music signal. The chord features computed from chord sequences, as well as the low-level features, are then utilized for high-level applications such as MER, music structure analysis, and music recommendation.

11.4 Performance Evaluation

We evaluate the performance of the aforementioned methods in terms of the accuracy of chord recognition and emotion classification.

11.4.1 Evaluation of Chord Recognition System

To evaluate the accuracy of the chord recognition system described in Section 11.1, we use the test set provided by the researchers Harte and Sandler [119], which contains 28 recordings from two albums, *Please Please Me* (CD1) and *Beatles for*

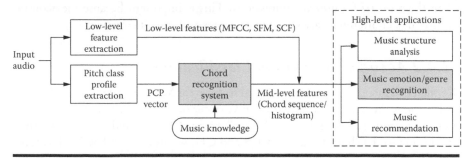

Figure 11.4   A schematic diagram of achieving high-level applications using mid-level features. Gray-colored blocks correspond to the ones described in this chapter.

Table 11.1 Accuracy and Time Complexity of Chord Recognition Systems

System		CD1	CD2	Overall	Complexity
Without *N*-gram		51.2%	68.7%	60.7%	$O(kn)$
Template matching [119]		53.9%	70.8%	62.4%	$O(kn)$
HMM / Viterbi [195]		61.0%	84.5%	72.8%	$O(k^2n)$
N-gram based	$N = 2$	56.3%	70.3%	63.9%	$O(kn)$
	$N = 3$	60.6%	73.0%	67.3%	$O(kn)$
	$N = 4$	60.9%	72.5%	67.2%	$O(kn)$

Sale (CD2), of the band Beatles. Evaluation is made on a frame-by-frame basis, and only the exact matches between the decoded chord sequences and the ground-truth transcriptions are counted as correct recognitions.

Table 11.1 shows that the best results are achieved by tri-gram and 4-gram models. The *N*-gram-based approach outperforms the typical HMM-based approach without *N*-gram by 7% in overall accuracy. This supports the claim that the *N*-gram model effectively learns the common rules of chord progression.

The same test set is used in [119] and [195]. The former uses template matching in chord decoding and yields 62.4% overall accuracy, which is inferior to the one described in this chapter (67.3%). The latter uses key-independent HMM and achieves an overall accuracy of 72.8%. However, this system is more complicated and computationally more expensive (cf. Section 11.1).

We can also see that the accuracy of CD1 increases significantly from 51.2% to 60.9% when 4-gram is used, whereas the improvement for CD2 is less salient, from 68.7% to 72.5%. Since more ambiguities are found to be present in the observed feature vectors of CD1 [195], we can infer that the *N*-gram model is very helpful when the acoustic features are ambiguous. This is important because the acoustic features of a chord often vary with music genres and instrumentation.

11.4.2 Accuracy of Emotion Classification

We then evaluate the use of the two chord features for MER. The data set used in this evaluation is the same as the one used in Chapter 6, which consists of 195 popular songs of various genres and artists from Western, Chinese, and Japanese albums. In addition to the chord features, LCCS and CH, we also extract low-level features including MFCCs, spectral flatness measure (SFM), and spectral crest factor (SCF), by Marsyas [324]. See Chapter 3 for more descriptions of these features.

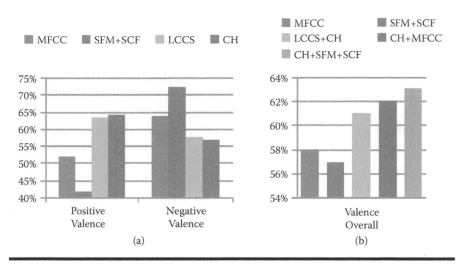

Figure 11.5 **Accuracy of valence prediction using different feature sets. The incorporation of chord features (LCCS, CH) improves the overall accuracy to 63%.**

Emotions are categorized to four classes — happy, angry, sad, and relaxing—corresponding to the four quadrants of the emotion plane. Because arousal classification has been shown easier (e.g., see Chapter 10), we focus on valence classification in this evaluation. That is, *happy* and *relaxing* are considered as positive valence, whereas *angry* and *sad* are considered as negative valence. We use the *k*-nearest neighbor (*k*-NN) algorithm to find the *k* most similar songs for each song and then set the valence label of the song by majority voting [78]. See Tables 6.1 and 6.2 for example MATLAB codes for fuzzy *k*-NN, a generalization of *k*-NN. The result of fuzzy *k*-NN is equivalent to that of *k*-NN when β is set to 1. See Section 6.2.1 for more details.

The results are shown in Figure 11.5. The overall accuracy of valence classification using low-level features is around 57%. The accuracy increases to 61.03% when only the two chord features are used. This result shows the strength of chord features for music emotion classification. Furthermore, it can be observed from Figure 11.5(a) that the chord features are useful for predicting positive valence, and the low-level features are helpful for negative valence. Consequently, by using an early-fusion to concatenate the chord features and the low-level feature vectors for classification, the overall accuracy can be improved to 63.08%, as shown in Figure 11.5(b). Note that although both LCCS and CH are more useful than low-level features, better results are achieved using CH instead of LCCS since the latter is more sensitive to errors in chord recognition. The advantage of LCCS may be more salient if one adopts a more accurate chord recognition system.

11.5 Summary

In this chapter, we have described the construction of mid-level chord features and their application to music emotion recognition. Specifically, we describe an effective and efficient N-gram-based chord recognition system and two chord features that can be computed from the output chord sequence: longest common chord subsequence and chord histogram. The use of these two features achieves 6% improvement in the accuracy of binary valence classification compared with the result of using only low-level features.

12

Genre Classification and Its Application to MER

Continuing the previous two chapters, this chapter describes the use of genre metadata to bridge the semantic gap between audio signal and emotion perception. While lyrics are complementary to music signal and chords describe the harmonic progression and the tonal structure of a song, genre metadata have been utilized to describe the intrinsic form of music. Genre and emotion provide complementary descriptions of music content and often correlate with each other. The two-layer emotion classification scheme introduced in this chapter exploits such correlation and improves the accuracy of emotion classification.

12.1 Motivation

Genre, by which a song is classified into classical, jazz, rock, hip-hop, country, etc., has been used to describe the intrinsic form of music for a long time [28]. A user study shows that genre is the most popular cue for searching music, in addition to other metadata such as artist name, song title, and lyrics [193]. Most music websites, such as Last.fm [6] and All Music Guide (AMG) [1], also provide the genre metadata of music recordings. A good deal of work has been done in automatic music genre classification; see [276] for a comprehensive review.

Emotion, as one of the preeminent functions of music [146], is also an important means for music classification. An emotion-based music retrieval system provides users the functionality for retrieving music according to emotion. Compared with genre classification, emotion classification is considered more challenging because of the subtlety of emotion and the difficulty of collecting (subjective) annotation of emotion.

197

Genre and emotion provide complementary descriptions of music content and often correlate with each other. For example, a rock song is often aggressive, whereas a rhythm and blues (R&B) song is more likely to be sentimental. Despite the salient correlation between genre and emotion, genre classification and emotion classification are often studied separately without considering the interrelation.

This chapter describes a two-layer music emotion classification scheme that exploits the correlation between genre and emotion [358]. The genre metadata are used to aid emotion classification because genre metadata are easier to collect and because genre classification is relatively easier. Specifically, the genre of a song is predicted in the first layer, and then the genre-specific emotion classification model is applied in the second layer to predict the emotion of the song, as shown in Figures 12.1(b) and (c). Experimental results are provided to show the superiority of the two-layer music emotion classification scheme over the traditional single-layer scheme.

12.2 Two-Layer Music Emotion Classification

The main idea of the two-layer emotion classification scheme is to group songs by genre and train an emotion classifier specifically for songs of each genre. The use of such genre-specific classifiers is motivated by the following two observations. First, since emotion and genre are correlated, we may set up different emotion priors for each genre-specific classifier. For example, a rap song is less likely to be relaxing than a jazz song. Second, as a happy song of rock music and a happy song of jazz music may sound substantially different, emotion classification may become easier if each genre-specific classifier only needs to focus on a single genre of music.

As shown in Figure 12.1(a), a typical single-layer emotion classification system is composed of two parts: feature extraction and emotion classification. An emotion

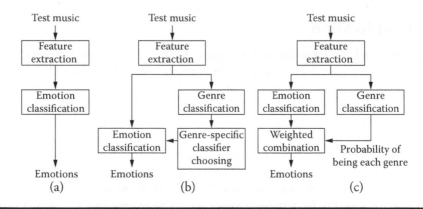

Figure 12.1 Schematic diagrams of (a) the traditional single-layer emotion classification scheme, (b) the proposed two-layer scheme hardGenre, and (c) the soft version of the two-layer scheme softGenre.

classifier learns the relationships between audio features and emotion labels in the training process. We denote this single-layer scheme as "single" hereafter.

Figure 12.1(b) shows the proposed two-layer emotion classification scheme, referred to as "hardGenre." In the training phase, a genre classifier is trained in the first layer. The training data set is then divided according to the genres, and the genre-specific multilabel emotion classifiers are trained separately using the songs of the corresponding genre in the second layer. In the testing phase, the system predicts the genre of a song in the first layer and then predicts the emotions of the song in the second layer using the (multilabel) emotion classifier specifically trained for that (predicted) genre. For example, if a song is predicted as rock in the first layer, the emotion classifier trained with rock songs will be employed in the second layer.

It is likely that the intrinsic form of some songs is mixed with the musical elements of more than two genres. For example, an R&B song may contain rap elements in its verse part. Therefore, assigning the genre label of a song in a deterministic way may be too restrictive. To deal with this issue, one may employ the soft version of the two-layer scheme, which is referred to as "softGenre" hereafter. As seen in Figure 12.1(c), softGenre utilizes soft-decision in the first layer and predicts the probability $P(g|x)$ of a song x being associated with each genre g. In the second layer, softGenre employs all the genre-specific emotion classifiers to compute the emotions of the song and aggregates the results of different emotion classifiers by a weighted combination. Each genre-specific emotion classifier is weighted in proportion to $P(g|x)$. That is, the result of emotion classification is dominated by the classifiers trained for the genres the song is most probably associated with. If the weighted combination for an emotion label is larger than a certain threshold (e.g., 0.5), that emotion label is assigned to the song. Note that hardGenre is a special case of softGenre, with total weight assigned to the most probable genre of a song.

12.3 Performance Evaluation

This section presents an empirical analysis of the correlation between genres and emotions and an evaluation of the two-layer emotion classification scheme.

12.3.1 Data Collection

To evaluate the performance of the two-layer scheme, we build a data set composed of genre and emotion labels downloaded from AMG [1]. This data set, referred to as the *whole* set hereafter, contains the annotation of 6490 albums. Each album is annotated with a single genre and multiple emotions. A total of 12 genres and 184 emotions are used. See Table 12.1 for a summary. This data set has been made publicly available [Online] http://mpac.ee.ntu.edu.tw/~vagante/genreEmo.

The audio files of a subset of the whole set are acquired from personal collections for the evaluation of music emotion classification. The data set, called the *cluster* set,

Table 12.1   Description of the Data Set

Data Set	Number of Albums	Number of Genres	Number of Emotions
Whole set	6490	12	184
Cluster set	300	6	12

is composed of 1535 songs collected from 300 albums. These albums are labeled with the following six genres: blues, country, jazz, R&B, rap, and rock. The number of albums per genre is roughly the same. For simplicity, the annotations of a song are directly inherited from the album that contains the song. Therefore, every song of an album would have the same emotion and genre labels.

Since 184 emotion labels contain several synonyms, a set of more representative emotion clusters is obtained by grouping. We measure the similarity $S(e_1, e_2)$ of two emotion labels, e_1 and e_2, by the frequency with which they co-occur as follows:

$$S(e_1, e_2) = \frac{|E_1 \cap E_2|}{|E_1 \cup E_2|}, \tag{12.1}$$

where E_1 is the set of albums annotated with e_1, E_2 is the set of albums annotated with e_2, and $|E|$ denotes the cardinality of a set. Note that we measure the similarity of emotion labels in the album levels instead of the song levels. Based on the similarity defined above, we construct an affinity matrix of emotion labels and employ spectral clustering [236, 360] to group them. The number of clusters is determined by the eigenGap technique described in [24]. After removing those emotion clusters that contain more than half of the albums in the data set, we obtain the 12 emotion clusters shown in Table 12.2. It can be found that the emotions in the same cluster are often synonyms of the same feeling, whereas emotions in different clusters share little similarity. For example, the fifth cluster contains emotions such as *carefree*, *cheerful*, and *happy*, whereas the third cluster contains emotions such as *acerbic*, *bitter*, and *ironic*. See Table 12.3 for an example MATLAB® code of spectral clustering.

In the performance evaluation, the whole data set and the cluster data set is used for analyzing the correlation between emotions and genres, whereas only the cluster data set is used for evaluating MER.

12.3.2 Analysis of the Correlation between Genre and Emotion

We begin with an empirical analysis of the correlation between genres and emotions using the chi-square test — one of the most widely used significance tests of association [17]. Based on a null hypothesis, the chi-square statistic χ^2 is computed to

Table 12.2 The 12 Emotion Clusters Derived from 184 All Music Guide Emotion Labels Using Spectral Clustering

Cluster	Associated Emotion Labels (Partial)			# Songs
1	Rustic	Self-conscious	Sparse	161
2	Bright	Reverent	Sparkling	269
3	Acerbic	Bitter	Ironic	330
4	Aggressive	Fiery	Manic	701
5	Carefree	Cheerful	Happy	729
6	Bleak	Brooding	Ominous	369
7	Delicate	Gentle	Intimate	704
8	Atmospheric	Ethereal	Hypnotic	326
9	Angry	Harsh	Hostile	463
10	Humorous	Quirky	Silly	440
11	Ambitious	Dramatic	Enigmatic	407
12	Hedonistic	Outrageous	Reckless	301

Source: Data from F. R. Bach and M. I. Jordan. *J. Machine Learning Research.* 7: 1963–2001, 2006 and A. Y. Ng et al. *Proc. Neural Information Processing Systems*, 849–856, 2002.

indicate how far the observed distribution departs from the expected distribution of the null hypothesis. If χ^2 is larger than the critical value χ_0^2 of a significance level, the null hypothesis is rejected. We test the null hypothesis that genres and emotions are independent at a significance level of 0.05 [232]. In addition to applying the test on the whole set, we also conduct the test without considering rock albums because about half of the whole set are rock and this bias may be unfavorable.

As shown in Table 12.4, the results of the chi-square test on all three data sets (whole, whole – rock, and cluster) reject the null hypothesis, suggesting that genre and emotion are correlated.

To estimate the associative strength, we also compute Cramer's V [17] for each of the data sets. The value of Cramer's V ranges from zero to one, and a larger value indicates stronger association. As seen in Table 12.4, the Cramer's V of the three data sets ranges from 0.225 to 0.353. Considering that not all genre-emotion pairs are correlated — for example, the passion of love is too general to be associated with a specific genre — the reported Cramer's V shows that a certain degree of correlation does exist between genres and emotions.

Note that the result presented here is not in line with the one described in [137], which claimed that genres and emotions are independent. The authors of [137] examined the correlation of genre-emotion pairs and found that those significantly correlated emotions are shared by all genres. They concluded that one can model

Table 12.3   An Example MATLAB® Code for Spectral Clustering [24, 236]

```
function [C, centroid] = spec_clus(A)
% perform spectral clustering
% input:  A -- affinity matrix (N by N)
% output: C -- cluster assignment (N by 1)
%           centroid -- cluster centroid

% parameters
Kmin = 2;  % the smallest possible number of clusters
Kmax = 10; % the largest  possible number of clusters

% compute the Laplacian matrix
N = size(A,1);    % number of data
D = ones(N,1)./(sqrt(sum(A,2))+eps);
D = diag(D);
L = D*A*D;

% determine the number of clusters by eigenGap
[LV LD] = eig(L); % compute eigenvalues and eigenvectors
eigGap = zeros(1,Kmax);
for j = Kmin:Kmax
    eigGap(j) = 1 - abs( LD(j+1,j+1)/LD(j,j) );
end
[dummy K] = max(eigGap);
LX = LV(:,1:K); % staking the top K eigenvectors in columns

% row normalization
LY=[];
for i=1:N
    LY(i,:) = LX(i,:)/(norm(LX(i,:))+eps);
end

% apply kmeans on the eigenvectors
[C, centroid] = kmeans(LY, K);
```

Source: Data from F. R. Bach and M. I. Jordan. *J. Machine Learning Research.* 7: 1963–2001, 2006 and A. Y. Ng et al. *Proc. Neural Information Processing Systems*, 846–856, 2002.

Table 12.4   Results of the Association Test

Data Set	χ^2	$\chi_0^2(0.05)$	Cramer's V
Whole set	9393.6	233.9	0.227
Whole set – rock	6057.6	177.4	0.353
Cluster set	1550.8	73.3	0.225

genre and emotion separately, even though the most co-occurred emotions of each genre are quite different. The experimental results reported in this chapter, however, show that the integral correlation between genre and emotion does exist and that such correlation can be utilized to improve MER.

12.3.3 Evaluation of the Two-Layer Emotion Classification Scheme

We then evaluate the performance of emotion classification using the cluster data set. In our implementation, each song is converted to a uniform format (22,050 Hz, mono channel PCM WAV) and normalized to the same volume level for fair comparison. Each song is represented by a total of 436 audio features extracted by Marsyas [324]: 68 timbre features, 48 pitch features, 8 rhythm features, 120 linear-prediction-based features, and 192 MPEG-7 features. These features represent the spectral attributes, temporal traits, and musical characteristics of songs.

12.3.3.1 Computational Model

Because a music recording can be associated with more than one emotion in AMG, we formulate emotion classification as a multilabel classification problem [318] and employ a multilabel variant of support vector classification (SVC) implemented in LIBSVM [54, 86] for emotion classification. That is, the emotion classifier may associate with a song multiple emotion labels instead of only one label. The multilabel SVC is extended from the one-against-all multiclass method [78]. For genre classification, the traditional multiclass SVC implemented in LIBSVM is adopted.

12.3.3.2 Evaluation Measures

We adopt 10-fold cross-validation and randomly partition the data set into 10 parts, nine for training and one for testing. The partition is performed iteratively until each fold is held out once. The above process is repeated 20 times to get an average result.

The standard evaluation measurements for multilabel classification problems are the macro-average F-measure ($\bar{F}$) and micro-average F-measure ($\tilde{f}$) [318], defined as

$$\bar{F} = \frac{2}{C} \sum_{j=1}^{C} \frac{\sum_{i=1}^{N_j} \hat{y}_{ij} y_{ij}}{\sum_{i=1}^{N_j} (\hat{y}_{ij} + y_{ij})}, \tag{12.2}$$

$$\tilde{f} = \frac{2 \sum_{j=1}^{C} \sum_{i=1}^{N_j} \hat{y}_{ij} y_{ij}}{\sum_{j=1}^{C} \sum_{i=1}^{N_j} (\hat{y}_{ij} + y_{ij})}, \tag{12.3}$$

where C denotes the number of class labels, N_j is the number of songs of label j, $\hat{y}_{ij}$ denotes the prediction result of song i for label j, and y_{ij} is the ground truth value. $\bar{F}$ is the equally weighted mean of the F-measure of each label, whereas $\tilde{f}$ accounts for the prediction of all samples and calculates the F-measure across all labels. Therefore, $\bar{F}$ accounts for each label equally, whereas $\tilde{f}$ accounts for the overall prediction result of all labels.

12.3.3.3 Results

We compare the performance of the following four emotion classification schemes. Single is the traditional single-layer scheme, while hardGenre and softGenre are the proposed two-layer schemes. To estimate the maximal improvement the two-layer scheme can make, we put an oracle genre classifier that predicts the genre of a song according to the ground truth in the first layer of the hardGenre scheme. We refer to this scheme as "trueGenre." Though the oracle genre classifier is not perfect in that we have approximated the song-level ground truth using album-level annotations, one may consider the performance of the trueGenre scheme as an upper bound that defines both the viability of the two-layer scheme and the F-measures that are reasonable for the implemented system to achieve.

Table 12.5 shows the performance of the four emotion classification schemes. It can be observed that the two-layer schemes greatly outperform the traditional single-layer scheme. The performance difference is significant at a significance level of 0.05. With the use of softGenre, the $\bar{F}$ and $\tilde{f}$ are improved to 0.43 and 0.56, which are very close to that of trueGenre. A closer look at Table 12.5 reveals that hardGenre outperforms single in $\tilde{f}$ but not in $\bar{F}$. This is because hardGenre performs worse in clusters 4, 5, and 7, which contain the largest number of songs among the 12 emotion clusters (see Table 12.2 and Figure 12.2). Even though hardGenre performs well for the rest of the emotion clusters, its worse performance in the three clusters greatly hampers the $\tilde{f}$. The softGenre is free of this drawback, improving both $\bar{F}$ and $\tilde{f}$ to a similar degree to those of trueGenre.

Figure 12.2 shows the F-measures of the 12 emotion clusters in the four emotion classification schemes. As trueGenre brings about improvement for all emotion

Table 12.5 Experiment Results of the Four Emotion Classification Schemes

System	Macro-avg $\bar{F}$	Micro-avg $\tilde{f}$
Single	0.31	0.52
hardGenre	0.40*	0.51
softGenre	0.43*	0.56*
trueGenre	0.46*	0.60*

Note: The symbol * denotes significant improvement over the single scheme at significant level 0.05.

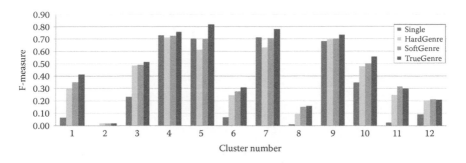

Figure 12.2 **Performance of (a) the traditional single-layer emotion classification scheme, (b) the proposed two-layer scheme hardGenre, and (c) the soft version of the two-layer scheme softGenre.**

clusters, we can see that the emotion classification can be much improved if genre classification has been done perfectly. When the genre of a song is predicted by the system and some incorrect predictions are made (the genre classification accuracy is about 58.98%), hardGenre still offers improvement for most emotion clusters, especially for emotion clusters whose F-measures are low under the single scheme. On the other hand, it can also be observed that the errors made in genre classification have negative impacts on the prediction of emotion clusters, such as clusters 4, 5, and 7.

In our evaluation, it is found that the misclassified songs often have two comparable likelihoods of the different genres, which is consistent with the observation mentioned in Section 12.2. For songs that are a mixture of two genres, using deterministic genre classification is not suitable. This problem is effectively mitigated by the use of soft decision in genre classification. As shown in Figure 12.2, softGenre compensates for the classification errors of the first layer and consistently improves the accuracy of emotion classification for all the emotion clusters.

12.4 Summary

In this chapter, we have presented a careful examination of the correlation between music genres and emotions and the application of such correlation to improve the performance of categorical MER. With the two-layer scheme, significant improvement of classification accuracy over the conventional single-layer scheme is achieved. Despite the errors made in the first layer genre classification of the two-layer scheme, the utilization of soft genre decisions helps the two-layer scheme achieve a similar accuracy as if the true genres are known.

13

Music Retrieval in the Emotion Plane

With MER, many novel emotion-based music retrieval and organization methods can be developed. One can search music by emotion, find music pieces that are similar to a given music piece in terms of perceived emotion, or browse a music collection in the emotion space. This chapter describes a music retrieval platform that organizes music pieces in the 2D valence-arousal emotion plane. Such a simple 2D user interface is useful for mobile devices that have a small display space and a limited input capability.

13.1 Emotion-Based Music Retrieval

The most appealing function of music is that it can convey emotion and modulate a listener's mood [90]. Past years have witnessed an increase of interests in emotion-based music organization and retrieval. In academia, more and more multimedia systems that involve emotion analysis of music signals have been developed, such as Mood Cloud [185, 187], Moody [141], MusicSense [45], LyQ [136], Mood-track [328], and *i*.MTV [370–372], to name a few. In the industry, many music companies, such as AMG [1], Gracenote [5], MoodLogic [12], Musicovery [13], Syntonetic [14], and Sourcetone [145], use emotion as a cue for music retrieval. Some of these systems view emotions from the categorical perspective, while others from the dimensional perspective. We have introduced two music retrieval systems that adopt the categorical conceptualization of emotion in Chapter 1.

This chapter describes an emotion-based music retrieval platform, called *Mr. Emo*, that views emotion from the dimensional perspective [357, 362]. Mr. Emo represents a good example showing how the dimensional conceptualization of emotion and the techniques developed for dimensional MER can be applied to music retrieval and management in the 2D emotion space.

13.2 2D Visualization of Music

Visualizing music in 2D space has been studied in the past. As conventional approaches that manage music pieces based on catalog metadata such as artist name, album name, and song name cannot provide enough information on music similarity, which the users highly expect from a music search tool [188], systems that help users to retrieve and browse music pieces in a content-based fashion have been developed. For example, an approach to visualizing a music collection based on two perceptual attributes, rhythm and timbre, has been developed in [373]. Other systems that present music pieces in 2D space include the *PocketSOM* [95] and the *Islands of Music* [247], which utilize the self-organizing map [172] to map the high-dimensional music features to a 2D map grid while preserving similarity relationships in the feature space. However, there is no semantic meaning associated with the resulting two dimensions.

As some sort of emotional experience is probably the main reason behind most people's engagement with music, a plausible way of visualizing music pieces is presenting them in the emotion plane. With Mr. Emo, one can easily retrieve music pieces of a certain emotion without knowing the titles or browse a personal collection in the emotion plane. One can also couple emotion-based retrieval with traditional keyword- or artist-based ones, to retrieve songs similar (in the sense of perceived emotion) to a favorite piece or to select the songs of an artist according to emotion. In addition, it is also possible to play back music that matches a user's current emotion state, which can be estimated from facial or prosodic cues [22, 192, 253]. Such a simple 2D user interface for content-based retrieval of music is particularly useful for tiny mobile devices such as MP3 players or cell phones that have a small display space and a limited input capability.

13.3 Retrieval Methods

In Mr. Emo, the critical task of predicting the VA values is accomplished by the regression techniques introduced in Chapter 4. Given the regression models, the valence and arousal (VA) values of an input song can be automatically computed without manual labeling. Associated with the VA values, each music piece is visualized as a point in the emotion plane, and the similarity between music pieces is measured by Euclidean distance. Many novel retrieval methods can be realized in the emotion plane, making music information access much easier and more effective. Below we describe four example music retrieval and organization methods that are performed in the emotion plane.

13.3.1 Query by Emotion Point (QBEP)

With Mr. Emo, a user can retrieve music of a certain emotion by simply specifying a point in the emotion plane. The system then returns the music pieces whose VA values are closest to the point. This retrieval method is functionally powerful since people's criterion of music selection is often related to the emotion state at the moment of music selection. In addition, a user can also easily discover previously unfamiliar songs, which are now organized and browsed according to emotion. Similarly, a user can also query by dragging a rectangle or clicking on multiple points in the emotion plane to retrieve music of different emotions.

13.3.2 Query by Emotion Trajectory (QBET)

A user can also generate a playlist by drawing a free trajectory representing a sequence of emotions in the emotion plane. This way, songs of various emotions corresponding to different points on the trajectory are added to the playlist and played back in order. As the trajectory goes from one point to another, the emotions of the songs in the playlist would vary accordingly. For example, in Figure 13.1 the trajectory goes from the first quadrant down to the lower emotion plane and creates a playlist that starts from "Laughing at You" by the artist Big Pun and "Penny Lane" by the Beatles to "To All the Girls I Love" by Willie Nelson and so on.

13.3.3 Query by Artist and Emotion (QBAE)

Associated with the artist metadata, a user can combine the emotion-based retrieval with the conventional artist-based retrieval. As shown in Figure 13.2, we can easily visualize the distribution of the music pieces of an artist and browse them. With QBAE, we get to know that the band Sex Pistols usually performs songs whose emotions are located in the second quadrant, whereas the artist Rod Stewart often sings songs whose arousal values are lower. We can also visualize the distribution of the music pieces sung by the band the Beatles and select the sad songs or happy songs sung by them. In addition, QBEP and QBAE can be used in a cooperative way: We can select a song and browse the other ones sung by the same artist by QBAE, or select a song and browse the other songs that sound similar to it using QBEP. The system can also recommend similar artists to us by modeling the distributions of music emotions as Gaussian mixture models (GMM) [232] and measuring similarity by the Kullback–Leibler divergence [176].

13.3.4 Query by Lyrics and Emotion (QBLE)

According to a user study [193], when people search for music or music information, 74% of people would like to search by some words of the lyrics, 33% of people would like to search by the main subject of music (theme), and 24% of them by

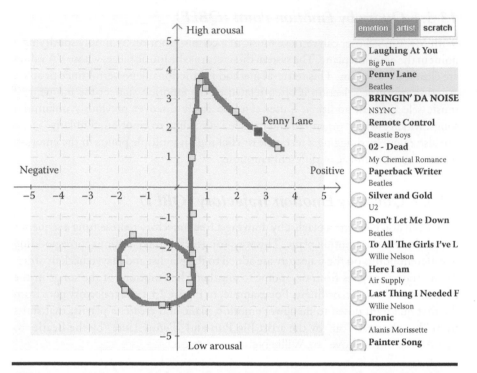

Figure 13.1 **Mr. Emo represents each song as a point in the 2D valence-arousal emotion plane [362]. A user can retrieve music of a certain emotion by simply specifying a point in the plane. The system then returns the songs whose VA values are close to the point. A user can also draw a trajectory and create a playlist of songs with various emotions corresponding to different points on the trajectory.**

the occasions of use (wedding, party, etc.) [360]. With standard natural language processing techniques [290], a lyrics-based music retrieval system can be realized, responding to user query by comparing the input text with the lyrics of songs. In practice, the query terms are typically short and may not be part of the lyrics, so query expansion techniques [61,350] can be adopted to enrich the semantics of the query. Furthermore, just like the artist metadata, we can also browse music pieces that contain a certain fragment of lyrics in the emotion plane.

13.4 Implementation

We train a computational model for dimensional MER using the 60 English songs described in Section 7.4.1 and implement the user interface Mr. Emo. We use 52 spectrum features (spectral centroid, spectral rolloff, spectral flux, and MFCCs) and

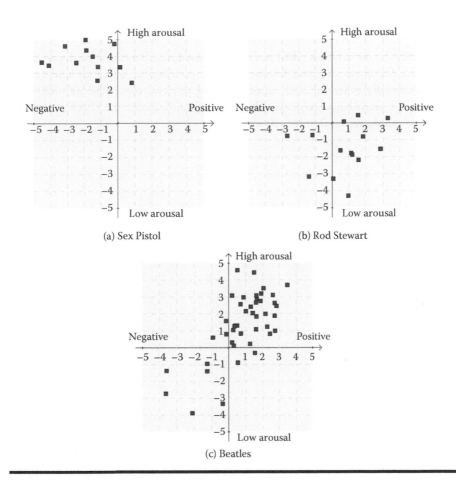

Figure 13.2 Distributions of the songs of three famous artists/bands in the emotion plane.

192 MPEG-7 features (spectral flatness measure and spectral crest factor) generated by Marsyas [324] for feature representation and the ϵ-support vector regression (SVR) [69, 301] algorithm described in Section 4.3.3.2 for model training. The R^2 statistics (cf. Eq. 4.13) of 10-fold cross-validation is 0.793 for arousal and 0.334 for valence. The trained regression models are applied to another 1000 English pop songs of 52 artists. Note, there is no overlapping between the training samples and the test samples. In our implementation, feature extraction and VA values computation are efficient and take less than five seconds per song on a regular dual-core Pentium PC. A video demonstration of the implemented system is available online: http://www.youtube.com/watch?v=ra55xO20UHU.

13.5 Summary

In this chapter, we have described an emotion-based music retrieval platform, called Mr. Emo, for organizing and browsing music collections. Being content-centric and functionally powerful, such emotion-based retrieval complements traditional keyword- or artist-based retrieval. This platform also shows the effectiveness and novelty of music retrieval in the emotion plane.

14

Future Research Directions

In the previous chapters, we have described several computational techniques that address some critical issues of MER and provide a basis for emotion-based music retrieval. This chapter describes some possible directions of future research that can be extended from the techniques introduced in this book. As Klaus R. Scherer concluded in the foreword of *Music and Emotion: Theory and Research* [159], we hope this book will inspire more multidisciplinary-minded researchers to study "a phenomenon that has intrigued mankind since the dawn of time."

14.1 Exploiting Vocal Timbre for MER

In Chapters 10–12, we have described the use of lyrics, chord sequence, and genre metadata to improve the accuracy of emotion prediction. Another source of information that is not touched upon in this book, however, is the singing voice of music. Typically, a pop song is composed of a singing voice, accompanying music, and lyrics. The timbre of the singing voice, such as *aggressive, breathy, falsetto, gravelly, high-pitched, rapping,* or *strong* [321], is usually related to our emotion perception of music. For example, a song with screaming and roaring voices usually expresses an angry emotion, whereas a song with sweet voices tends to express positive emotions. Therefore, it should be beneficial to incorporate vocal timbre into the MER system.

An essential step before analyzing the vocal timbre of a song is the suppression or reduction of the accompanying music [108]. Because the music track and the vocal track have been mixed in most popular songs sold in the market, separating one track from the other before audio signal processing techniques is a required step. While the human auditory system has a remarkable capability to separate one source of sound from many others, it has been found considerably difficult for a machine to do so [108, 135, 177, 255, 327]. A great amount of effort has been put forth on melodic source separation; see [334] for a review.

A simple approach is to apply a bandpass filter that preserves the frequency components corresponding only to the singing voice (sometimes referred to as *vocal range*) [307]. Many professional music editing software tools such as GoldWave [4] also adopt such an approach. However, this approach may easily fail when the accompanying instruments have frequency responses in the vocal range.

If the accompanying music can be (partially) reduced, one can employ speech signal analysis to extract descriptors of the vocal timbre. Speech features that have been found useful for speech emotion recognition [91, 105, 253, 289, 329] or singer identification [98, 238, 295, 317] include linear predictive Mel cepstrum coefficients (LPMCC), Δf_0 [97], vibrato, harmonics, attack-delay [239], voice source features [91], zero-crossing rate, RMS energy, pitch frequency, and harmonics-to-noise ratio [289], to name a few. A multimodal music emotion recognition system can then be built to aggregate the information obtained from the accompanying music, lyrics, and singing voice.

14.2 Emotion Distribution Prediction Based on Rankings

We have described a ranking-based method that simplifies the emotion annotation process in Chapter 5 and a computational model that predicts the emotion distribution of music pieces from music features in Chapter 9. However, it remains to be explored how the ranking-based emotion annotations can be utilized to emotion distribution prediction, which requires emotion ratings to compute the emotion mass at a discrete sample of the emotion plane. This study is important because the generality of training samples is essential to the performance of a computational model and because building a large-scale data set by ranking is much easier.

One direction is to improve the strategy of converting emotion rankings to emotion ratings, such that the ranking-based annotation method can be directly applied to ground truth collection. As we have discussed in Section 5.7, one may consider using a small number of emotion ratings to regulate the conversion—for example, to determine which songs have neutral valence or arousal values.

Another direction is to investigate the *contradiction* of emotion rankings to obtain clues regarding emotion distribution. A contradiction occurs when a user ranks song a higher than song b but another user ranks contrarily. Intuitively, the emotion distribution of a song that causes more contradictions should be sparser (i.e., the emotion perception of the song is more subjective). In Chapter 9, the pairwise comparisons are directly incorporated into a binary preference matrix without considering the contradiction. For future work one may consider using a real-valued preference matrix or explicitly taking the contradiction into account to measure the subjectivity of the emotion perception of a song.

14.3 Personalized Emotion-Based Music Retrieval

As discussed, Chapter 9 only deals with the *indexing* part of MER (i.e., predicting the probabilistic emotion distribution $P(\mathbf{e}|d)$ of a song d over the emotion plane), but not the *retrieval* part (i.e., when a user u clicks on a point e^{ij}, the return is a list of songs ranked in the descending order of $P(d|e^{ij}, u)$.* One may regard an emotion distribution $P(\mathbf{e}|d)$ as a collection of users' perceived emotions of a song and the perceived emotion of the user $P(\mathbf{e}|d, u)$ as a sample from the distribution. By doing so, music emotion recognition and emotion-based music retrieval can be treated under a unified *probabilistic* framework rather than separately as was done in Chapters 7 and 8.

Moreover, according to Bayes' rule we have

$$P(d\,|\mathbf{e}, u) = \frac{P(\mathbf{e}|d, u)\, P(d\,|u)}{P(\mathbf{e}|u)}, \qquad (14.1)$$

where $P(\mathbf{e}|d, u)$ is a term of personal perception of music emotion, $P(d|u)$ indicates the preference of the user with respect to music type, and $P(\mathbf{e}|u)$ refers to the emotion preference of the user. Both $P(d|u)$ and $P(\mathbf{e}|u)$ can be learned from the user's listening history. Therefore, it is possible to incorporate personal information to the probabilistic framework.

14.4 Situational Factors of Emotion Perception

According to psychological studies, the emotion response to a music piece is dependent on an interplay between the musical, personal, and situational factors of the music piece. Because of the influence of the situational factors, one may perceive different emotions from a music piece in a different listening context. For example, when we are in a sad mood, a happy song may not be perceived as happy for us. Our emotion perception of a music piece may change when listening alone or with others, in everyday context or in a special event. Consequently, it would be beneficial for an MER system to detect the listening context such as the listening mood or the listening environment and modify the emotion predictions accordingly. The

---

* Here $e^{ij} = [v^i, a^j]^\top$ is a discrete sample (associated with specific valence and arousal values) of the emotion plane and $\mathbf{e}$ denotes a set of discrete samples.

former can be approached by utilizing prosodic cues, facial expression, body movements, or physiological signals of the user [149, 192, 208, 209, 253], whereas the latter can be approached by monitoring the background volume or ambient light of the environment or using the GPS (global positioning system) receiver, time clock, kinetic sensor, or Internet RSS (really simple syndication) feed receiver on a mobile device [58, 77, 84, 264]. An MER system can also utilize the information of the listening context to actively *recommend* music to the listeners.

14.5 Connections between Dimensional and Categorical MER

As we have described in Section 2.2, the categorical approach and the dimensional approach to MER offer complementary advantages; the former offers an atomic description of music that is easy to incorporate into conventional text-based retrieval systems, whereas the latter offers a simple means for 2D user interface. It is therefore interesting to combine the two approaches to improve the performance of MER and to build a more effective and user-friendly emotion-based music retrieval system.

From the model training perspective, as collecting emotion labels is relatively easier (e.g., by crawling AMG or Last.fm), it is interesting to develop a method that utilizes the categorical emotion labels as the ground truth for training a dimensional MER system. For example, one can map the affective terms (e.g., *peaceful, romantic, sentimental*) to points in the emotion plane (cf. Figure 2.2) and consider the corresponding VA values as the ground truth ratings of the corresponding music pieces. Though there could be a tie (many music pieces are associated with the same emotion value), learning-to-rank algorithms such as RBF-ListNet can be employed to resolve it. This way, constructing a large-scale database for training and evaluating dimensional MER would be easier.

From the music retrieval perspective, because users may be unfamiliar with the essence of the valence and arousal dimensions, it would be helpful to add affective terms in the emotion plane to give users some cues. Moreover, we can allow a user to choose which affective terms to be displayed and to change the placement of the affective terms in the emotion plane. Such user inputs can be further utilized to personalize the MER system.

14.6 Music Retrieval and Organization in 3D Emotion Space

As described in Section 2.1.2, the 2D valence-arousal conceptualization of emotions has been criticized by some researchers because it blurs important psychological distinctions between emotions [191]. Describing our emotion perception in terms of these two dimensions may not differentiate emotions such as anger and fear. In consequence, it may be needed to extend the emotion space to 3D, using additional emotion dimensions such as potency (dominant–submissive) to obtain a more complete picture of emotion [33, 67, 337]. Although some efforts have been made along this direction (e.g., [80]), it remains to be seen what the best third emotion dimension is, how to effectively annotate the emotions of music pieces in 3D, and how to retrieve and organize music pieces in 3D emotion space, especially for mobile devices. Alternatively, one may build a computational system that computes the emotion values of music pieces for more than two or three dimensions and lets the users decide which emotion dimensions to be used in music navigation or retrieval.

References

[1] All music guide. [Online] http://www.allmusic.com/.

[2] Cool edit pro. [Online] http://www.adobe.com/products/audition/.

[3] GOASEMA – semantic description of musical audio. [Online] http://www.ipem. ugent.be.

[4] Goldwave: Audio editor, recorder, converter, restoration, & analysis software. [Online] http://www.goldwave.com/.

[5] Gracenote. [Online] http://www.gracenote.com/.

[6] Last.fm. [Online] http://www.last.fm/.

[7] Lingpipe. [Online] http://alias-i.com/lingpipe/.

[8] Lyricwiki. [Online] http://lyrics.wikia.com/.

[9] MATLAB® optimization toolbox. [Online] http://www.mathworks.com/products/optimization/.

[10] MATLAB wavelet toolbox. [Online] http://www.mathworks.com/products/ wavelet/.

[11] MIREX: Music information retrieval evaluation exchange. [Online] http://www. music-ir.org/mirex/.

[12] Moodlogic. [Online] http://www.moodlogic.com.

[13] Musicovery: Interactive Web radio. [Online] http://www.musicovery.com/.

[14] Syntonetic. [Online] http://www.syntonetic.com/.

[15] A. Abbasi, H. Chen, S. Thoms, and T. Fu. Affect analysis of Web forums and blogs using correlation ensembles. *IEEE Trans. Knowledge & Data Engineering*, 20(9):1168–1180, 2008.

[16] H. F. Abeles and J. W. Chung. *Responses to Music*, pages 285–342. IMR Press, San Antonio, TX, 1996.

[17] A. Agresti. *Categorical Data Analysis*. John Wiley & Sons Publications, Hoboken, New Jersey, 2002.

[18] A. Aizawa. An information-theoretic perspective of tf-idf measures. *Information Processing and Management*, 39:45–65, 2003.

[19] S. O. Ali. Songs and emotions: are lyrics and melodies equal partners. *Psychology of Music*, 34(4):511–534, 2006.

[20] S. O. Ali and Z. F. Peynircioğu. Songs and emotions: are lyrics and melodies equal partners. *Psychology of Music*, 34(4):511–534, 2006.

[21] E. Allamanche, J. Herre, O. Helmuth, B. Fröba, T. Kasten, and M. Cremer. Content-based identification of audio material using MPEG-7 low level description. In *Proc. Int. Conf. Music Information Retrieval*, pages 197–204, 2001.

[22] K. Anderson and P. W. McOwan. A real-time automated system for the recognition of human facial expressions. *IEEE Trans. System, Man & Cybernetics*, 36(1):96–105, 2006.

[23] S. Arifin and P. Y. K. Cheung. Affective level video segmentation by utilizing the pleasure-arousal-dominance information. *IEEE Trans. Multimedia*, 10(7):1325–1341, 2008.

[24] F. R. Bach and M. I. Jordan. Learning spectral clustering, with application to speech separation. *J. Machine Learning Research*, 7:1963–2001, 2006.

[25] S. A. Banawan and N. M. Zeidat. A comparative study of load sharing in heterogeneous multicomputersystems. In *Proc. Annual Simulation Symposium*, pages 22–31, 1992.

[26] L. Barrington, D. O'Malley, D. Turnbull, and G. Lanckriet. Herd the music—a social music annotation game. In *Proc. Int. Conf. Music Information Retrieval*, 2008.

[27] M. Bartoszewski, H. Kwasnicka, U. Markowska-Kaczmar, and P. B. Myszkowski. Extraction of emotional content from music data. In *Proc. Computer Information Systems and Industrial Management Applications*, pages 293–299, 2008.

[28] D. Beard and K. Gloag. *Musicology: the Key Concepts*. Routledge, New York, 2005.

[29] J. P. Bello, L. Daudet, S. Abdallah, C. Duxbury, M. Davies, and M. B. Sandler. A tutorial on onset detection in music signals. *IEEE Trans. Speech and Audio Processing*, 13(5):1035–1047, 2005.

[30] J. P. Bello and J. Pickens. A robust mid-level representation for harmonic content in music signals. In *Proc. Int. Conf. Music Information Retrieval*, pages 304–311, 2005.

[31] E. Benetos, M. Kotti, and C. Kotropoulos. Large scale musical instrument identification. In *Proc. Int. Conf. Music Information Retrieval*, 2007. [Online] http://www.ifs.tuwien.ac.at/mir/muscle/del/audio_tools.html#Sound DescrToolbox.

[32] L. Bergroth, H. Hakonen, and T. Raita. A survey of longest common subsequence algorithms. In *Proc. Int. Symp. String Processing Information Retrieval*, pages 322–336, 2000.

[33] E. Bigand, S. Vieillard, F. Madurell, J. Marozeau, and A. Dacquet. Multidimensional scaling of emotional responses to music: The effect of musical expertise and of the duration of the excerpts. *Cognition and Emotion*, 19(8):1113–1139, 2005.

[34] K. Bischoff, C. S. Firan, R. Paiu, W. Nejdl, C. Laurier, and M. Sordo. Music mood and theme classification - a hybrid approach. In *Proc. Int. Conf. Music Information Retrieval*, pages 657–662, 2009.

[35] L. Bo and C. Sminchisescu. Twin Gaussian processes for structured prediction. *Int. J. Computer Vision*, 87(1–2):28–52, 2010.

[36] E. V. Bonilla, K. M. A. Chai, and C. K. I. Williams. Multi-task Gaussian process prediction. In *Proc. Conf. Neural Information Processing Systems*, pages 164–170, 2008.

[37] A. Bosch, A. Zisserman, and X. M. noz. Scene classification using a hybrid generative discriminative approach. *IEEE Trans. Pattern Analysis & Machine Intelligence*, 30(4):712–727, 2008.

[38] Z. I. Botev, J. F. Grotowski, and D. P. Kroese. Kernel density estimation via diffusion. *Annals of Statistics*, 2009. Submitted.

[39] A. W. Bowman and A. Azzalini. *Applied Smoothing Techniques for Data Analysis*. Oxford University Press, New York, 1997.

[40] S. P. Boyd and L. Vandenberghe. *Convex Optimization*. Cambridge University Press, Cambridge, UK, 2004.

[41] P. Boyle and M. Frean. Dependent Gaussian processes. In *Proc. Conf. Neural Information Processing Systems*, pages 217–224, 2004.

[42] C. J. Burges, T. Shaked, E. Renshaw, A. Lazier, M. Deeds, N. Hamilton, and G. Hullender. Learning to rank using gradient descent. In *Proc. IEEE Int. Conf. Machine Learning*, pages 89–96, 2005.

[43] R. Burkard. Sound pressure level measurement and spectral analysis of brief acoustic transients. *Electroencephalography and Clinical Neurophysiology*, 57(1):83–91, 1984.

[44] D. Cabrera. Psysound: A computer program for psycho-acoustical analysis. In *Proc. Australian Acoustic Society Conf.*, pages 47–54, 1999. [Online] http://psysound. wikidot.com/.

[45] R. Cai, C. Zhang, C. Wang, L. Zhang, and W.-Y. Ma. MusicSense: Contextual music recommendation using emotional allocation modeling. In *Proc. ACM Int. Conf. Multimedia*, pages 553–556, 2007.

[46] A. Camacho. *SWIPE: A Sawtooth Waveform Inspired Pitch Estimator for Speech and Music.* PhD thesis, Univ. Florida, 2007.

[47] W. M. Campbell, J. P. Campbell, D. A. Reynolds, E. Singer, and P. A. Torres-Carrasquillo. Support vector machines for speaker and language recognition. *Computer Speech & Language*, 20(2–3):210–229, 2006.

[48] C. Cao and M. Li. Thinkit's submissions for MIREX2009 audio music classification and similarity tasks. In *MIREX task on Audio Mood Classification*, 2009.

[49] Z. Cao, T. Qin, T.-Y. Liu, M.-F. Tsai, and H. Li. Learning to rank: from pairwise approach to listwise approach. In *Proc. IEEE Int. Conf. Machine Learning*, pages 129–136, 2007.

[50] M. A. Casey, R. Veltkamp, M. Goto, M. Leman, C. Rhodes, and M. Slaney. Content-based music information retrieval: Current directions and future challenges. *Proceedings of the IEEE*, 96(4):668–696, 2008.

[51] W. B. Cavnar and J. M. Trenkle. N-gram-based text categorization. In *Proc. Annual Symp. Document Analysis and Information Retrieval*, pages 181–196, 1994.

[52] W. Chai and B. Vercoe. Using user models in music information retrieval systems. In *Proc. Int. Symp. Music Information Retrieval*, 2000.

[53] J. Chalupper and H. Fastl. Dynamic loudness model for normal and hearing-impaired listeners. 88:378–386, 2002.

[54] C.-C. Chang and C.-J. Lin. *LIBSVM: A library for support vector machines*, 2001. [Online] http://www.csie.ntu.edu.tw/ cjlin/libsvm.

[55] C.-H. Chen, M.-F. Weng, S.-K. Jeng, and Y.-Y. Chuang. Emotion-based music visualization using photos. In *Proc. Multimedia Modeling*, 2008.

[56] J.-C. Chen, W.-T. Chu, J.-H. Kuo, C.-Y. Weng, and J.-L. Wu. Tiling slideshows. In *Proc. ACM Int. Conf. Multimedia*, pages 25–34, 2006.

[57] T. Chen and H. Chen. Approximation capability to functions of several variables, nonlinear functionals, and operators by radial basis function neural networks. *IEEE Trans. Neural Networks*, 6(4):904–910, 1995.

[58] X. Y. Chen and Z. Segall. XV-Pod: An emotion aware, affective mobile video player. In *Proc. World Congress on Computer Science and Information Engineering*, pages 277–281, 2009.

[59] H.-T. Cheng, Y.-H. Yang, Y.-C. Lin, and H.-H. Chen. Multimodal structure segmentation and analysis of music using audio and textual information. In *Proc. IEEE Int. Symp. Circuits and Systems*, pages 1677–1680, 2009.

[60] H.-T. Cheng, Y.-H. Yang, Y.-C. Lin, I.-B. Liao, and H.-H. Chen. Automatic chord recognition for music classification and retrieval. In *Proc. IEEE Int. Conf. Multimedia and Expo.*, pages 1505–1508, 2008.

[61] P. A. Chirita, C. S. Firan, and W. Nejdl. Personalized query expansion for the Web. In *Proc. ACM Int. Conf. Information Retrieval*, pages 7–14, 2007.

[62] Y.-H. Cho and K.-J. Lee. Automatic affect recognition using natural language processing techniques and manually built affect lexicon. *IEICE Trans. Information Systems*, E89(12):2964–2971, 2006.

[63] B. Y. Chua and G. Lu. Perceptual rhythm determination of music signal for emotion-based classification. In *Proc. Multimedia Modeling*, 2006.

[64] Z. Chuang and C. Wu. Emotion recognition using audio features and textual contents. In *Proc. IEEE Int. Conf. Multimedia and Expo.*, pages 53–56, 2004.

[65] R. Cohen and M. Swerdlik. *Psychological Testing and Assessment: An Introduction to Tests and Measurement.* Mayfield Publishing Company, Mountain View, CA, 2002.

[66] W. W. Cohen, R. E. Schapire, and Y. Singer. Learning to order things. *J. Artificial Intelligence Research,* 10:243–270, 1999.

[67] G. Collier. Beyond valence and activity in the emotional connotations of music. *Psychology of Music,* 35(1):110–131, 2007.

[68] T. H. Cormen, C. E. Leiserson, R. L. Rivest, and C. Stein. *Introduction to Algorithms.* McGraw-Hill, 2001.

[69] C. Cortes and V. Vapnik. Support vector networks. *Machine Learning,* 20(3):273–297, 1995.

[70] R. Cowie, E. Douglas-Cowie, S. Savvidou, E. McMahon, M. Sawey, and M. Schröer. Feeltrace: An instrument for recording perceived emotion in real time. In *Proc. Speech and Emotion, ISCA Tutorial and Research Workshop,* pages 19–24, 2000.

[71] N. Cressie. *Statistics for Spatial Data.* Wiley, New York, 1993.

[72] A. Damasio. *Descartes' Error. Emotion, Reason, and the Human Brain.* Grosset/Putnam, New York, 1994.

[73] S. Davis and P. Mermelstein. Comparison of parametric representations for monosyllabic word recognition in continuously spoken sentences. *IEEE Trans. Acoustics, Speech & Signal Processing,* 28(4):357–366, 1980.

[74] A. P. Dempster, N. M. Laird, and D. B. Rubin. Maximum likelihood from incomplete data via the EM algorithm. *J. Royal Statist. Society B,* 39:1–38, 1977.

[75] R. Dietz and A. Lang. Affective agents: Effects of agent affect on arousal, attention, liking and learning. In *Proc. Int. Cognitive Technology Conf.,* 1999.

[76] S. Dixon. Evaluation of the audio beat tracking system BeatRoot. *J. New Music Research,* 36(1):39–50, 2007. [online] http://www.elec.qmul.ac. uk/people/simond/beatroot/.

[77] S. Dornbush, K. Fisher, K. Mckay, A. Prikhodko, and Z. Segall. XPOD: A human activity and emotion aware mobile music player. In *Proc. Int. Conf. Mobile Technology, Applications and Systems,* 2005.

[78] R. O. Duda, P. E. Hart, and D. G. Stork. *Pattern Classification.* John Wiley & Sons, Inc., New York, 2000.

[79] P. Dunker, S. Nowak, A. Begau, and C. Lanz. Content-based mood classification for photos and music. In *Proc. ACM Int. Conf. Multimedia Information Retrieval,* pages 97–104, 2008.

[80] T. Eerola, O. Lartillot, and P. Toiviainen. Prediction of multidimensional emotional ratings in music from audio using multivariate regression models. In *Proc. Int. Conf. Music Information Retrieval,* pages 621–626, 2009.

[81] T. Eerola, P. Toiviainen, and C. L. Krumhansl. Real-time prediction of melodies: Continuous predictability judgments and dynamic models. In *Proc. Int. Conf. Music Perception and Cognition,* pages 473–476, 2002.

[82] P. Ekman. An argument for basic emotions. *Cognition and Emotion,* 6(3):169–200, 1992.

[83] M. S. El-Nasr, J. Yen, and T. Ioerger. FLAME—fuzzy logic adaptive mode of emotions. In *Proc. Autonomous Agents and Multi-Agent Systems,* pages 219–257, 2000.

[84] G. T. Elliott and B. Tomlinson. PersonalSoundtrack: Context-aware playlists that adapt to user pace. In *Proc. ACM Int. Conf. Human Factors in Computing Systems,* pages 736–741, 2006. extended abstract.

[85] J. Ellson, E. R. Gansner, E. Koutsofios, S. C. North, and G. Woodhull. Graphviz – open source graph drawing tools. In *Proc. Graph Drawing,* pages 483–484, 2001.

[86] R.-E. Fan and C.-J. Lin. A study on threshold selection for multi-label classification. Technical report, National Taiwan University, 2007.

[87] P. R. Farnsworth. A study of the Hevner adjective list. *J. Aesthetics and Art Criticism,* 13:97–103, 1954.

[88] P. R. Farnsworth. *The Social Psychology of Music.* Dryden Press, 1958.

[89] H. Fastl. Fluctuation strength and temporal masking patterns of amplitude-modulated broad-band noise. 8(1):59–69, 1982.

[90] Y. Feng, Y. Zhuang, and Y. Pan. Popular music retrieval by detecting mood. In *Proc. ACM Int. Conf. Information Retrieval,* pages 375–376, 2003.

[91] R. Fernandez and R. W. Picard. Classical and novel discriminant features for affect recognition from speech. In *Proc. INTERSPEECH,* 2005.

[92] J. Fontaine, K. Scherer, E. Roesch, and P. Ellsworth. The world of emotions is not two-dimensional. *Psychological Science,* 18(12):1050–1057, 2007.

[93] J. Fornari and T. Eerola. The pursuit of happiness in music: Retrieving valence with high-level musical descriptors. In *Proc. Computer Music Modeling and Retrieval,* 2008.

[94] J. Fornäs. Songs and emotions: Are lyrics and melodies equal partners. *Psychology of Music,* 34(4):511–534, 2006.

[95] J. Frank, T. Lidy, P. Hlavac, and A. Rauber. Map-based music interfaces for mobile devices. In *Proc. ACM Int. Conf. Multimedia,* pages 981–982, 2008.

[96] Y. Freund, R. Iyer, R. E. Schapire, and Y. Singer. An efficient boosting algorithm for combining preferences. In *Proc. IEEE Int. Conf. Machine Learning,* pages 170–178, 1998.

[97] H. Fujihara and M. Goto. A music information retrieval system based on singing voice timbre. In *Proc. Int. Conf. Music Information Retrieval,* 2007.

[98] H. Fujihara, T. Kitahara, M. Goto, K. Komatani, T. Ogata, and H. G. Okuno. Singer identification based on accompaniment sound reduction and reliable frame selection. In *Proc. Int. Conf. Music Information Retrieval,* 2005.

[99] I. Fujinaga and K. McMillan. Realtime recognition of orchestral instruments. In *Proc. Int. Computer Music Conf.,* pages 141–143, 2000.

[100] A. Gabrielsson. Emotion perceived and emotion felt: Same or different? *Musicae Scientiae,* pages 123–147, 2002. special issue.

[101] A. Gabrielsson and E. Lindström. The influence of musical structure on emotional expression. In P. N. Juslin and J. A. Sloboda, editors, *Music and Emotion: Theory and Research.* Oxford University Press, New York, 2001.

[102] W. W. Gaver and G. Mandler. Play it again, Sam: On liking music. *Cognition and Emotion,* 1:259–282, 1987.

[103] G. Geleijnse and J. Korst. Efficient lyrics extraction from the Web. In *Proc. Int. Conf. Music Information Retrieval,* 2006.

[104] X. Geng, T.-Y. Liu, T. Qin, and H. Li. Feature selection for ranking. In *Proc. ACM Int. Conf. Information Retrieval,* pages 407–414, 2007.

[105] T. Giannakopoulos, A. Pikrakis, and S. Theodoridis. A dimensional approach to emotion recognition of speech from movies. In *Proc. IEEE Int. Conf. Acoustics, Speech, and Signal Processing,* pages 65–68, 2009.

[106] L. R. Goldberg. The structure of phenotypic personality traits. *American Psychologist,* 48(1):26–34, 1993.

[107] E. Gómez. *Tonal Description of Music Audio Signal.* PhD thesis, Universitat Pompeu Fabra, Barcelona, 2006.

[108] M. Goto. A real-time music-scene-description system: Predominant-f0 estimation for detecting melody and bass lines in real-world audio signals. *Speech Communication,* 43:311–329, 2004.

[109] M. Goto, H. Hashiguchi, T. Nishimura, and R. Oka. RWC music database: Music genre database and musical instrument sound database. In *Proc. Int. Conf. Music Information Retrieval,* pages 229–230, 2003.

[110] M. Grimaldi and P. Cunningham. Experimenting with music taste prediction by user profiling. In *Proc. ACM Int. Workshop on Multimedia Information Retrieval*, pages 173–180, 2004.

[111] F. E. Grubbs. Procedures for detecting outlying observations in samples. *Technometrics*, 11(1):1–21, 1969.

[112] I. Guyon and A. Elisseeff. An introduction to variable and feature selection. *J. Machine Learning Research*, 3:1157–1182, 2003.

[113] S. Hallam, I. Cross, and M. Thaut. *The Oxford Handbook of Music Psychology*. Oxford University Press, New York, 2008.

[114] B.-J. Han, S. Rho, R. B. Dannenberg, and E. Hwang. SMERS: Music emotion recognition using support vector regression. In *Proc. Int. Conf. Music Information Retrieval*, pages 651–656, 2009.

[115] J. H. Han and Y. K. Kim. A fuzzy k-nn algorithm using weights from the variance of membership values. In *Proc. IEEE Conf. Computer Vision and Pattern Recognition*, 1999.

[116] A. Hanjalic. Extracting moods from pictures and sounds: towards truly personalized TV. *IEEE Signal Processing Magazine*, 23(2):90–100, 2006.

[117] A. Hanjalic and L.-Q. Xu. Affective video content representation and modeling. *IEEE Trans. Multimedia*, 7(1):143–154, 2005.

[118] D. J. Hargreaves. *The Developmental Psychology of Music*. Cambridge Univ. Press, Cambridge, UK, 1986.

[119] C. Harte and M. Sandler. Automatic chord identification using a quantised chromagram. In *Proc. AES Convention*, pages 245–250, 2005.

[120] C. Harte, M. Sandler, and M. Gasser. Detecting harmonic change in musical audio. In *Proc. ACM Workshop on Audio and Music Computing Multimedia*, pages 21–26, 2006.

[121] W. M. Hartmann. *Signals, Sound, and Sensation*. Springer, New York, 1998.

[122] S. Haykin. *Neural Networks: A Comprehensive Foundation*. Prentice Hall, Englewood Cliffs, NJ, 1999.

[123] R. Herbrich, T. Graepel, and K. Obermayer. Support vector learning for ordinal regression. In *Proc. Int. Conf. Artificial Neural Networks*, pages 97–102, 1999.

[124] P. Herrera, A. Yeterian, and F. Gouyon. Automatic classification of drum sounds: A comparison of feature selection methods and classification techniques. In *Proc. Int. Conf. Music and Artificial Intelligence*, pages 69–80, 2002.

[125] H. M. Hersh and A. Caramazza. A fuzzy set approach to modifiers and vagueness in natural language. *J. Experimental Psychology: General*, 105:251 – 276, 1976.

[126] K. Hevner. Expression in music: A discussion of experimental studies and theories. *Psychological Review*, 48(2):186–204, 1935.

[127] K. Hevner. Experimental studies of the elements of expression in music. *American J. Psychology*, 48:246–268, 1936.

[128] K. Hoashi, K. Matsumoto, and N. Inoue. Personalization of user profiles for content-based music retrieval based on relevance feedback. In *Proc. ACM Int. Conf. Multimedia*, pages 110–119, 2003.

[129] T. Hofmann. Probabilistic latent semantic indexing. In *Proc. ACM Int. Conf. Information Retrieval*, pages 50–57, 1999.

[130] T. Hofmann. Collaborative filtering via Gaussian probabilistic latent semantic analysis. In *Proc. ACM Int. Conf. Information Retrieval*, pages 259–266, 2003.

[131] T. HOFMANN. Latent semantic models for collaborative filtering. *ACM Trans. Information Systems,*, 22(1):89–115, 2004.

[132] M. B. Holbrook and R. M. Schindler. Some exploratory findings on the development of musical tastes. *J. Consumer Research*, 16:119 –124, 1989.

[133] M. Hollander and D. A. Wolfe. *Nonparametric Statistical Methods*. John Wiley & Sons Inc., Hoboken, NJ, 1999.

[134] E. Hörster, R. Lienhart, and M. Slaney. Continuous visual vocabulary models for pLSA-based scene recognition. In *Proc. ACM Int. Conf. Image and Video Retrieval*, pages 319–328, 2008.

[135] C.-L. Hsu and J.-S. R. Jang. On the improvement of singing voice separation for monaural recordings using the MIR-1K dataset. *IEEE Trans. Audio, Speech, & Language Processing*, 18(2):310–319, 2010.

[136] D. C.-W. Hsu and J. Y.-J. Hsu. LyQ: An emotion-aware music player. In *Proc. AAAI Workshop on Computational Aesthetics: Artificial Intelligence Approaches to Beauty and Happiness*, 2006.

[137] X. Hu and J. S. Downie. Exploring mood metadata: Relationships with genre, artist and usage metadata. In *Proc. Int. Conf. Music Information Retrieval*, 2007.

[138] X. Hu and J. S. Downie. When lyrics outperform audio for music mood classification: A feature analysis. In *Proc. Int. Conf. Music Information Retrieval*, 2010.

[139] X. Hu, J. S. Downie, and A. F. Ehmann. Lyric text mining in music mood classification. In *Proc. Int. Conf. Music Information Retrieval*, 2009.

[140] X. Hu, J. S. Downie, C. Laurier, M. Bay, and A. F. Ehmann. The 2007 MIREX audio mood classification task: Lessons learned. In *Proc. Int. Conf. Music Information Retrieval*, pages 462–467, 2008.

[141] X. Hu, V. Sanghvi, B. Vong, P. J. On, C. Leong, and J. Angelica. Moody: A Web-based music mood classification and recommendation system. In *Proc. Int. Conf. Music Information Retrieval*, 2008.

[142] Y. Hu, X. Chen, and D. Yang. Lyric-based song emotion detection with affective lexicon and fuzzy clustering method. In *Proc. Int. Conf. Music Information Retrieval*, 2009.

[143] T.-K. Huang, R. C. Weng, and C.-J. Lin. Generalized Bradley-Terry models and multi-class probability estimates. *J. Machine Learning Research*, 7:85–115, 2006.

[144] X. Huang, A. Acero, and H.-W. Hon. *Spoken Language Processing: A Guide to Theory, Algorithm and System Development*. Prentice Hall, 2001.

[145] A. Huq, J. P. Bello, A. Sarroff, J. Berger, and R. Rowe. Sourcetone: An automated music emotion recognition system. In *Proc. Int. Conf. Music Information Retrieval*, 2009. demo/late-breaking.

[146] D. Huron. Perceptual and cognitive applications in music information retrieval. In *Proc. Int. Conf. Music Information Retrieval*, 2000.

[147] D. Huron. *Sweet Anticipation: Music and the Psychology of Expectation*. MIT Press, Cambridge, Massachusetts, 2006.

[148] A. Jaimes and N. Sebe. Multimodal human computer interaction: A survey. In *Proc. IEEE Int. Workshop on HCI in Conj. with Int. Conf. Computer Vision*, pages 1–15, 2005.

[149] A. Jaimes, N. Sebe, and D. Gatica-Perez. Human-centered computing: A multimedia perspective. In *Proc. ACM Int. Conf. Multimedia*, pages 855–864, 2006.

[150] D. J. Jargreaves and A. C. North. *The Social Psychology of Music*. Oxford University Press, Oxford, UK, 1997.

[151] Jensen. Timbre models of musical sounds. Technical report, University of Copenhagen, 1999.

[152] D. N. Jiang, L. Lu, H. J. Zhang, J. H. Tao, and L. H. Cai. Music type classification by spectral contrast features. In *Proc. IEEE Int. Conf. Multimedia Expo.*, pages 113–116, 2002.

[153] T. Joachims. Optimizing search engines using clickthrough data. In *Proc. ACM Int. Conf. Knowledge Discovery and Data Mining*, pages 133–142, 2002.

[154] K. Jonghwa and E. Ande. Emotion recognition based on physiological changes in music listening. *IEEE Trans. Pattern Analysis & Machine Intelligence*, 30(12):2067–2083, 2008.

[155] S. Jun, S. Rho, B.-J. Han, and E. Hwang. A fuzzy inference-based music emotion recognition system. In *Proc. Visual Information Engineering*, pages 673–677, 2008.

[156] P. N. Juslin. Emotional expression in music performance: Between the performer's intention and the listener's experience. *Psychology of Music*, 24:68–91, 1996.

[157] P. N. Juslin. Cue utilization in communication of emotion in music performance: Relating performance to perception. *J. Experimental Psychology: Human Perception and Performance*, 16(6):1797–1813, 2000.

[158] P. N. Juslin and P. Laukka. Expression, perception, and induction of musical emotions: A review and a questionnaire study of everyday listening. *J. New Music Research*, 33(3):217–238, 2004.

[159] P. N. Juslin and J. A. Sloboda. *Music and Emotion: Theory and Research*. Oxford University Press, New York, 2001.

[160] R. Kamien. *Music: An Appreciation*. New York: McGraw-Hill, 1992.

[161] N. B. Karayiannis and W. Mi. Growing radial basis neural networks: Merging supervised and unsupervised learning with network growth techniques. *IEEE Trans. Neural Networks*, 8(6):1492–1506, 1997.

[162] N. B. Karayiannis and M. Randolph-Gips. On the construction and training of reformulated radial basis function neural networks. *IEEE Trans. Neural Networks*, 14(4):835–846, 2003.

[163] S. O. Karl F. MacDorman and C.-C. Ho. Automatic emotion prediction of song excerpts: Index construction, algorithm design, and empirical comparison. *J. New Music Research*, 36(4):281–299, 2007.

[164] H. Katayose, M. Imai, and S. Inokuchi. Sentiment extraction in music. In *Proc. Int. Conf. Pattern Recognition*, pages 1083–1087, 1998.

[165] J. M. Keller, M. R. Gray, and J. A. Givens. A fuzzy k-nearest neighbor algorithm. *IEEE Trans. Systems, Man, and Cybernetics*, 15(4):580–584, 1985.

[166] D. Keltner and P. Ekman. The psychophysiology of emotion. *Handbook of Emotions*, M. Lewis and J.M. Haviland-Jones, eds., pages 236–249, 2000.

[167] H.-J. Kim, M.-J. Yoo, J.-Y. Kwon, and I.-K. Lee. Generating affective music icons in the emotion plane. In *Proc. ACM Int. Conf. Human Factors in Computing Systems*, pages 3389–3394, 2009. extended abstract.

[168] Y. E. Kim, E. Schmidt, and L. Emelle. Moodswings: A collaborative game for music mood label collection. In *Proc. Int. Conf. Music Information Retrieval*, pages 231–236, 2008.

[169] Y. E. Kim, D. S. Williamson, and S. Pilli. Towards quantifying the "album effect" in artist identification. In *Proc. IEEE Int. Conf. Acoustics, Speech, and Signal Processing*, pages 393–394, 2006.

[170] J. Kittler, M. Hatef, R. Duin, and J. Matas. On combining classifiers. *IEEE Trans. Pattern Analysis and Machine Intelligence*, 20(3):226–239, 1998.

[171] A. Klapuri. Sound onset detection by applying psychoacoustic knowledge. In *Proc. Int. Conf. Acoustics, Speech, and Signal Processing*, pages 3089–3092, 1999.

[172] T. Kohonen. *Self-Organizing Maps*. Springer, Berlin, 2001.

[173] M. D. Korhonen, D. A. Clausi, and M. E. Jernigan. Modeling emotional content of music using system identification. *IEEE Trans. System, Man & Cybernetics*, 36(3):588–599, 2006.

[174] J. Krimphoff, S. McAdams, and S. Winsberg. Caracterisation du timbre des sons complexes. 4(C5):625–628, 1994.

[175] C. Krumhansl. Music: A link between cognition and emotion. *Current Directions Psychological Science*, 11(2):45–50, 2002.

[176] S. Kullback and R. A. Leibler. On information and sufficiency. *The Annals of Mathematical Statistics*, 22(1):79–86, 1951.

[177] M. Lagrange, L. Martins, J. Murdoch, and G. Tzanetakis. Normalized cuts for predominant melodic source separation. *IEEE Trans. Audio, Speech, & Language Processing*, 16(2):278–290, 2008.

[178] P. Lamere. Social tagging and music information retrieval. *J. New Music Research*, 37(2):101–114, 2008.

[179] M. Lan, C. L. Tan, J. Su, and Y. Lu. Supervised and traditional term weighting methods for automatic text categorization. *IEEE Trans. Pattern Analysis & Machine Intelligence*, 31(4):721–735, 2009.

[180] Y. Lan, T.-Y. Liu, Z. Ma, and H. Li. Generalization analysis of listwise learning-to-rank algorithms. In *Proc. IEEE Int. Conf. Machine Learning*, pages 32–47, 2009.

[181] P. J. Lang. The emotion probe. *American Psychologist*, 50(5):372–290, 1995.

[182] O. Lartillot and P. Toiviainen. MIR in MATLAB (II): A toolbox for musical feature extraction from audio. In *Proc. Int. Conf. Music Information Retrieval*, pages 127–130, 2007. [Online] http://users.jyu.fi/ lartillo/mirtoolbox/.

[183] C. Laurier, J. Grivolla, and P. Herrera. Multimodal music mood classification using audio and lyrics. In *Proc. Int. Conf. Machine Learning and Applications*, pages 105–111, 2008.

[184] C. Laurier and P. Herrera. Audio music mood classification using support vector machine. In *MIREX task on Audio Mood Classification*, 2007.

[185] C. Laurier and P. Herrera. Mood cloud: A real-time music mood visualization tool. In *Proc. Computer Music Modeling and Retrieval*, 2008.

[186] C. Laurier, O. Meyers, J. Serra, M. Blech, P. Herrera, and X. Serra. Indexing music by mood: Design and integration of an automatic content-based annotator. *Multimedia Tools and Applications*, 2009.

[187] C. Laurier, M. Sordo, and P. Herrera. Mood cloud 2.0: Music mood browsing based on social networks. In *Proc. Int. Conf. Music Information Retrieval*, 2009. demo/late-breaking.

[188] C. Laurier, M. Sordo, J. Serrà, and P. Herrera. Digital music interaction concepts: A user study. In *Proc. Int. Conf. Music Information Retrieval*, pages 415–420, 2004.

[189] C. Laurier, M. Sordo, J. Serrà, and P. Herrera. Music mood representations from social tags. In *Proc. Int. Conf. Music Information Retrieval*, pages 381–386, 2009.

[190] E. L. M. Law, L. von Ahn, R. B. Dannenberg, and M. Crawford. TagATune: A game for music and sound annotation. In *Proc. Int. Conf. Music Information Retrieval*, 2007.

[191] R. S. Lazarus. *Emotion and Adaptation*. Oxford University Press, New York, 1991.

[192] C.-M. Lee and S. S. Narayanan. Toward detecting emotions in spoken dialogs. *IEEE Trans. Speech and Audio Processing*, 13(2):293–303, 2005.

[193] J. H. Lee and J. S. Downie. Survey of music information needs, uses, and seeking behaviours: Preliminary findings. In *Proc. Int. Conf. Music Information Retrieval*, pages 441–446, 2004.

[194] K. Lee. Identifying cover songs from audio using harmonic representation. In *MIREX task on Audio Cover Song Identification*, 2006.

[195] K. Lee and M. Slaney. A unified system for chord transcription and key extraction from audio using hidden markov models. In *Proc. Int. Conf. Music Information Retrieval*, pages 245–250, 2007.

[196] M. Leman, V. Vermeulen, L. D. Voogdt, and D. Moelants. Using audio features to model the affective response to music. In *Proc. Int. Symp. Musical Acoustics*, pages 74–77, 2004.

[197] M. Leman, V. Vermeulen, L. D. Voogdt, D. Moelants, and M. Lesaffre. Prediction of musical affect using a combination of acoustic structural cues. *J. New Music Research*, 34(1):39–67, 2005.

[198] M. Lesaffre, M. Leman, and J.-P. Martens. A user-oriented approach to music information retrieval. In *Content-Based Retrieval, Dagstuhl Seminar Proceedings*, 2006.

[199] G. Leshed and J. Kaye. Understanding how bloggers feel: Recognizing affect in blog posts. In *Proc. ACM Int. Conf. Computer Human Interaction*, 2006.

[200] M. Levy and M. Sandler. A semantic space for music derived from social tags. In *Proc. Int. Conf. Music Information Retrieval*, pages 411–416, 2007.

[201] M. Lew, N. Sebe, C. Djeraba, and R. Jain. Content-based multimedia information retrieval: State-of-the-art and challenges. *ACM Trans. Multimedia Computing, Communications and Applications*, 2:1–19, 2006.

[202] D. D. Lewis, Y. Yang, T. G. Rose, and F. Li. RCV1: A new benchmark collection for text categorization research. *J. Machine Learning Research*, 5:361–397, 2004.

[203] T. Li and M. Ogihara. Detecting emotion in music. In *Proc. Int. Conf. Music Information Retrieval*, pages 239–240, 2003.

[204] T. Li and M. Ogihara. Content-based music similarity search and emotion detection. In *Proc. IEEE Int. Conf. Acoustics, Speech, and Signal Processing*, pages 17–21, 2004.

[205] T. Li and M. Ogihara. Toward intelligent music information retrieval. *IEEE Trans. Multimedia*, 8(3):564–574, 2006.

[206] T. Lidy and A. Rauber. Evaluation of feature extractors and psycho-acoustic transformations for music genre classification. In *Proc. Int. Conf. Music Information Retrieval*, pages 34–41, 2005. [Online] http://www.ifs.tuwien.ac. at/mir/audiofeatureextraction.html.

[207] Y.-C. Lin, Y.-H. Yang, and H.-H. Chen. Exploiting genre for music emotion classification. In *Proc. IEEE Int. Conf. Multimedia and Expo.*, pages 618–621, 2009.

[208] Y.-P. Lin, T.-P. Jung, and J.-H. Chen. EEG dynamics during music appreciation. In *Proc. IEEE Int. Conf. Engineering in Medicine and Biology Society*, 2009.

[209] Y.-P. Lin, C.-H. Wang, T.-L. Wu, S.-K. Jeng, and J.-H. Chen. Support vector machine for EEG signal classification during listening to emotional music. In *Proc. IEEE Int. Workshop on Multimedia Signal Processing*, pages 127–130, 2008.

[210] Y.-P. Lin, C.-H. Wang, T.-L. Wu, S.-K. Jeng, and J.-H. Chen. Eeg-based emotion recognition in music listening: A comparison of schemes for multiclass support vector machine. In *Proc. IEEE Int. Conf. Acoustics, Speech, and Signal Processing*, pages 489–492, 2009.

[211] C. C. Liu, Y.-H. Yang, P.-H. Wu, and H. H. Chen. Detecting and classifying emotion in popular music. In *Proc. Joint Int. Conf. Information Sciences*, pages 996–999, 2006.

[212] D. Liu, L. Lu, and H.-J. Zhang. Automatic music mood detection from acoustic music data. In *Proc. Int. Conf. Music Information Retrieval*, pages 81–87, 2003.

[213] T.-Y. Liu. Learning to rank for information retrieval. *Foundations and Trends in Information Retrieval*, 3(3):225–331, 2009.

[214] S. R. Livingstone and A. R. Brown. Dynamic response: A real-time adaptation for music emotion. In *Proc. Australasian Conf. Interactive Entertainment*, pages 105–111, 2005.

[215] L. Ljung. *System Identification: Theory for the User*. Prentice-Hall, Upper Saddle River, NJ, 1999.

[216] B. Logan, A. Kositsky, and P. Moreno. Semantic analysis of song lyrics. In *Proc. IEEE Int. Conf. Multimedia and Expo.*, pages 827–830, 2004.

[217] L. Lu, D. Liu, and H. Zhang. Automatic mood detection and tracking of music audio signals. *IEEE Trans. Audio, Speech & Language Processing*, 14(1):5–18, 2006.

[218] L. Lu, H.-J. Zhang, and H. Jiang. Content analysis for audio classification and segmentation. *IEEE Trans. Speech and Audio Processing*, 10(7):504–516, 2002.

[219] Q. Lu, X. Chen, D. Yang, and J. Wang. Boosting for multi-modal music emotion classification. In *Proc. Int. Conf. Music Information Retrieval*, 2010.

[220] K. F. MacDorman, S. Ough, and C.-C. Ho. Automatic emotion prediction of song excerpts: Index construction, algorithm design, and empirical comparison. *J. New Music Research*, 36(4):281–299, 2007.

[221] N. C. Maddage, C. Xu, M. S. Kankanhalli, and X. Shao. Content-based music structure analysis with applications to music semantics understanding. In *Proc. ACM Int. Conf. Multimedia*, pages 112–119, 2004.

[222] J. P. G. Mahedero, Àlvaro Martìnez, P. Cano, M. Koppenberger, and F. Gouyon. Natural language processing of lyrics. In *Proc. ACM Int. Conf. Multimedia*, pages 475–478, 2005.

[223] D. Maier. The complexity of some problems on subsequences and supersequences. *J. ACM*, 25(2):322–336, 1978.

[224] M. I. Mandel and D. P. W. Ellis. A Web-based game for collecting music metadata. In *Proc. Int. Conf. Music Information Retrieval*, 2007.

[225] C. D. Manning and H. Schütze. *Foundations of Statistical Natural Language Processing*. MIT Press, Cambridge, Massachusetts, 2000.

[226] R. Mayer, R. Neumayer, and A. Rauber. Combination of audio and lyrics features for genre classification in digital audio. In *Proc. ACM Int. Conf. Multimedia*, pages 159–168, 2008.

[227] C. McKay, D. McEnnis, and I. Fujinaga. A large publicly accessible prototype audio database for music research. In *Proc. Int. Conf. Music Information Retrieval*, pages 160–163, 2006.

[228] A. Meng, P. Ahrendt, J. Larsen, and L. K. Hansen. Temporal feature integration for music genre classification. *IEEE Trans. Audio, Speech & Language Processing*, 15(5):1654–1663, 2007.

[229] L. B. Meyer. *Emotion and Meaning in Music*. University of Chicago Press, Chicago, 1956.

[230] L. C. Molina, L. Belanche, and A. Nebot. Feature selection algorithms: A survey and experimental evaluation. In *Proc. IEEE Int. Conf. Data Mining*, pages 306–313, 2002.

[231] F. Monay and D. Gatica-Perez. Modeling semantic aspects for cross-media image indexing. *IEEE Trans. Pattern Analysis & Machine Intelligence*, 29(10):1802–1817, 2007.

[232] D. C. Montgomery, G. C. Runger, and N. F. Hubele. *Engineering Statistics*. Wiley, New York, 1998.

[233] A. Moschitti and R. Basili. Complex linguistic features for text classification: A comprehensive study. In *Proc. European Conf. Information Retrieval Research*, pages 161–175, 2004.

[234] F. Nagel, R. Kopiez, O. Grewe, and E. Altenmüller. EMuJoy: Software for continuous measurement of perceived emotions in music. *Behavior Research Methods*, 39(2):283–290, 2007.

[235] T. Nakagawa. Chinese and Japanese word segmentation using word-level and character-level information. In *Proc. Int. Conf. Computational Linguistics*, pages 466–472, 2004.

[236] A. Y. Ng, M. I. Jordan, and Y. Weiss. On spectral clustering: Analysis and an algorithm. In *Proc. Neural Information Processing Systems*, pages 849–856, 2002.

[237] F. V. Nielsen. Musical "tension" and related concepts. In *Semiotic Web*, pages 491 – 513, 1986.

[238] T. L. Nwe and H. Li. Exploring vibrato-motivated acoustic features for singer identification. *IEEE Trans. Audio, Speech, & Language Processing*, 15(2):519–530, 2007.

[239] T. L. Nwe and H. Li. Singing voice detection using perceptually-motivated features. In *Proc. ACM Int. Conf. Multimedia*, pages 309–312, 2007.

[240] I. Nyklicek, J. F. Thayer, and L. J. P. van Doornen. Cardiorespiratory differentiation of musically-induced emotions. *J. Psychophysiology*, 11:304 –321, 1997

[241] A. P. Oliveira and A. Cardoso. Controling music affective content: A symbolic approach. In *Proc. Conf. Interdisciplinary Musicology*, 2008.

[242] A. P. Oliveira and A. Cardoso. Automatic manipulation of music to express desired emotions. In *Proc. Sound and Music Computing Conf.*, pages 265–270, 2009.

[243] C. E. Osgood, G. J. Suci, and P. H. Tannenbaum. *The Measurement of Meaning*. Univ. Illinois Press, Urbana, IL, 1957.

[244] S. Ovadia. Ratings and rankings: Reconsidering the structure of values and their measurement. *Int. J. Social Research Methodology*, 7(5):403–414, 2004.

[245] F. Pachet and P. Roy. Improving multilabel analysis of music titles: A large-scale validation of the correction approach. *IEEE Trans. Audio, Speech & Language Processing*, 17(2):335–343, 2009.

[246] E. Pampalk. A MATLAB toolbox to compute music similarity from audio. In *Proc. Int. Conf. Music Information Retrieval*, 2004. [Online] http://www.ofai.at/ elias.pampalk/ma/.

[247] E. Pampalk, A. Rauber, and D. Merkl. Content-based organization and visualization of music archives. In *Proc. ACM Int. Conf. Multimedia*, pages 570–579, 2002.

[248] H. Papadopoulos and G. Peeters. Large-scale study of chord estimation algorithms based on chroma representation. In *Proc. Int. Workshop on Content-Based Multimedia Indexing*, pages 53–60, 2007.

[249] G. Peeters. A large set of audio features for sound description (similarity and classification) in the CUIDADO project. Technical report, IRCAM, 2004.

[250] G. Peeters. A generic training and classification system for MIREX08 classification tasks: Audio music mood, audio genre, audio artist and audio tag. In *MIREX task on Audio Mood Classification*, 2008.

[251] F. Peng, X. Huang, D. Schuurmans, and S. Wang. Text classification in asian languages without word segmentation. In *Proc. Int. Workshop on Information Retrieval with Asian Languages*, pages 41–48, 2003.

[252] R. W. Picard. *Affective Computing*. MIT Press, 1997.

[253] R. W. Picard, E. Vyzas, and J. Healey. Toward machine emotional intelligence: Analysis of affective physiological state. *IEEE Trans. Pattern Analysis & Machine Intelligence*, 23(10):1175–1191, 2001.

[254] J. C. Platt. *Probabilities for Support Vector Machines*. MIT Press, 1999.

[255] M. D. Plumbley, S. A. Abdallah, J. P. Bello, M. E. Davies, G. Monti, and M. B. Sandler. Automatic music transcription and audio source separation. *Cybernetics and Systems*, 33(6):603–627, 2002.

[256] R. Plutchik. *Emotion: A Psychoevolutionary Synthesis*. Harper & Row, New York, 1980.

[257] T. Pohle, E. Pampalk, and G. Widmer. Evaluation of frequently used audio features for classification of music into perceptual categories. In *Proc. Int. Workshop on Content-Based Multimedia Indexing*, 2005.

[258] H. F. Pollard and E. V. Jansson. A tristimulus method for the specification of musical timbre. *Acustica*, 51:162–171, 1982.

[259] M. F. Porter. An algorithm for suffix stripping. *Program*, 14(3):130–137, 1980. [Online] http://tartarus.org/ martin/PorterStemmer/.

[260] J. Posner, J. A. Russell, and B. Peterson. The circumplex model of affect: An integrative approach to affective neuroscience. *Development and Psychopathology*, 17(3):715–734, 2005.

[261] Q. Pu and G.-W. Yang. Short-text classification based on ica and lsa. In *Proc. Advances in Neural Networks*, pages 265–270, 2006.

[262] T. Qin, X.-D. Zhang, M.-F. Tsai, D.-S. Wang, T.-Y. Liu, and H. Li. Query-level loss functions for information retrieval. *Information Processing and Management*, 44(2):838–855, 2007.

[263] C. E. Rasmussen and C. K. I. Williams. *Gaussian Processes for Machine Learning*. MIT Press, 2006. [Online] http://www.gaussianprocess.org/gpml/.

[264] S. Reddy and J. Mascia. Lifetrak: music in tune with your life. In *Proc. Human-Centered Multimedia*, pages 25–34, 2006.

[265] N. A. Remington, L. R. Fabrigar, and P. S. Visser. Reexamining the circumplex model of affect. *J. Personality & Social Psychology*, 79:286–300, 2000.

[266] B. H. Repp. A microcosm of musical expression. i. Quantitative analysis of pianists' timing in the initial measures of chopin's etude in e major. *J. Acoustical Society of America*, 104:1085–1100, 1998.

[267] J. Ricard. *Towards Computational Morphological Description of Sound*. PhD thesis, Univ. Pompeu Fabra, Barcelona, 2004.

[268] M. G. Rigg. The mood effects of music: A comparison of data from four investigators. *J. Psychology*, 58:427–438, 1964.

[269] M. Rokeach. *The Nature of Human Values*. New York: Free Press.

[270] R. T. Ross. A statistics for circular scales. *J. Educational Psychology*, 29:384 – 389, 1938.

[271] Y. Rubner, C. Tomasi, and L. J. Guibas. The Earth Mover's distance as a metric for image retrieval. *Int. J. Computer Vision*, 40(2):99–121, 2000.

[272] J. A. Russell. A circumplex model of affect. *J. Personality & Social Psychology*, 39(6):1161–1178, 1980.

[273] J. A. Russell. Core affect and the psychological construction of emotion. *Psychological Review*, 110(1):145–172, 2003.

[274] J. A. Russell, A. Weiss, and M. G. A. Affect grid: A single-item scale of pleasure and arousal. *J. Personality & Social Psychology*, 57(3):493–502, 1989.

[275] J. Saunders. Real-time discrimination of broadcast speech/music. In *Proc. IEEE Int. Conf. Acoustics, Speech, and Signal Processing*, pages 993–996, 1996.

[276] N. Scaringella, G. Zoia, and D. Mlynek. Automatic genre classification of music content: A survey. *IEEE Signal Processing Magazine*, 23(2):133–141, 2006.

[277] S. Schaefer, T. McPhail, and J. Warren. Image deformation using moving least squares. *ACM Trans. Graphics*, 25(3):533 –540, 2006.

[278] K. R. Scherer. Which emotions can be induced by music? what are the underlying mechanisms? and how can we measure them. *J. New Music Research*, 33(5):239–251, 2004.

[279] E. M. Schmidt and Y. E. Kim. Projection of acoustic features to continuous valence-arousal mood. In *Proc. Int. Conf. Music Information Retrieval*, 2009. demo/late-breaking.

[280] E. M. Schmidt and Y. E. Kim. Prediction of time-varying musical mood distributions from audio. In *Proc. Int. Conf. Music Information Retrieval*, 2010.

[281] B. Schölkopf, A. J. Smola, R. C. Williamson, and P. L. Bartlett. New support vector algorithms. *Neural Computation*, 12:1207–1245, 2000.

[282] E. Schubert. *Measurement and Time Series Analysis of Emotion in Music*. PhD thesis, School of Music Education, Univ. New South Wales, Sydney, Australia, 1999.

[283] E. Schubert. Measuring emotion continuously: Validity and reliability of the two-dimensional emotion space. *Aust. J. Psychology*, 51(5):154–165, 1999.

[284] E. Schubert. Correlation analysis of continuous response to music: Correcting for the effects of serial correlation. *Musicae Scientiae*, pages 213–236, 2001.

[285] E. Schubert. Update of the Hevner adjective checklist. *Perceptual and Motor Skills*, 96:1117–1122, 2003.

[286] B. Schuller, J. Dorfner, and G. Rigoll. Determination of nonprototypical valence and arousal in popular music: Features and performances. *EURASIP J. Audio, Speech, and Music Processing*, 2010. Article ID 735854, 19 pages.

[287] B. Schuller, F. Eyben, and G. Rigoll. Tango or waltz? Putting ballroom dance style into tempo detection. *EURASIP J. Audio, Speech, and Music Processing*, 2008. Article ID 846135, 12 pages.

[288] B. Schuller, C. Hage, D. Schuller, and G. Rigoll. "Mister D.J., Cheer Me Up!": Musical and textual features for automatic mood classification. *J. New Music Research*, 39(1):13–34, 2010.

[289] B. Schuller, S. Steidl, and A. Batliner. The INTERSPEECH 2009 emotion challenge. In *Proc. INTERSPEECH*, 2009.

[290] F. Sebastiani. Machine learning in automated text categorization. *ACM Computing Surveys*, 34(1):1–47, 2002.

[291] A. Sen and M. Srivastava. *Regression Analysis: Theory, Methods, and Applications*. Springer, New York, 1990.

[292] W. A. Sethares. *Tuning, Timbre, Spectrum, Scale*. Springer-Verlag, 1998.

[293] H. Sever. *Knowledge Structuring for Database Mining and Text Retrieval Using Past Optimal Queries*. PhD thesis, Univ. Southwestern Louisiana, 1995.

[294] B. Shao, T. Li, and M. Ogihara. Quantify music artist similarity based on style and mood. In *Proc. ACM Workshop on Web Information and Data Management*, pages 119–124, 2008.

[295] J. Shen, B. Cui, J. Shepherd, and K.-L. Tan. Towards efficient automated singer identification in large music databases. In *Proc. ACM Int. Conf. Information Retrieval*, pages 59–66, 2006.

[296] C. Simmermacher, D. Deng, and S. Cranefield. Feature analysis and classification of classical musical instruments: An empirical study. In *Proc. Advances in Data Mining*, pages 444–458, 2006.

[297] J. Skowronek, M. F. McKinney, and S. van de Par. Ground truth for automatic music mood classification. In *Proc. Int. Conf. Music Information Retrieval*, pages 395–396, 2006.

[298] J. Skowronek, M. F. McKinney, and S. van de Par. A demonstrator for automatic music mood estimation. In *Proc. Int. Conf. Music Information Retrieval*, 2007.

[299] J. A. Sloboda and P. N. Juslin. Psychological perspectives on music and emotion. In P. N. Juslin and J. A. Sloboda, editors, *Music and Emotion: Theory and Research*. Oxford University Press, New York, 2001.

[300] J. A. Sloboda, S. A. O'Neill, and A. Ivaldi. Functions of music in everyday life: An exploratory study using the experience sampling methodology. *Musicae Scientiae*, 5(1):9–32, 2001.

[301] A. J. Smola and B. Schölkopf. A tutorial on support vector regression. *Statistics and Computing*, 14(3):199–222, 2004.

[302] C. Snoek, M. Worring, and A. W. M. Smeulders. Early versus late fusion in semantic video analysis. In *Proc. ACM Int. Conf. Multimedia*, pages 399–402, 2005.

[303] D. Solomatine and D. Shrestha. AdaBoost.RT: A boosting algorithm for regression problems. In *Proc. IEEE Int. Joint Conf. Neural Networks*, pages 1163–1168, 2004.

[304] StatSoft. *Electronic Statistics Textbook*. StatSoft, Tulsa, OK, 2010. [Online] http://www.statsoft.com/textbook/.

[305] A. Stolcke. SRILM – an extensible language modeling toolkit. In *Proc. Int. Conf. Spoken Language Processing*, 2002. [Online] http://www-speech.sri.com/projects/srilm/.

[306] M.-Y. Su, Y.-H. Yang, Y.-C. Lin, and H.-H. Chen. An integrated approach to music boundary detection. In *Proc. Int. Conf. Music Information Retrieval*, pages 705–710, 2009.

[307] J. Sundberg. *The Science of the Singing Voice*. DeKalb, Ill: Northern Illinois University Press, 1987.

[308] P. Synak and A. Wieczorkowska. Some issues on detecting emotions in music. In *Rough Sets, Fuzzy Sets, Data Mining, and Granular Computing, Int. Conf*, pages 314–322, 2005.

[309] O. R. Terrades, E. Valveny, and S. Tabbone. Optimal classifier fusion in a non-Bayesian probabilistic framework. *IEEE Trans. Pattern Analysis and Machine Intelligence*, 31(9):1630–1644, 2009.

[310] R. E. Thayer. *The Biopsychology of Mood and Arousal*. Oxford University Press, New York, 1989.

[311] W. F. Thompson and B. Robitaille. Can composers express emotions through music? *Empirical Studies of the Arts*, 10:79–89, 1992.

[312] P. Toiviainen and C. L. Krumhansl. Measuring and modeling real-time responses to music: The dynamics of tonality induction. *Perception*, 32(6):741–766, 2003.

[313] T. Tolonen and M. Karjalainen. A computationally efficient multipitch analysis model. *IEEE Trans. Speech Audio Processing*, 8(6):708–716, 2000.

[314] M. Tolos, R. Tato, and T. Kemp. Mood-based navigation through large collections of musical data. In *Proc. IEEE Consumer Communications & Network Conf.*, pages 71–75, 2005.

[315] D. Tran, M. Wagner, and T. Zheng. Fuzzy nearest prototype classifier applied to speaker identification. In *Proc. ESIT*, 1999.

[316] K. Trohidis, G. Tsoumakas, G. Kalliris, and I. Vlahavas. Multi-label classification of music into emotions. In *Proc. Int. Conf. Music Information Retrieval*, pages 325–330, 2008.

[317] W.-H. Tsai and H.-M. Wang. Automatic singer recognition of popular music recordings via estimation and modeling of solo vocal signals. *IEEE Trans. Audio, Speech & Language Processing*, 14(1):330–341, 2006.

[318] G. Tsoumakas and I. Katakis. Multi-label classification: An overview. *Int. J. Data Warehousing and Mining*, 3(3):1–13, 2007.

[319] M. Turk and A. Pentland. Face recognition using eigenfaces. In *Proc. Int. Conf. Computer Vision and Pattern Recognition*, pages 586–591, 1991.

[320] B. A. Turlach. Bandwidth selection in kernel density estimation: A review. Technical report, Univ. Catholique de Louvain, 1993.

[321] D. Turnbull, L. Barrington, D. Torres, and G. Lanckriet. Semantic annotation and retrieval of music and sound effects. *IEEE Trans. Audio, Speech & Language Processing*, 16(2):467–476, 2008.

[322] D. Turnbull, R. Liu, L. Barrington, and G. Lanckriet. A game-based approach for collecting semantic annotations of music. In *Proc. Int. Conf. Music Information Retrieval*, 2007.

[323] G. Tzanetakis. MARSYAS submissions to MIREX 2007. In *MIREX Task on Audio Mood Classification*, 2007.

[324] G. Tzanetakis and P. Cook. Musical genre classification of audio signals. *IEEE Trans. Speech & Audio Processing*, 10(5):293–302, 2002. [Online] http://marsyas.sness. net/.

[325] B. van de Laar. Emotion detection in music, a survey. In *Proc. Twente Student Conf. IT*, 2006.

[326] M. van Zaanen and P. Kanters. Automatic mood classification using tf*idf based on lyrics. In *Proc. Int. Conf. Music Information Retrieval*, 2010.

[327] S. Vembu and S. Baumann. Separation of vocals from polyphonic audio recordings. In *Proc. Int. Conf. Music Information Retrieval*, 2005.

[328] G. S. Vercoe. Moodtrack: Practical methods for assembling emotion-driven music. Master's thesis, Massachusetts Institute of Technology, 2006.

[329] D. Ververidis and C. Kotropoulos. Emotional speech recognition: Resources, features, and methods. *Speech Communication*, 48(9):1162–1181, 2006.

[330] P. Viola and M. J. Jones. Robust real-time face detection. *Int. J. Computer Vision*, 57(2):137–154, 2004.

[331] A. J. Viterbi. Error bounds for convolutional codes and an asymptotically optimum decoding algorithm. *IEEE Trans. Information Theory*, 13(2):260–269, 1967.

[332] M. N. Volkovs and R. S. Zemel. Boltzrank: Learning to maximize expected ranking gain. In *Proc. IEEE Int. Conf. Machine Learning*, page 137, 2009.

[333] M. R. Šikonja and I. Kononenko. Theoretical and empirical analysis of ReliefF and RReliefF. *Machine Learning*, 53:23–69, 2003.

[334] D. Wang and G. J. Brown. *Computational Auditory Scene Analysis: Principles, Algorithms and Applications*. Wiley, 2006.

[335] H. L. Wang and L. F. Cheong. Affective understanding in film. *IEEE Trans. Circuits and Systems for Video Technology*, 16(6):689–704, 2006.

[336] M.-Y. Wang, N.-Y. Zhang, and H.-C. Zhu. User-adaptive music emotion recognition. In *Proc. IEEE Int. Conf. Signal Processing*, pages 1352–1355, 2004.

[337] C. M. Whissell, M. Fournier, R. Pelland, D. Weir, and K. Makarec. A dictionary of affect in language: IV. reliability, validity, and applications. *Perceptual and Motor Skills*, 62:875–888, 21986.

[338] A. Wieczorkowska. Towards extracting emotions from music. In *Proc. Int. Workshop on Intelligent Media Technology for Communicative Intelligence*, pages 228–238, 2004.

[339] A. Wieczorkowska, P. Synak, R. A. Lewis, and Z. W. Raś. Extracting emotions from music data. In *Proc. Int. Symp. Intelligent Systems*, pages 456–465, 2005.

[340] A. Wieczorkowska, P. Synak, and Z. W. Raś. Multi-label classification of emotions in music. In *Proc. Intelligent Information Processing and Web Mining*, pages 307–315, 2006.

[341] T.-L. Wu and S.-K. Jeng. Automatic emotion classification of musical segments. In *Proc. Int. Conf. Music Perception and Cognition*, 2006.

[342] T.-L. Wu and S.-K. Jeng. Extraction of segments of significant emotional expressions in music. In *Proc. Int. Workshop Comput. Music Audio Technology*, pages 76–80, 2006.

[343] T.-L. Wu and S.-K. Jeng. Regrouping of expressive terms for musical qualia. In *Proc. Int. Workshop Computer Music Audio Technology*, 2007.

[344] T.-L. Wu and S.-K. Jeng. Probabilistic estimation of a novel music emotion model. In *Proc. Int. Multimedia Modeling Conf.*, pages 487–497, 2008.

[345] T.-L. Wu, Y.-P. Lin, S.-K. Jeng, and J.-H. Chen. Automatic movie themes playlist generation through gaps across emotion loci and curve of GAEL versus preference. In *Proc. Int. Conf. Music Perception and Cognition*, 2008.

[346] T.-L. Wu, H.-K. Wang, C.-C. Ho, Y.-P. Lin, T.-T. Hu, M.-F. Weng, L.-W. Chan, C.-H. Yang, Y.-H. Yang, Y.-P. Hung, Y.-Y. Chuang, H.-H. Chen, H. H. Chen, J.-H. Chen, and S.-K. Jeng. Interactive content presenter based on expressed emotion and physiological feedback. In *Proc. ACM Int. Conf. Multimedia*, pages 1009–1010, 2008.

[347] F. Xia, T.-Y. Liu, J. Wang, W.-S. Zhang, and H. Li. Listwise approach to learning to rank: Theory and algorithm. In *Proc. IEEE Int. Conf. Machine Learning*, pages 1192–1199, 2008.

[348] Z. Xiao, E. Dellandrea, W. Dou, and L. Chen. What is the best segment duration for music mood analysis. In *Proc. IEEE Int. Workshop on Content-Based Multimedia Indexing*, pages 17–24, 2008.

[349] C.-S. Xu, N. C. Maddage, and X. Shao. Automatic music classification and summarization. *IEEE Trans. Speech and Audio Processing*, 13(3):441–450, 2005.

[350] J. Xu and W. B. Croft. Query expansion using local and global document analysis. In *Proc. ACM Int. Conf. Information Retrieval*, pages 4–11, 1996.

[351] N. Xue. Chinese word segmentation as character tagging. *Int. J. Computational Linguistics and Chinese*, 8(1):29–48, 2003.

[352] D. Yang and W.-S. Lee. Disambiguating music emotion using software agents. In *Proc. Int. Conf. Music Information Retrieval*, 2004.

[353] D. Yang and W.-S. Lee. Music emotion identification from lyrics. In *Proc. IEEE Int. Symp. Multimedia*, pages 624–629, 2009.

[354] Y.-H. Yang and H. H. Chen. Predicting the distribution of perceived emotions of a music signal for content retrieval. *IEEE Trans. Audio, Speech & Language Processing*. Submitted.

[355] Y.-H. Yang and H. H. Chen. Ranking-based emotion recognition for music organization and retrieval. *IEEE Trans. Audio, Speech & Language Processing*. Submitted.

[356] Y.-H. Yang and H. H. Chen. Music emotion ranking. In *Proc. IEEE Int. Conf. Acoustics, Speech, and Signal Processing*, pages 1657–1660, 2009.

[357] Y.-H. Yang and H. H. Chen. Searching music in the emotion plane. *IEEE MMTC E-Letter,* (November issue), 2009. Invited position paper.

[358] Y.-H. Yang and W.-H. Hsu. Video search reranking via online ordinal reranking. In *Proc. IEEE Int. Conf. Multimedia and Expo.,* pages 285–288, 2008.

[359] Y.-H. Yang, W.-H. Hsu, and H.-H. Chen. Online reranking via ordinal informative concepts for context fusion in concept detection and video search. *IEEE Trans. Circuits and Systems for Video Technology,* 19(12):1880–1890, 2009.

[360] Y.-H. Yang, Y.-C. Lin, and H.-H. Chen. Clustering for music search results. In *Proc. IEEE Int. Conf. Multimedia and Expo.,* pages 874–877, 2009.

[361] Y.-H. Yang, Y.-C. Lin, and H. H. Chen. Personalized music emotion recognition. In *Proc. ACM Int. Conf. Information Retrieval,* pages 748–749, 2009.

[362] Y.-H. Yang, Y.-C. Lin, H.-T. Cheng, and H. H. Chen. Mr. Emo: Music retrieval in the emotion plane. In *Proc. ACM Int. Conf. Multimedia,* pages 1003–1004, 2008. [online] http://www.youtube.com/watch?v=ra55xO20UHU.

[363] Y.-H. Yang, Y.-C. Lin, H.-T. Cheng, I.-B. Liao, Y.-C. Ho, and H.-H. Chen. Toward multi-modal music emotion classification. In *Proc. Pacific-Rim Conf. Multimedia,* pages 70–79, 2008.

[364] Y.-H. Yang, Y.-C. Lin, Y.-F. Su, and H. H. Chen. A regression approach to music emotion recognition. *IEEE Trans. Audio, Speech & Language Processing,* 16(2):448–457, 2008.

[365] Y.-H. Yang, C. C. Liu, and H. H. Chen. Music emotion classification: A fuzzy approach. In *Proc. ACM Int. Conf. Multimedia,* pages 81–84, 2006.

[366] Y.-H. Yang, Y.-F. Su, Y.-C. Lin, and H. H. Chen. Music emotion recognition: The role of individuality. In *Proc. ACM Int. Workshop on Human-Centered Multimedia,* pages 13–21, 2007. [Online] http://mpac.ee.ntu.edu.tw/ yihsuan/MER/hcm07/.

[367] C.-C. Yeh, S.-S. Tseng, P.-C. Tsai, and J.-F. Weng. Building a personalized music emotion prediction system. In *Proc. Pacific-Rim Conf. Multimedia,* pages 730–739, 2006.

[368] K. Yu, S. Yu, and V. Tresp. Multi-label informed latent semantic indexing. In *Proc. ACM Int. Conf. Information Retrieval,* pages 258–265, 2005.

[369] M.-L. Zhang and Z.-H. Zhou. ML-knn: A lazy learning approach to multi-label learning. *Pattern Recognition,* 40(7):2038–2048, 2007.

[370] S. Zhang, Q. Huang, Q. Tian, S. Jiang, and W. Gao. *i.*MTV—an integrated system for MTV affective analysis. In *Proc. ACM Int. Conf. Multimedia,* pages 985–986, 2008.

[371] S. Zhang, Q. Tian, Q. Huang, W. Gao, and S. Li. Utilizing affective analysis for efficient movie browsing. In *Proc. IEEE Int. Conf. Image Processing,* 2009.

[372] S. Zhang, Q. Tian, S. Jiang, Q. Huang, and W. Gao. Affective MTV analysis based on arousal and valence features. In *Proc. IEEE Int. Conf. Multimedia and Expo.,* pages 1369–1372, 2008.

[373] J. Zhu and L. Lu. Perceptual visualization of a music collection. In *Proc. IEEE Int. Conf. Multimedia and Expo.,* pages 1058–1061, 2005.

[374] E. Zwicker. Subdivision of the audible frequency range into critical bands. *J. Acoustical Society of America,* 33, 1961.

[375] E. Zwicker and H. Fastl. *Psychoacoustics: Facts and Models.* Springer, New York, 1999.

Index